THE LAW AS GOSPEL:

Revival and Reform in the Theology of Charles G. Finney

by

DAVID L. WEDDLE

Studies in Evangelicalism, No. 6

The Scarecrow Press, Inc.
Metuchen, N.J., & London
1985

Material reprinted from Charles G. Finney's <u>Lectures</u> <u>on</u>
<u>Systematic</u> <u>Theology</u> (Oberlin: E. J. Goodrich, 1878; reprint
edition, Grand Rapids, Michigan: Eerdmans, 1964). Used by
permission of Wm. B. Eerdmans Publishing Company.

BX
7260
.F47
W4
1985

Library of Congress Cataloging in Publication Data

Weddle, David L. (David Leroy), 1942-
   The law as gospel.

   (Studies in evangelicalism ; no. 6)
   Includes bibliographical references and index.
   1. Finney, Charles Grandison, 1792-1875. I. Title.
II. Series.
BX7260.F47W4 1985   230'.58'0924   85-8303
ISBN 0-8108-1819-1

STUDIES IN EVANGELICALISM
edited by
Kenneth E. Rowe &
Donald W. Dayton

1. Melvin E. Dieter. *The Holiness Revival of the Nineteenth Century.* 1980.

2. Lawrence T. Lesick. *The Lane Rebels: Evangelicalism and Antislavery in Antebellum America.* 1980.

3. Edward H. Madden and James E. Hamilton. *Freedom and Grace: The Life of Asa Mahan.* 1982.

4. Roger H. Martin. *Evangelicals United: Ecumenical Stirrings in Pre-Victorian Britain, 1795-1830.* 1983.

5. Donald W. Dayton. *Theological Roots of Pentecostalism.* 1985.

6. David L. Weddle. *The Law as Gospel: Revival and Reform in the Theology of Charles G. Finney.* 1985.

To Sharon,
Dan, and Lisa

The current resurgence of Evangelical religion has high-lighted the important role of this force in the formation of American and British culture. This series will explore its roots in the Evangelical Revival and Awakenings of the eighteenth century, its nineteenth-century blossoming in revivalism and social reform, and its twentieth-century developments in both sectarian and "mainline" churches. We will be particularly concerned to emphasize the diversity within Evangelicalism--the search for holiness, the Millennial traditions, Fundamentalism, Pentecostalism, and so forth. We are pleased to publish David Leroy Weddle's study of one of America's preeminent evangelists, Charles G. Finney, as number six in our series.

A graduate of Hope College, Holland, Michigan, Dr. Weddle took the doctorate in religious studies at Harvard University, and began his academic career at Westmont College, Santa Barbara, California. Since 1973 Dr. Weddle has taught in the Department of Religion at Cornell College, Mount Vernon, Iowa.

Donald W. Dayton
Northern Baptist
 Theological Seminary
Lombard, Illinois

Kenneth E. Rowe
Drew University
Madison, New Jersey

CONTENTS

The sects that exist in the United States are innumerable. They all differ in respect to the worship which is due to the Creator; but they all agree in respect to the duties which are due from man to man. Each sect adores the Deity in its own peculiar manner, but all sects preach the same moral law in the name of God.

Alexis de Tocqueville
Democracy in America

For me the Law and the Gospel have but one rule of life; and every violation of the spirit of the law, is also a violation of the spirit of the Gospel.

Charles G. Finney
Memoirs

Following the Revolution and the establishment of the fledgling government in Washington, expansion to the West began
in earnest. The decades around the turn of the nineteenth
century saw large numbers of emigrants make their way from
the planned elegance of New England towns to the uncivilized
forests and valleys of central and western New York State.
These emigrants were not pioneers, in Sidney Mead's terms,
but settlers, people concerned to "stake out" a place on the
land, to cultivate and order it.[1] They achieved their
purpose in the land by the plow and fence wire; they created
order in their society by laws and courts. At first a
simple matter of "common sense equity," the legal order grew
into an ever more complex system of courts, laws, and judicial processes. Unlike the pioneers who were rankled by any
restrictions on their movements, the settlers respected the
law as a means of both confining the violent and greedy and
also directing the energies of the constructive and ambitious. The law provided guidelines for the legitimate exercise of human initiative.

The religious tradition of New England, however, especially as restated by Jonathan Edwards with such force
during the Great Awakening, did not allow for human autonomy. Indeed, the Mysterious Sovereign of New England theology directed human destiny in his own strange ways to bring
about his kingdom. Yet the settlers' very move westward was
an admission that New England had not met their expectations; the God of the covenant had not provided the abun-
dance of the promised kingdom. Thus, while they maintained
many of the traditional religious practices of New England,
and almost all their parish ministers were trained in the
East, they were dissatisfied with a theology which denied

them knowledge of the divine laws governing their lives and
condemned their claim to "a self-determining power in the
will" as an illusion.[2]

Therefore, when a preacher appeared in the settlements
with a version of Christian faith which preserved both
reason and volition, the settlers were prepared to listen;
and when he carried his campaign east, to Philadelphia and
Boston and New York City, the urban capitalists, who shared
the belief in the self-determining power of the will, also
heard him gladly. To Charles Grandison Finney the principles of divine government were as intelligible as the
Science of Law was to William Blackstone, as the system of
Nature was to Isaac Newton, or as the Laws of Mind were to
John Locke.[3] He promised his hearers that God governs human
affairs according to laws that can be known by any person
possessed of common sense. It was a promise, like those of
American jurists and scientists of the period, made in the
name of "Nature and Nature's God"--a God who ruled his
universe by principles which any person can learn and to
which all people are obligated.

Charles Finney was a son of the settlements; his family
had been among the more ambitious of the early emigrants.
He received little religious training as a youth, and after
a few years in Connecticut for secondary education, he
returned to western New York and began training as a lawyer.
His practice was cut short by a dramatic conversion to
Christianity which marked the beginning of a remarkable
career as evangelist, theologian, teacher, and finally president of Oberlin College. In his preaching Finney often
used the story of his own conversion as a model of the way
to find salvation: a willed effort to bring one's life into
conformity with the laws of God. The model was a convincing
one for thousands of his contemporaries in the settlements,
and Finney's revivals spread like wildfire over an area
which had felt the flames of religious enthusiasm so often
by the 1820's that it was already called the "burned-over
district."[4]

The primary purpose of this study is to explain Finney's contribution to American theology, a contribution which consists of a consistent set of doctrinal views, informed by principles of legal order, which justified and promoted both revivals and reforms. Finney is generally recognized as the first "modern" revivalist, who developed a wide repertoire of techniques to promote religious convictions; and as a supporter of reform movements, who believed in perfecting the social order through "moral means." But he also deserves notice as a theologian. In the midst of a strenuous schedule of preaching and teaching Finney thought about what he was doing, perhaps not with the sophistication and broad learning of his contemporaries in academic posts at New Haven and Princeton, but with a singular passion for clarity and what he called "common sense" interpretation. He appealed directly to the reason and conscience of his hearers and sought not only to state the truth, but to persuade them to honor its moral demands. As the condition of his agreeing to go to Oberlin, Finney insisted on the freedom to conduct revivals for several months each year. Thus, he was in the remarkable position of not only formulating the policy of divine government in his classroom and study, but also directing its operations from his pulpit and on the campaign trail. No revivalist since his time has come close to matching the range of theological arguments set out in his published lectures; all later revivalists have profited from the aid and comfort given their cause by Finney's statement of what was then called the "New Divinity."[5]

For half a century Finney devoted himself to extending the authority of moral government over human life through revival and reform. His career provides a valuable case study in American theology which, since the Puritans, has taken its first test of adequacy from experience. Consequently, as Daniel Day Williams has shown, American theologians have adjusted themselves to major shifts in cultural values and social awareness.[6] Such adjustments often appear to those whose experience is still informed by the old ways as heretical novelties. Reflecting upon a lifetime of

raising revivals by "new measures," Finney rightly saw himself as one who spoke a new language for a new era:

> I am aware that by a certain portion of the church
> I have been considered an innovator, both in
> regard to doctrine and measures; and that many
> have looked upon me as rather prominent, especial-
> ly in assailing some of the old forms of theologi-
> cal thought and expression, and in stating the
> doctrines of the gospel in many respects in new
> language.[7]

The "old forms" were the doctrines of New England Calvinism,
grounded in the Westminster Confession of 1647, impressed
early upon the American conscience by awesome Puritan
divines, defended by the most profound thinker in American
religious history, Jonathan Edwards, and rather unimagina-
tively systematized by his disciples, such as Joseph Bellamy
and Samuel Hopkins.[8]

In opposition to the Old School Calvinists' claim that
God's ways are not our ways and that salvation is entirely
beyond human control, Finney announced that God's ways are
perfectly understandable and that salvation in fact depends
upon informed efforts at moral reformation. One of Finney's
first published sermons contains in its title a challenge to
the theology of New England: "Sinners Bound to Change Their
Own Hearts" (1834). For the religious mind restless within
the confined limits of Puritan life, Finney's announcement
that God governs human affairs by a rational, consistent,
and fully revealed body of laws meant that one need not feel
guilty about seeking spiritual prosperity with the same
energy and forceful means employed in commercial transactions. Civil laws, as the sublime instrument of social
improvement, found their religious counterparts in the spiritual laws of Finney's gospel by which sinners' efforts to
"change their own hearts" and to reform society were encouraged and directed.

The impressive achievement of Finney's revival preaching is that he provided a set of guidelines for the exercise

of initiative in religious life. His theology excised from
the spiritual realm all uncertainty and mystery, even as
civil laws sought to eliminate insecurity in the political
realm. Finney assured the readers of his famous Lectures on
Revivals of Religion that "there is nothing in religion
beyond the ordinary powers of nature. It consists entirely
in the right exercise of the powers of nature."[9] Finney was
doing nothing less than shifting the basis of theology from
mystery to law. In one of those sweeping pronouncements
with which Finney's work is liberally supplied, he declared:
"What is religion? Obedience to God's law."[10] Proceeding
on that conviction, Finney reduced the complicated formulae
of Christian orthodoxy to a straight forward set of moral
demands, intelligible to any person of reason and common
sense. He took the mystery out of theology, and in so doing
deprived sinners of all excuses for not repenting and submitting to divine government on the spot. He took the
mystery out of psychology, and in so doing reduced the
question of religious faith and moral virtue to a simple
exercise of will, unaffected by an evil disposition or some
hidden work of grace. He took the mystery out of the drama
of history itself by guaranteeing the fulfillment of millennial hopes through "the right use of means."

The new language in which Finney stated his doctrinal
innovations was not, as might be expected, derived directly
from religious experience. Finney came to Christianity as a
mature adult, with a clearly defined sense of identity and a
well-formed world view, possessing a professional vocabulary. As Bernard Weisberger notes, "He was a unique candidate in divinity, a grown man, furiously independent, and
already trained in another discipline."[11] That discipline
was the law; and when Finney entered the ranks of Christian
preachers, he retained a deep loyalty, not only to the
methods of courtroom advocacy but also to the classic metaphysical vision and contemporary cultural ambitions of what
Perry Miller called "the legal mentality."[12] In restating
"the doctrines of the Gospel" Finney borrowed heavily and
often from his early investment in the study of law.

The appeal of Finney's revival theology lay in his use
of the principles of legal order to interpret the relation
of the individual to God. Finney learned these principles
during his brief apprenticeship as a lawyer. He applied
both the techniques and principles of the legal profession
to his vocation as a revivalist. The result was an innovative practice of evangelism, called the "new measures," many
of which were adaptations of the methods used by attorneys
to plead their cases before the bar. Finney's measures
included a dramatic appeal for immediate decision; use of
the "anxious seat" to elicit public commitment to faith;
protracted meetings to promote the spread of revival in an
area; public prayers for sinners by name; and enlistment of
all converts in the work of the revival, including women.[13]

Finney developed his system of theology through the
application of legal reasoning to the text of the Bible.
The key to his theology is the unshakeable conviction,
gained in the study of law, confirmed in his own conversion,
and strengthened by his success in revival work, that conversion is a reasoned decision to submit to God's moral
government, an act of will entirely within the sinner's
natural powers. From the premise that each person possesses
all the powers and responsibilities belonging to a free
moral agent, Finney works out a thorough revision of Calvinism. Finney argues that sin is voluntary disobedience of
law, not an inherited moral defect; that Christ provides
atonement through his death, which so upholds respect for
God's moral government that God may forgive sinners without
weakening his moral authority; that grace is the provision
of truth to the sinner's mind and heart through preaching,
not a supernatural transformation of human nature; that
faith is a voluntary submission to the truth of the gospel
(and, in principle, capable of being extended throughout
life to attain entire sanctification); that the vocation of
the believer is to practice benevolence toward others, by
seeking their conversion and supporting their moral rights.

Once the foundation of Finney's theology in the principles of legal order is laid bare, it is clear how he came to

accept the possibility of perfection both for individuals
and the society of which they are members. In words remini-
scent of John Wesley, Finney declares that "total abstinence
from all known sin is the only practicable rule of life."[14]
The Christian is to miss no opportunity to obey the moral
law, in social policies as well as in private piety. Thus,
while bringing another soul to conversion is the highest
duty of the Christian, the true believer should also be
active in social reform, from temperance and Sabbatarianism
to abolition. In his Lectures on Revivals Finney hangs
exalted hopes on the voluntary diligence of his congregation: "If the Church will do all her duty, the millennium
may come in this country in three years."[15] For Finney
nothing stands in the way of millennium except the rebellious, but convertible, human will. Thus, while social
reforms are morally praiseworthy, they are utterly unable to
create the kingdom of God on earth without the soul-shaking
power of revival. Finney, as Edwards before him, understood
the revival as the central movement in the history of salvation. Through the conversion of nations the entire world
would be brought to the saving acknowledgment of the divine
moral government. Then would the biblical promises of a
kingdom of perfect peace and righteousness be fulfilled.

Finney is generally considered the first of the modern
revivalists, those fiercely independent itinerants whose
earnest pleadings are now more often heard from television
sets and car radios than from the tents and tabernacles of
an earlier day. His successors have retained his fervor for
"saving souls," but few have the courage to retain his hope
in the coming of the kingdom of God to earth. Yet it is
precisely Finney's belief in the evangelistic enterprise
that led him, logically he would add, to millennial optimism. For if the individual is capable of repentance, then
is it not possible for groups of individuals to agree to
govern their common life by that same law? If so, then
universal obedience, elicited by the persuasive power of
reason and love, is the final goal of history, the fulfillment of the promise of salvation in the Christian gospel.
What follows is an analysis of Finney's systematic revival

theology which begins with the premise of human freedom, proceeds by means of legal reasoning informed by the vision of universal moral government, and ends with exhortations to social and political action.

A thorough acquaintance with Finney's work is a necessary condition for understanding American revivalism. No other popular evangelist has thought so clearly and carefully about the meaning of revivals; Finney's theology is a report from the field and has the authenticity of a battle diary. That he emphasizes the role of reason in judging religious beliefs, the importance of a just order of conduct in both individual and cultural life, and the necessity of working for political and social reforms is sufficient reason for both supporters and critics of revivalism to pay attention to his remarkable career. Both groups may have something to learn about the Christian gospel from the preacher "who was bred a lawyer."

NOTES

1. Sidney Mead, "The American People: Their Space, Time and Religion," Journal of Religion 34 (1953), 247.

2. The greatest defender of the Calvinist theology of absolute divine sovereignty and utter human impotence was Jonathan Edwards. He devoted his mighty exercise in logic, Enquiry into the Modern Prevailing Notion, of that Freedom of Will which is supposed to be Essential to Moral Agency (Boston, 1754), to a complete dismantling of the notion of "a self-determining power in the will."

3. Cf. Daniel J. Boorstin, The Mysterious Science of the Law: An Essay on Blackstone's Commentaries Showing How Blackstone, Employing Eighteenth-Century Ideas of Science, Religion, History, Aesthetics, and Philosophy, Made of the Law at Once a Conservative and a Mysterious Science (Cambridge, Mass.: Harvard University Press, 1941), p. 12: "Blackstone was, in a sense, doing for the English legal system what Newton had done for the physical world, and what

Locke had done for the world of the mind." As a systema-
tizer of mysteries, Finney was in good company.

4. The classic study of the area from which Finney, as
well as many other creative and eccentric figures, emerged
is Whitney R. Cross, The Burned-over District: The Social
and Intellectual History of Enthusiastic Religion in Western
New York, 1800-1850 (Ithaca, N.Y.: Cornell University
Press, 1950).

5. In the afterword to Finney's Memoirs, his successor
to the presidency of Oberlin, James H. Fairchild, rightly
predicted that Finney's efforts to develop "a true Christian
philosophy" would not be recognized. Nevertheless, "other
generations will reap the benefits, without knowing the
source whence they have sprung" [Charles G. Finney, Memoirs
(New York: A. S. Barnes, 1876), p. 477]. A recent sustained attempt to analyze the salient features of Finney's
theology is a series of articles by James E. Johnson. See
"Charles G. Finney and a Theology of Revivalism," Church
History 36 (Spring, 1969), 338-358; "Charles G. Finney and
Oberlin Perfectionism," Journal of Presbyterian History 46
(March-June, 1968), 42-57, 128-138. Johnson both summarizes
Finney's views and gathers much of the contemporary response
to the sensation Finney's career created. I have attempted
to supplement his work, as well as that of more well-known
scholars, on Finney's role in the drama of American revivalism by illuminating the pervasive and persistent influence
of his early training in the law on his theological development.

6. See his insightful survey of American Protestant
thought, "Tradition and Experience in American Theology,"
The Shaping of American Religion, ed. J. W. Smith and A.
Leland Jamison, Religion in American Life (Princeton, N.J.:
Princeton University Press, 1961), Vol. I, pp. 443-495.

7. Charles G. Finney, Memoirs, pp. 1-2. Hereinafter
referred to as MF.

8. The nineteenth-century defenders of Presbyterian
orthodoxy were called the "Old School" to distinguish their
views from the "New School" Calvinism of Nathaniel W. Taylor, Lyman Beecher, and Finney. These latter evangelicals
were closely associated with the revival movement, and

emphasized freedom of human agency in conversion. Joseph Haroutunian provided a detailed account of the transition from Old School to New School views in Piety Versus Moralism: The Passing of the New England Theology, original edition, 1932 (New York: Harper Torchbooks, 1970).

9. Charles G. Finney, Lectures on Revivals of Religion, ed. William G. McLoughlin, Jr. (Cambridge, Mass.: Harvard University Press, 1960), p. 13. The lectures were originally given by Finney in 1833-34, and subsequently published in the New York Evangelist.

10. Lectures on Revivals, p. 317.

11. Bernard A. Weisberger, They Gathered at the River: The Story of the Great Revivalists and Their Impact upon Religion in America (Chicago: Quadrangle Books, 1966), p. 94.

12. Perry Miller, The Life of the Mind in America from the Revolution to the Civil War (New York: Harcourt, Brace & World, 1965), Book Two: The Legal Mentality, pp. 99-265.

13. The "new measures" are described and defended by Finney in Lectures on Revivals, pp. 250-276. Cf. Cross, Burned-over District, pp. 173-184.

14. "When Sin is Fatal," The Guilt of Sin (Grand Rapids, Mich.: Kregel Publication, n.d.), p. 121. This volume is part of a seven-volume reprint edition of selected sermons and lectures, "The Charles G. Finney Memorial Library."

15. Lectures on Revivals, p. 306.

Chapter I

THE CRISIS OF CONSCIENCE

In the early nineteenth century two movements of the American spirit converged toward the common end of the creation of a just social order for the happiness of humankind and the glory of God. The revival and the institution of legal order grew and flourished from a common root: the conviction that renewed national community could be formed only on the basis of respect for law. The biblical promise of millennial bliss fervently extended by the revivalists and the constitutional promise of domestic tranquillity recited by the lawyers were both dependent for their fulfillment on the people's submission to regulations, whether religious or civil. The interest in law as the basis of "settling things" with both God and one's neighbors implied a confidence in the human ability to understand and to honor the principles by which the affairs of God and his creatures are rightfully ordered.

Such confidence, however, was inconsistent with the limits set on human insight and moral power by the Puritan theology which both Yankees and Yorkers had been taught in their fathers' homes. The law stimulated, as well as regulated, individual initiative in the realms of politics and economics; however, in the realm of religion initiative was condemned as pride, and resignation to an inscrutable Governor was demanded. The crisis in religious consciousness, while intensified in those who emigrated from New England, disturbed that entire generation, including those who did not venture out into the West. As confidence grew in their

own abilities to build a society in which life, liberty and
the pursuit of happiness would be enjoyed as inalienable
rights by every citizen, the children of the Puritans,
whether transplanted to the settlements or tending to business in the cities, found increasingly less practical use
for the Calvinist ideology of their fathers. The problem
they faced can be analyzed in theological terms as apostasy,
and in psychological terms as the tension between initiative
and guilt. In both cases the fundamental question was how
to exercise autonomy without the guilt of violating the
higher laws of civil and cosmic order and without the shame
of failing to fulfill one's own nature and responsibilities
as a moral agent.

The answer, which resolved the crisis on both levels,
is that individual freedom may flourish within the limits of
law. As one ministerial orator proclaimed in 1839: "The
soul, constructed upon the model of God's law, can be free
only in obeying it."[1] The law was offered by both evangelists and lawyers as the means of directing the flow of
vital energies in the maturing republic. Appropriately, as
Edwin Starbuck would demonstrate in the latter part of the
century, the population among whom the revivalists' message
found its most enthusiastic adherents were young people in
the turbulent passage from childhood to adult life; conversion, one of America's earliest psychologists discovered, is
an "adolescent phenomenon."[2] The appeal of revival preaching to the adolescent mind, struggling for some way to break
forth legitimately into individual expression, was the clear
emphasis on the law as a reliable and authoritative guide
for successful action in the world. To the extent that in
the early nineteenth century large groups of influential
people--enterprising settlers in the country and ambitious
merchants and craftsmen in the cities--were grappling with a
similar problem in larger cultural forms, the revivalists
who preached the "evangelical law" and the attorneys who
practiced "civil law" as the instruments of individual and
social reform found themselves allied by virtue of the
widespread interest in their common vision of legal order.

The alliance did not survive the century; but, for a time, the search for a rational system of eternal laws, rooted in human nature, reflected in the cosmic order, discovered by common sense and good will, and revealed as the ultimate basis of the Christian religion, fired the Protestant imagination with visions of a national polity and settled the restless hearts of a generation. Both the crisis and its resolution are sharply focused in the life and preaching of the most creative religious personality among the sons of the settlers: Charles Grandison Finney, who combined in his personal history the roles of lawyer and revivalist and who worked out a theology of legal order that sanctified human initiative.

Emigration

Charles Finney was born on August 29, 1792, in the town of Warren, Connecticut, in Litchfield County, home of the first law school in America. He was the seventh child of Sylvester and Rebecca Rice Finney; of his siblings Finney mentions only his "youngest brother" in the Memoirs.[3] When Charles was two years old, the family emigrated to Oneida County, in central New York State. In a description of the area in 1836, Thomas Gordon expressed doubt "whether a greater sum of happiness can be found on the face of the globe, than is apparent here."[4] In 1794, however, the county had been established only five years and was still, as Finney remembered much later, "to a great extent, a wilderness" (MF, p. 4). It would be a decade before enough New England emigrants had poured into these promising valleys to justify Whitney Cross' claim that "Oneida was the new Connecticut."[5] The Finney household was slightly ahead of its time in leaving Litchfield County, and that fact reflects well on the intuition of its head. In Oneida County, according to its historians in the next generation, "Hardly a farm is without perpetual streams and brooks . . . the soil is of various qualities, but everywhere rich and productive."[6] It is not known why the elder Finney removed his family from the security of Connecticut but it seems

safe to assume that he was one of those who hoped, by industry or speculation, to find themselves, in a few years, "in
comfortable, if not in affluent circumstances."[7]

The Memoirs do not specify where in Oneida County the
Finney household settled, but it was apparently in the area
of Whitestown, "the first permanent settlement of the
county, or in the state, west of the Dutch settlement in the
valley of the Mohawk."[8] Finney returned to this area in the
summer of 1830, during the Western revivals, to visit his
wife's family (MF, p. 272) and often spent summers there
throughout his itinerancy, resting and planning new campaigns. It was here that he conducted his well-known tour
through a "cotton manufactory" on the Oriskany creek, just
north of Whitestown. The superintendent of the factory was
Finney's brother-in-law, who invited him to preach; but, as
Finney strode up and down the aisles in a preliminary tour,
the women at the looms burst into tears; and revival was on:
"in the course of a few days nearly all in the mill were
hopefully converted" (MF, p. 184). Apparently, Finney
received more spiritual encouragement from his wife's family
than from his own; this sense of kinship may indicate an
association extending back to the years when Finney was
growing up in Oneida County. The conditions of this area
accord with Finney's description in the Memoirs: largely
wilderness, with a notable indifference to religious observance among the populace.

Further, the ambitious motives of the first settlers
seem to correspond to those of Sylvester Finney. As a
contemporary historian of the area wrote, "Soon after the
close of the Revolutionary contest, the attention of the
'sons of the Pilgrims' in New England, was called towards
western New York, as an excellent field for the display of
Yankee enterprise."[9] The founder of Whitestown, one Hugh
White, arrived in 1784, at fifty-one years of age. Jones
observes that it was not "the ardor and restlessness of
youth which induced him to emigrate, but that spirit of
enterprise and perseverance which looked forward to the
future prosperity of himself and family."[10] An area which

encouraged such "Yankee enterprise" would be attractive to
the emigrating Finney family. Further, it may be that the
area held particular advantages for a predominately female
household. In the church records of Westmoreland (taken
from Whitestown in 1792) there is an entry for the marriage
of Samuel Cornwell and Hannah Finney, on August 17, 1794.[11]

Whatever may not be known of Finney's parents, they
were, no doubt, strong-willed and ambitious people, willing
to exchange the comforts of home, family, and tradition for
the challenge, and possible profit, of the wilderness. Not
quite pioneers (they stopped in central New York and not
Ohio); yet, like their fellow emigrants, they were "possessed of an enterprising character," fortified by the
"intelligence" that was the fruit of an eastern "common
school education."[12] For their children as well, these
settlers desired the advantages of primary education. A
year after the Finneys arrived, a common school system was
established in the state, on behalf of what the Regents of
the University of New York called in their petition to the
legislature, "the many infant settlements . . . chiefly
composed of families in very indigent circumstances, and
placed in the most unfavorable situations for instruction."[13]

Young Charles attended a common school until about the
age of fourteen, and then studied for two years at the
Hamilton Oneida Academy. Such academies were of great value
in providing competent teachers for the common schools.
Besides the standard curriculum of English, writing, arithmetic, history, and natural and moral philosophy, students
at the academies studied the "principles of teaching," and
"the constitution of the United States, and the constitution
of the state of New York."[14] The interest in the law was
early cultivated in those who would convey the wisdom of
civilization to the "infant settlements." The first news-
paper in the wilderness of neighboring Ostego County had, as
its motto, the verse, "Historic truth our Herald shall
proclaim, the law our guide, the public good our aim."[15]

As Finney modestly recalled, he "advanced so far as to
be supposed capable of teaching a common school myself, as
common schools were then conducted" (MF, p. 4). He had his
opportunity to experiment with the highly respected vocation
of teacher[16] when his family moved once more, west and
north, into Jefferson County, to the newly established village of Henderson, on the shores of Lake Ontario. In his
Memoirs Finney makes the significant association of this
move with the fact that his

> parents were neither of them professors of relig-
> ion, and, I believe, among our neighbors there
> were very few religious people. In the neighbor-
> hood of my father's residence we had just erected
> a meeting house and settled a minister, when my
> father was induced to remove again into the wil-
> derness skirting the southern shore of Lake Ontar-
> io, a little south of Sackett's Harbor. Here
> again I lived for several years, enjoying no bet-
> ter religious privileges than I had in Oneida
> county [MF, p. 5].[17]

The restless parental energies contrast dramatically with
the stabilizing power of the meeting house and a "settled"
minister. One wonders if the young Charles so clearly
identified himself with the forces of faith and order as
does the aging Finney in the words, "we had just erected a
meeting house. . . when my father was induced to remove
again. . . " Probably the old ambition to occupy greener
pastures near a harbor town[18] was part of the "inducement"
for Sylvester Finney; however, for his son the revivalist
the demonic impulse to intrude further into the wilderness,
leaving behind the regulation of civil and religious community, had an association with a more sinister propensity of
human nature. His father's initiative had again deprived
his children of religious instruction and brought a greater
guilt upon himself. To Finney's mind, a half-century later,
the memory which lingers is the conflict between the energy
of self-determination and the civilizing order of religion.
The elder Finney consistently failed to reconcile these

values for himself and his offspring; his salvation, like
that of many other settlers, awaited the message of his own
son.

During a brief respite in the Western revivals, Charles
returned to Henderson, and in answer to his father's greet-
ing at the gate, he replied, "I am well, father, body and
soul. But, father, you are an old man; all your children
are grown up and have left your house; and I never heard a
prayer in my father's house" (MF, p. 29). In response, "the
old man, " in a pattern that was to be repeated in Finney's
revivals, "dropped his head, and burst into tears." Finney
had "broken down" his own father. The energy of independence, the fierce autonomy, had proven an inadequate defense
against the hidden accumulation of shame and guilt, exposed
by the light of "evangelical law." Rebecca Finney joined in
the ensuing time of prayer; "and in a very short time there-
after they were both hopefully converted" (MF, p. 30). The
son had brought both his parents through a new birth. It
would be difficult to imagine more impressive evidence of
the authority of his new identity and vocation.

What is the ground of such generative power in the
religious message Finney brought first to the settlements?
The answer lies in understanding the two-fold crisis that
emigration posed for the conscience of the early settlers:
in religious terms, the problem is apostasy; in psychological terms, it is the conflict between initiative and guilt.

Apostasy

Sylvester Finney, like many others in his generation of
displaced Yankees, suffered from a divided mind. On the one
hand, they retained, at least, vestigial respect for traditional Calvinist beliefs in the absolute sovereignty of God
and the total impotence of human beings to achieve any good
on their own--in short, the faith of their Puritan fore-
bears. On the other hand, they could not avoid feeling an

intense pride in their own strength and resolution that had
enabled them to achieve a very great deal of good indeed.
The conflict was intensified, in many cases, by the realization that they had, for the sake of ambition, forsaken home
and family in the East. Had their bold initiative and proud
insistence on autonomy led them to transgress the limits of
decency and piety? Passing by the meeting house which some
of the more devout had established, the thoughtful emigrant
might well be reminded of a tearful parent in Connecticut,
or hear the threatening rumble of the Lord coming over the
Berkshires from Massachusetts.[19]

For many of them anxiety over the conflict between
individual will and traditional order was nothing new for
they had been in New England during the revivals of the
1790's. In that phase of the Second Great Awakening, "the
young were torn between an outmoded Calvinism and deistic
infidelity."[20] The intellectual challenge was met in a
straight forward manner by the likes of Timothy Dwight, the
newly established president of Yale, who defeated in public
debate the skeptics among the student body. But the practical challenge was not so easily turned aside. For the heart
of skepticism beat on, even after its mind had been momen-
tarily subdued; at its heart was a passionate conviction
that individual freedom of thought and expression should not
be conditioned by any authority other than one's reason
itself. It is not surprising that all guardians of established order should assume that skepticism and anarchy, hand
in hand, were threatening to go on a moral rampage. Richard
Birdsall notes that, in the period immediately preceding the
Second Awakening, there had been growing concern among orthodox clergymen and Federal politicians over the "post-revolutionary trend toward a looser, more individualistic society" and its threat to the stability of the social order and
the coherence of national aims.

The liberals in both religion and politics, of course,
dismissed the rhetoric of the disintegration of American
society as the predictably exaggerated fears of "fevered
imaginations."

These liberals would have found much to applaud in
Adam Smith's idea that if people would all pursue
their private interests, the public interest would
take care of itself. They would have subscribed
also to that aspect of the common law which implied that society as a corporate entity did not
exist but was merely the sum of John Does and
Richard Roes. Laissez-faire, not the "union of
hearts" in a community of worship, was the proper
goal for politics. The great task of the age was
to free the individual from a too restrictive
social and moral order.[21]

Birdsall argues that the revivals themselves "can best be
seen as a kind of revolt against a social system that made
demands on people far beyond any personal commitment they
felt to it and against a religion grown too institutional-
ized and secured."[22] The result of conversion was to release the individual from "the broad and somewhat abstract
social pattern of the formal law" and initiate him into a
new "community of belief in which he was encouraged to make
a decision that would be a positive organizing principle for
his own life."[23]

The problem was how to provide institutional forms in
New England for the egalitarian movements of the early
nineteenth century, among which the revival was foremost,
corresponding to the Calvinist Church and the Federalist
State of the late eighteenth century. Birdsall concludes
that the voluntary associations for reform provided

new institutions that were attuned to democracy,
capitalism, and nationalism. The Second Great
Awakening remains the moment of institutional and
ideological flux out of which grew the characteristic liberal-protestant-bourgeois synthesis of
nineteenth-century America.[24]

But it was also a "moment" in which many chose to absent
themselves from the drama of New England life.

The emigrants left precisely at the time of intense spiritual renewal; whatever their needs or desires, they were fulfilled by neither the old wineskins of the established order nor the new wine of revival ferment. For the emigrants in western New York, faced with the demanding labor of the field and forest, and widely separated from one another, neither the righteous company of reform societies nor the intimate communion of revived congregations could serve as adequate institutional safeguards of their private opinions or public order. A historian of the time noted that, unlike the pilgrims in New England, the settlers in western New York were not forced into compact villages for the sake of safety. They were at peace with the Indians and set out, family by family, to locate in the most favorable places. "In many instances a single family lived at a distance of some miles from any other family for a year or tow. Under these circumstances, it was not practicable to form religious societies."[25] For the earliest of the settlers, like Sylvester Finney, their removal in effect was a voluntary withdrawal from both the theological system and the cultural order of New England. The emigration itself, then, was an admission that for them, New England had not proven to be the promised land. The God of the covenant, in whose name the Puritans had run their "errand into the wilderness" of the New World, had not rewarded their children with prosperity. Now those "sons of the Pilgrims" had taken their destinies into their own hands. In religious terms, their movement west was "apostasy" from the land, and the God, of their fathers.

As in any large-scale movement, the motives for emigration were mixed. Hotchkin's judgement, certainly supported by common sense, is that "emigrants to Western New York were generally drawn thither by a regard to temporal circumstances," particularly cheap land and an expanding market. Some "were moved by a spirit of romance," while some demonstrated "that one principal object in their removal was to get rid of the restraints which civil law and public sentiment, connected with religious institutions, imposed upon them in the Eastern States from which they emigrated." The

connection between law and religious institutions was
rightly perceived; often the first community building in a
village was a meeting house, the visible symbol of the
civilizing power the settlers intended to bring to bear upon
the wilderness and, at least in a formal way, upon their own
lives. Within this mixed multitude, some were "openly irreligious," and usually not too accepting of other institutional restraints either; but many were merely "thoughtless
on the subject of religion, immersed in the concerns of this
life, and regardless of the institution of the Gospel,"
although under the pressure of revival preaching, "they
would acknowledge a belief in the reality and importance of
Christianity."[26] In fact, as Cross fully documents, the
missionaries sent out from New England, especially Connecticut, worked hard at keeping the Yorker conscience tender.
As a result,

> An overwhelming majority of western New Yorkers
> sympathized with the churches and attended meet-
> ings regularly. Relatively few, however, "profes-
> sed" religion, attended Communion, or belonged in
> a legal or religious sense to the church proper.[27]

Though they did not publicly testify to faith themselves, this "allied population" provided a great deal of
financial support for religious activities, especially Sabbath instruction for their children. Thus the Yorkers
worked out their own, typically commercial, version of the
Half Way Covenant. Like nominal Christians in all ages they
invested heavily in the social morality and visible equip-
ment of the church, even though their deposits of theology
and piety were embarrassingly low.[28]

The ambivalence of the settlers toward religious matters is clearly illustrated in the autobiography of Thomas
Sheardown, a Baptist itinerant from England who settled in
central New York in 1826:

> Perhaps there never was a more friendly, congenial
> class of people, than those who became settlers on

> that new tract. Although most of them were uncon-
> verted people, yet they were a kind, frank,
> sympathetic class of men and women. Aristocracy
> was unknown . . . and seldom had an evening gath-
> ering but that religion was a topic of conver-
> sation.[29]

He notes particularly the "tender love" of the women for
their children, clearly moved by the degree to which these
people preserved the moral values of traditional Christian
civilization, while not professing a personal commitment to
the gospel. One imagines that Sheardown was a welcome
addition to their company, allowing the topic of religion,
which was never entirely absent from their memory, to be
introduced into their conversation. The Baptist minister
had apparently not yet learned to bring pressure to bear
upon their consciences in the way the Presbyterian missionaries from New England did. Whereas the Methodist circuit riders and Baptist lay exhorters developed adaptive
strategies in both message and means for evangelizing folks
on the frontier, the Presbyterians and Congregationalists
sought to move, essentially unchanged, both the form and
substance of New England church life westward. Thus the
most prominent symbol of Calvinist continuity in the settlements was the educated minister himself, who reminded the
emigrants of their Sunday School lessons.

The settlers who had learned their theology early in
Massachusetts and Connecticut had been taught that mere
civil virtue was not sufficient to earn the favor of the
Almighty and that the damnable corruption of the soul could
not be forever disguised by the pleasant outward appearance
of good works. To "own the covenant" aright required "visible sainthood," specifically, public testimony to an experience of saving grace, sustained prayer, and evident holiness
of life.[30] It was a lesson they did not wholly believe, nor
could they entirely ignore.

It is important to understand that the covenant which
God makes with his people, in Puritan theology, is not a

contract between equally responsible partners in a transaction, whose fulfillment depends upon both parties keeping
its conditions, but a unilateral promise which God makes to
those he has chosen. Although the waywardness of either the
old or the new Israel might delay the fulfillment of the
covenant by transgressing its terms, the saint can take
comfort from the faith that the promises of God are finally
inviolable. As St. Paul assured his Gentile converts in
Rome regarding the election of Israel, "the gifts and calling of God are without repentance." God will never change
his mind about what he has done or what he has promised. In
the fragile conditions of their existence, threatened by
disease, famine, and the resentful native occupants of the
land, the colonists found a solid rock of consolation in the
belief that the sovereign Lord himself guaranteed the meaningfulness of their hopes, their labors, and their terrible
sacrifices. Their confidence in God, their dependence upon
his deliverance, was in direct proportion to their sense of
vulnerability and weakness.[31] The correlation was as much
theological as psychological for the Bible is a book written
by, and for, endangered minorities.

Yet there is also, in the language of covenant, a
recognition that, as God has spoken, humans at least have
listened to his words, and as God has acted, humans at least
have praised his deeds. The "man-ward" side of the covenant
came more clearly into focus as the daunting mission of the
Pilgrims began to appear more manageable to later generations, and the marvelous obscurity of the divine sovereign
was increasingly illumined by reason and law.[32] If the
covenant is seen less as a terrible wonder, calling for
strenuous self-denial, and more as a reasonable compact,
allowing for the greatest amount of self-fulfillment within
the limits of moral government, then the legitimate basis of
social order is a system of laws by which the actions of God
and humans can be intelligibly directed. Understood in this
way, law supplants covenant as the mediating term between
God and his people; the ideal form of society is no longer
theocracy, but nomocracy.

Thus, while the settlers were beginning to break away
from the theology of New England, they could not survive
without some basis of cultural order. The fact was not lost
on those who labored in western New York to lay "deep and
broad foundations for a religious community." The report of
the American Home Missionary Society of 1835 claims
considerable success in building civil order on a spiritual
base:

> The society has done much to promote the virtue,
> intelligence, and consequent prosperity of this
> part of the state, and to make it a delightful
> residence for the Christian, and for the lover of
> order.[33]

The statement is remarkable not only as a boast of sanctified ambition, but also as a recognition of the allied
interests of both Christians and the irreligious in maintaining the love of order. Inasmuch as the settlers sought
to build a new community, then, they carried with them into
the forests and valleys the same concern for civil order the
Pilgrims brought to the coastline of New England--but with a
very great difference. The settlers were substituting their
own laws for the legislation of the theocracy, and exercising their own autonomy rather than submitting to the
divinely sanctioned order of things.

The problem was how to balance the two sides of the
covenant so that human responsibility could be acknowledged
as an authentic condition of religious life. Could the
settlers find new terms in the law for their relationship
with God to replace the unilateral covenant between the
sovereign Lord and his elect? Clearly they could not construct a new civilization without either establishing some
new ground rules with the Deity or abandoning the faith of
their fathers altogether and accepting the threatened consequence of "apostasy."

The crisis, furthermore, was not only theological. It
is also helpful to think of the problem in the psychological

terms of Erik Erikson, as the tension between autonomy and initiative, on the one hand, and shame, doubt, and guilt, on the other. The settlers had struck out into the wilderness, leaving fathers and the Father behind, and now they were faced with the anxiety of being "on their own," risking the loss of order and authority which the parental tradition of Calvinism offered.[34]

Initiative

In his outline of the "eight ages of man" Erik Erikson offers a heuristic diagram of the "psycho-social" development of the individual.[35] The hyphenated adjective emphasizes what is the genius of Erikson's modification of Freudian theory, viz., the insistence that psychological development is integrally bound up with the individual's participation in the institutions of society.[36] The stage of development to which Erikson has given greatest attention in his studies of youth, particularly of the "young man Luther" is that in which the individual faces the crisis of "identity versus role confusion." The resolution of this crisis in "the healthy personality" finds concrete social form in the choice of vocation. Erikson describes this crisis of identity as the process in which the individual makes a selection among the variety of images of the self (and of the world) with which he or she is confronted. The selection calls for commitment to the expression of a coherent image of the world in an "ideology." Thus identity and ideology are "two aspects of the same process" which provides "a coherent, if systematically over-simplified, over-all orientation in space and time."[37]

The basic problem which arises in the formation of identity is the question of fidelity: what can be trusted, and what proves trustworthy, as a guide of action? The primary desire of reflective young people is to find a rationally consistent and emotionally satisfying understanding of what it means to be a responsible agent in a "universe," that is, in a complex but ordered system of reality.

(There is, of course, a certain ambivalence in this desire
inasmuch as the adolescent mind often resists all premature
attempts by society to give it answers or to assign it
limits, and sometimes runs to the paradoxical extreme of
total fanaticism.)

Erikson, properly recognizing the inadequacy of a chart
of sequential stages to grasp the complexity of human matur-
ation, points out that in the crisis of identity one or more
of the earlier crises may represent unresolved conflicts
which again become the focus of attention. This recurrence
is especially true of the first three crises, which he calls
"basic trust versus mistrust," "autonomy versus shame," and
"initiative versus guilt." These categories emerged from
Erikson's work with children, but he insists that "every
adult carries these conflicts with him in the recesses of
his personality."[38] The conflicts surface in different
ways, according to the mystery of individuality; but there
is a demonstrable parallel between the type of crisis which
is most significant in early adulthood and the ideas and
values--in short, the "ideology"--which one accepts as a
trustworthy interpretation of reality.

Further, the ideology that one acknowledges as a faithful articulation of the new sense of identity will quite
likely reflect an interest in the social institution which
provides a means of resolving the recurrent crisis. For
example, as Erikson argued in the case of Martin Luther, one
who has never fully established a sense of "basic trust" in
the world, and in himself, finds the recapturing of such
trust the central question in his crisis of identity.[39]
Since religion is the social institution that offers to the
individual a sense of trust in an infallible Provider, it is
appropriate that Luther would turn to theology for the
resources to renew his faith, in himself and the world.

For Finney, however, theology is more modified by,
rather than a source of aid in, the resolution of the crisis
of identity. By the time of his conversion, at age twenty-
nine, he had already weathered the storms of "role

confusion" and chosen an image of the self and a role in
society from among the alternatives which his education and
interests offered. That he had, four years earlier, decided
to enter the "fraternity" of lawyers suggests that his
crisis of identity involved a struggle with the question of
moral agency and the legitimate forms and limits of autono-
mous action. That is, Finney's crisis of identity involved
what Erikson calls the second and third "ages of man."
Thus, in its resolution, Finney utilized the strength and
direction of the social institution appropriate to the problem of autonomy: the law.

Erikson has suggested,

The lasting need of the individual to have his
will reaffirmed and delineated within an adult
order of things which at the same time reaffirms
and delineates the will of others has an institutional safeguard in the principles of law and
order. In daily life as well as in the high
courts of law--domestic and international--this
principle apportions to each his privileges and
his limitations, his obligations and his rights.
. . . Thus the sense of autonomy . . . serves (and
is served by) the preservation in economic and
political life of a sense of justice.[40]

This concern to establish the limits of acceptable
behavior arises in early childhood. The child seeks a way
to exercise his or her own will--"holding on or letting
go"--without feeling "exposed" as an ungrateful rebel
against the authorities which had hitherto defined the
limits of conduct. Such shame may be accompanied by a
profound uncertainty about one's own trustworthiness as an
independent agent. The problem is exacerbated when the
individual begins not only to exercise independent control
over his or her own body, but also to initiate "intrusive"
action into the bodies, or space, of others. At this point,
the individual becomes aware (perhaps painfully so) of the
restrictions on conduct which the area of the other imposes.

With the obligations of territorial limits comes the full
development of conscience. St. Paul, who was no mean
observer of the human condition, noted long ago that it is
the knowledge of the limits of conduct which awakens moral
consciousness:

> . . . except through law I should never have
> become acquainted with sin. For example, I should
> never have known what it was to covet, if the law
> had not said, 'Thou shalt not covet' [Romans 7:7,
> N.E.B.]

It is important to note here--especially since St. Paul
is often misrepresented as overlooking the point--that law
presents to the conscience a knowledge of right, as well as
of wrong. The law of God has a positive use, as theologians
have long insisted, in directing one in the path of righteousness, in addition to forbidding one's walking in the way
of the ungodly. It is the duty of society to support its
newly matured members by governing in a way that encourages
morality, as well as punishes vice. At the very least,
civil legislation ought to provide the legitimation of certain exercises of constructive energy.

Thus law in the social order can provide a satisfactory
means of encouraging the autonomy and initiative necessary
for the growth of "healthy personality," without the shame
and doubt which accompanies action in the absence of clear
guidelines, and without the guilt that arises from an exaggerated conscience which questions the legitimacy of every
independent action.

What is proposed here is that Charles Finney's choice
of the law as a vocation is a strong indication that the
crises which Erikson describes as the second and third "ages
of man" were central to his search for a satisfying sense of
identity. The evidence is admittedly scarce for an analysis
of Finney's "psycho-social" development; but such as is
available clearly points in this direction. Inasmuch as

these crises seem also to constitute the central concerns of
his contemporaries, Finney's successful resolution of them
in his own experience makes available an interpretation of
personal identity which rings true to what Calvin Colton
called "the public mind."[41]

The question of shame and doubt confronted the Yorker
each time he attended meeting and was reminded, by the
minister who had also emigrated from New England, of his
"apostasy." Thus, when a preacher appeared in the wilderness with a version of Christian faith that reconciled the
language of the Bible with the language of moral agency and
legal order, and whose theology interpreted spiritual life
in terms of that universal law which supported both the
civil and religious orders of civilized society, the settlers were prepared to listen. In his own experience, and
in his preaching, Charles Finney accomplished the momentous
feat of establishing individual initiative, under law, as
religious value. An eyewitness of Finney's early revivals
reported that

> his intellectual force attracted many citizens who
> would not have listened to a less gifted expounder
> of the divine law. His exposition of that law was
> original and bold . . . in the religious world he
> inaugurated a brief reign of terror. His stern
> methods were oftentimes as necessary as they were
> wholesome; but it was a singular fact that among
> those whose hearts most failed them for fear were
> found many who had adorned years of religious
> profession by lives unspotted from the world.[42]

The lesson is clear: for those who pass through the terrors
of the law the narrow, but well-marked, path to righteousness is opened.

For Finney, and those among whom he first exercised
religious leadership, the knowledge of the laws of divine
government provided the assurance that God not only

tolerates human initiative, but encourages and directs it.
A theology of legal order defines the rules by which people
can exercise their potentially anarchic freedom without
incurring guilt or running the risk of spiritual and civil
chaos. In the most general terms Finney replaced covenant
with law as the "root metaphor" of the Protestant world
view. The implications of the shift are many and reach far
beyond the somewhat special circumstances of those early
"infant settlements." The generation of New Englanders
whose minds were early steeped in the condemnatory phrases
of Puritan Calvinism were everywhere beginning to replace
heroic faith in the threatening Unknown with a hearty acceptance of reasonable duties, as defined by a system of laws.

Law

The villages of Jefferson and Oneida counties, in the early
nineteenth century, were neither frontier outposts nor
cities, but groups of families who were "settling down" in
the process of becoming civilized again. Their problem, in
the words of Sidney Mead, was that of transforming "eager
pioneers" into "settlers," people who recognized that "human
freedom must work itself out within the context of stable,
traditional patterns."[43] The settlers had a keen interest
in the power of the law to secure the unruly space they were
prepared to occupy and to legitimate their aggressive intrusion into that space. As the historian Anton-Hermann
Chroust commented, the founders of the early settlements
were "thoughtful, earnest, and independent people who not
only possessed a natural genius for self-government, but
also recognized the necessity as well for the authority of
law and order."[44]

Although viewed with some suspicion by the more rugged
adventurers, the law provided the social institution by
which the values of personal initiative and communal order
could be balanced to the relative satisfaction of all parties. Thus, despite the primitive settings of the early
courts and the intemperate habits of judges and counsellors

alike,[45] the use of, and respect for, the judicial system
rose steadily in the early nineteenth century.[46] What complaints there were among the populace in "the age of Jackson" were mainly directed at the lawyers themselves and
reflected a general suspicion of the vested interests of any
professional class. When Stanley Matthews addressed the
State Bar Association of New York on the inspiring subject,
"The Function of the Legal Profession in the Progress of
Civilization," he ruefully acknowledged that the "common
opinion" of the legal system was that it is

> a science, if one at all, intricate, complex, and
> hard to understand, full of uncertainties, confu-
> sions, and contradictions; a trap for the unwary;
> a net whose meshes are strong enough to catch only
> small fish, while the strong break through and
> escape.[47]

Further, not only did the law seem to lend itself sometimes
to unjust manipulations, it also seemed to serve the social
and financial ambitions of the members of the bar, who kept
its inner secrets tightly wrapped in language known only to
the initiated.[48]

Yet for all the distrust of attorneys and their arcane
jargon, the settlers could not organize the new space which
they occupied without recourse to the social institution of
law and order. They resented any intrusion on their freedom
to move through their space, yet survival required a means
of settling disputes over claims. The settlers of the Pike
River Valley in southeastern Wisconsin, for example, found
it necessary to organize a Claimants Union in 1836 in order
to secure

> . . . those homes, to obtain which we left our
> friends, deprived ourselves of the many blessings
> and privileges of society, have borne the expen-
> ses, and encountered the hardships of a perilous
> journey, advancing into a space beyond the bounds
> of civilization, and having the many difficulties

> and obstructions of a state of nature to overcome,
> and on the peaceable possession of which our all
> is depending.[49]

In these phrases can be detected the transition from the
interests of the pioneer to the concerns of the settler:
the chaotic "space" beyond the defining, but confining,
forms of the civilizing imagination is now claimed and
bounded for the purposes of "peaceable possession." In the
words of Sidney Mead, the pioneer character was shaped by a
sense of "space---organic, pragmatic space--the space of
action," whereas the settler accepted the responsibility of
establishing historical continuity within a given space.[50]
In order to establish that continuity, the settlers employed
the ancient instrument of civilization that had regulated
the possession of the cramped area of Western Europe for
centuries: the law.

    In the "wide open spaces" of nineteenth-century Amer-
ica, however, law was used not only to establish a static
balance of energies as in Europe, but also to legitimate and
promote individual initiative. In this "formative era of
American law" Roscoe Pound concludes that juridical thought
"regards state and law as existing only to guarantee the
security and development of the individual." Indeed, American theorists drew from "the nineteenth-century historical-
metaphysical thinking which puts free individual self-assertion as the end of the legal order."[51] James Hurst discovers two working principles in the use of law in this
period:

> (1) the legal order should protect and promote the
> release of individual creative energy to the
> greatest extent compatible with the broad sharing
> of opportunity for such expression . . . (2) the
> legal order should mobilize the resources of the
> community to help shape an environment which would
> give men more liberty by increasing the practical
> range of choices open to them and minimizing the
> limiting force of circumstances.[52]

The purpose of the legal order, to the mind of western
settlers and eastern capitalists alike, was to enhance the
individual's creative energies; the law was a resource which
society provided for its more ambitious members "to bring
things about." Hurst concludes from his research that "in
this country the nineteenth-century legal order emphasized
individualism, in contrast to a sharper eighteenth-century
concern for the integrity of the community. To the nineteenth century liberty meant liberty for individuals."[54]

It must be remembered, however, that the happy premise
of most nineteenth-century thought was that, rightly guided,
individual creativity would in the long run serve the best
interests of the social whole. What is good for the individual is good for the country. Accordingly, the laws of
this period exhibit "a characteristic pattern of time preference in favor of a quick tempo of change so long as it
seemed to promise rapid growth."[55] Those who succeeded were
encouraged to flourish on the assumption that everyone bene-
fitted in a situation where as many as possible prospered.
The underlying premise, of course, was that human nature is
fundamentally good and needs only to be allowed to fulfill
its potential for virtue and industry, with as few restrictions as possible.

Thus, even though laws were enacted ostensibly to
"restrain the vicious," as George Ritter, a St. Louis attorney wrote,[56] in fact the legal system served to encourage
entrepreneurs and adventurers in their pursuit of the American dream: a life that is righteous and profitable at the
same time. They enthusiastically accepted the task of civilizing space and sanctifying time in the new world: property claims and Sabbath laws were both part of the grand
ambition to achieve a peaceful and holy legacy for their
children. Ritter quotes the old maxim, "order is Heaven's
first law," and earnestly informs his audience that "it
becomes our Christian duty to obey the laws of our country,
for the welfare of society." While such sentiments could
reflect the stolid conservatism one finds behind later calls

for "law and order," the legal system of the early nineteenth century was quite liberal in its allowance of individual initiative in the name of national progress.

Such liberality was as consistent with the settlers' intentions as with the ambitions of their city cousins. The bright hopes and progressive spirit of the time is recalled with enthusiasm by James Fairchild in his account of the building of the colony at Oberlin in central Ohio. In the beginning the site was "an unbroken wilderness, but the restless energy and aggressive habits in crowding back the forests and cutting high-ways to neighboring towns" soon rearranged every feature of the landscape, except a small grove of trees "under which Fathers Shiperd and Pease [founders of the colony] first knelt to pray; and that was preserved simply as the connecting link between the old and the new." Certainly in Fairchild's time "the conservatism of older societies, found here no material or scope."

> To pull down the old and build anew, was the only work at hand . . . the men who undertook such an enterprise, was strongly impressed with the conviction that the world was capable of improvement, and they had strong faith that they should live to see it move.[57]

As Charles Cole says, what was characteristic of Americans "in this age was their boundless optimism, their faith in the future and their assumption, common to the Western world of the nineteenth century, of an inevitable progress."[58] Indeed, the entire fabric of American life in this period was woven with deep confidence in human power and virtue. Progressive legislation, egalitarian politics, laissez-faire economic theory, evangelical religion, and the millennial hope in the destiny of America to assume the moral leadership of the world--all are rooted in the faith that history will reward the diligent, whether in commerce or piety.[59] It was a civic faith shared by populist and capitalist, farmer, craftsman, and shopkeeper; and it found

institutional form in laws which allowed for the greatest
possible freedom of opportunity. The widespread enthusiasm
for individual liberty was not the peculiar possession of
any particular political party, nor was it incompatible with
a conservative interest in legal order, nor did it flourish
only in the mildly anarchic conditions of the wilderness.
From the settlements to the expanding cities, there was
growing demand for both egalitarian politics and more liberal legal codes.[60] The two interests are perfectly harmonious, for the law was regarded primarily as an instrument
best-suited to help the industrious, the talented, and the
lucky "bring things about." Indeed, it is the widespread
faith in, and use of, the law as a means of directing and
encouraging individual initiative which serves as the common
denominator for the various audiences which responded to
revival preachers like Finney.[61]

If the analysis thus far is correct, then it might be
expected that Finney's greatest success would be among those
people, with a strong New England heritage, who enjoyed
sufficient status and power to achieve the aims they set
themselves. In the settlements such a description applies
to whole villages of self-reliant and self-governing emigrants, the solid folk who built Brownville, Rutland, Rome,
Auburn, and many other towns awakened to religious concerns
in Finney's early revivals. In the cities, where he found
larger, but more selective, audiences, Finney drew his converts largely from those in professional classes of society,
as he often notes in his Memoirs. While he claims that this
effect was a deliberate "measure" to convert the leaders of
a community first so that others of lower station would be
persuaded to follow their example, it is also clear that it
was precisely the educated and enterprising who had the
greatest stake in a religious vision which supported individual initiative within the familiar and stabilizing framework of "moral law."

Paul Johnson, in his admirable study of Finney's
revival in Rochester in 1830-31, demonstrates that the
greatest gains in converts were among master craftsmen, with

ambitions of owning their own shops; grocers and forwarding
merchants, who supplied the fiscal fuel for various reform
causes; lawyers, most of whom were also politicians ("and in
the 1830's resistance to the churches was political
suicide"); and "urban entrepreneurs who retained the social
practices and moral vision of village storekeepers."[62] All
of these were people whose aims could best be fulfilled in
stable and ordered communities; their business was conducted
on a co-operative basis, and they frowned on "ungoverned
personal ambition." The greatest problem they faced was the
loss of social control over the transient and intemperate
labor force from which they were increasingly alienated in
the movement from a household economy to the development of
little factories. Finney's preaching of "evangelical law"
as the basis of a just and happy society provided a religious solution to their social-political problem: owners and
workers together should voluntarily submit to the values of
sobriety and hard work proclaimed in the revival and
approved by God himself. The revival, then, while calling
for the radical inversion of personal values, at the same
time firmly grounded the social order, in which those values
were to be realized, in immutable divine law. Thus, there
is a curious mixture in revival preaching of the rhetoric of
revolutionary change and the platitudes of traditional
morality.

This productive partnership of law and religion had
been formed early in the western revivals. As William
Warren Sweet observed, even before the settlers arrived the
evangelical churches had been working to establish law and
order; thus revivalism was the lone representative of civilization in the unsettled areas. In what Sweet called the
struggle of "barbarism versus revivalism," the churches
often served as "frontier moral courts."[63] The churches
proclaimed certain principles of community life in preparation for the system of civil laws developed by the settlers.
In Finney's preaching the long engagement between religion
and law was consummated in a most fruitful marriage. His
commanding intellect, dramatic but restrained style, and his

stern emphasis on responsibility conveyed to his hearers an
impression of authority and respectability equalled only by
the sobering dignity of the courtroom.   When Finney announced the terms of God's government, the settlers, who had
already learned the necessity and benefits of temporal government, recognized that he was speaking their language.
Their astounding welcome of Finney's revisions of the theology of the Westminster Confession is in part an expression
of relieved gratitude for a religious position that allowed
them to retain their faith in God along with a high sense of
their own worth and abilities.   It was a relief felt also by
their contemporaries in the cities, whose loyalty to the
faith of Puritan New England was strained to the breaking
point by the demands and opportunities of a social order
based on individual freedom.

The key to resolving the crisis of conscience is the
emphasis new theologians like Taylor and Finney placed on
law as calling forth and dependably regulating human will.
By obedience to God's moral government the provisions of
which were detailed but reasonable, one could exercise initiative boldly in both spiritual and temporal affairs, free
from shame and guilt.   Far from apostasy, such action is
precisely what God requires of the faithful.

NOTES

1.   Jonathan Blanchard, "A Perfect State of Society,"
address before the "Society of Inquiry" in Oberlin Collegiate Institute, September 3, 1839 (Oberlin: James Steele,
1839), p. 11.

2.   Edwin Starbuck, The Psychology of Religion: An
Empirical Study of the Growth of Religious Consciousness
(New York: Charles Scribner's Sons, 1901).   Hillel Schwartz
offers evidence to suggest that even if the majority of
converts were not, in fact, teen-agers, the general expectation of both the revivalists and their opponents was that
the sudden conversions in revivals would manifest the contrary emotions of youth.   The revivalists sought to arouse

those emotions--"Were not the conflicts and paradoxes of
youth but a poor metaphor for the straits of the sinner
before God?"--then settle the convert into a life of "greater constancy and maturity." Opponents of revivals "refused
to become part of a 'machinery' that evoked the supposedly
in-between position of the adolescent, for fear of having to
cope with the contrary and sexual emotions of youth"
[Schwartz, "Adolescence and Revivals in Ante-bellum Boston,"
Journal of Religious History 8 (December 1974), 144-158].
Schwartz draws heavily from the various excitements, insani-
ties, suicides, associated with the work of the Baptist
intinerant, Elder Knapp. There is much less unsavory effect
in Finney's case because the antidote he offered for the
anxieties and tensions his preaching evoked was the strict
control of "evangelical law." Further, he did not encourage
inquirers to undergo protracted periods of despondency, but
to enter the glad ranks of the committed immediately.

3. In the census of 1790, two heads of families with
the name Finney appear in the list for Warren: Sylvester
and Jonah. Sylvester records six free white females, one
free white male over the age of sixteen and no free white
males under sixteen. Sylvester lists no slaves, but there
were only six in the whole town. At the time of his birth,
then, Charles had five sisters. See Heads of Families at
the First Census of the United States Taken in the Year
1790: Connecticut (Washington: Government Printing Office,
1908).

4. Thomas F. Gordon, Gazetteer of the State of New
York (Philadelphia: Collins, 1836), p. 567.

5. Cross, The Burned-over District, p. 6.

6. John W. Barber and Henry Howe, Historical Collections of the State of New York (New York: S. Tuttle, 1842),
p. 360.

7. James H. Hotchkin, A History of the Purchase and
Settlement of Western New York, and the Rise, Progress, and
Present State of the Presbyterian Church in That Section
(New York: M. W. Dodd, 1848), p. 25.

8. Pomroy Jones, Annals and Recollections of Oneida
County (Rome, 1851), p. 782.

9. Jones, Annals, p. 782.

10. <u>Ibid.</u>, p. 783.

11. <u>Ibid.</u>, p. 735.

12. Hotchkin, <u>History of the Purchase and Settlement of Western New York</u>, p. 26.

13. Gordon, <u>Gazetteer</u>, p. 193.

14. <u>Ibid.</u>, p. 197.

15. Levi Beardsley, <u>Reminiscences: personal and other incidents: early settlement of Ostego county; notices and anecdotes of public men; judicial, legal, and legislative matters: field sports: dissertations and discussions</u> (New York: Charles Vinten, 1852), p. 65.

16. Levi Beardsley recalled that in those days school teachers were accorded high respect and the best accommodations by the folks in the settlements with whom they boarded: "In truth, the master and mistress were regarded as distinguished personages" (<u>Reminiscences</u>, p. 58).

17. Cf. James E. Johnson, "Charles G. Finney and a Theology of Revivalism," <u>Church History</u> 38 (September 1969), 343: "From most accounts of his early life it does not appear that Finney received any teaching regarding theological issues from his family background--this in spite of the fact that some felt that he was by nature 'unusually susceptible to moral and religious impressions,' and that susceptibility must have been fostered to some extent 'by the Puritan notions which came with the family from their New England home.'" Johnson is quoting here from an article by Hiram Mead in the <u>Congregational Quarterly</u> (January 1877).

18. Henderson was located on Hungry Bay in Lake Ontario and provided harborage for ships up to one hundred tons. Sackett's Harbor, ten miles north, was the scene of several vigorous battles with the British in 1813-14 not long after the Finneys' arrival. "After the declaration of war this spot became an important military and naval position." Also, "a considerable trade is carried on here by the lake and St. Lawrence river and by the Oswego, Erie, and Welland canals" (Barber and Howe, <u>Historical Collections</u>, pp. 202-203).

19. Pomroy Jones captures something of the mood in one anecdote. "A portion of the first settlers were not very strict in their observance of the Lord's Day, and a number

of them used to congregate on this day . . . to talk over
the news of the day, etc. Two lads, of about fourteen years
old, took a rather novel way to cure the evil." Concealing
themselves in the thick foliage of a tall pine, the boys
took "testament in hand," and "in a loud but sepulchral
tone, commenced reading from the sacred volume texts against
the desecration of the day," with an occasional "admonition
to desist from the bad example they were setting their
children. The hearers strained their optics to see from
whence came the warnings, but no discovery was made. They,
however, very soon left, and the cure was most perfect"
(Annals, pp. 241f.).

20. William G. McLoughlin, Revivals, Awakenings, and
Reform: An Essay on Religion and Social Change, 1607-1977
(University of Chicago Press, 1978), p. 109.

21. Richard D. Birdsall, "The Second Great Awakening
and the New England Social Order," Church History 39 (1970),
351.

22. Ibid., 355.

23. Ibid., 357.

24. Ibid., 363.

25. Hotchkin, History of the Purchase and Settlement
of Western New York, pp. 24f.

26. Ibid., p. 26.

27. Cross, The Burned-over District, p. 41.

28. Henry O'Reilly, writing in 1838, indignantly rejected British warning that the Western settlements were
threatened with moral anarchy because they had forsaken "law
and gospel." On the contrary, he maintained that the settlers retained the ideals and values of their fathers, and
adduced as proof the rapid increase in "the PERFECTION OF
SOCIAL INSTITUTIONS" in Rochester since the construction of
the first church in 1815. Settlement in the West. Sketches
of Rochester; with Incidental Notices of Western New-York
(Rochester, N.Y.: William Alling, 1838), p. 277.

29. Thomas S. Sheardown, An Autobiography. Half a
Century's Labors in the Gospel, Including Thirty-Five Years
of Back-Woods' Mission Work and Evangelizing in New York and
Pennsylvania (Philadelphia: O. N. Warden and E. B. Case,
1866), p. 89.

30. See Edmund S. Morgan, Visible Saints: The History
of a Puritan Idea (Ithaca, N.Y.: Cornell University Press,
1963).

31. One of the most dramatic expressions of the sense
of the precariousness of existence and the call for absolute
surrender to God as one's only hope, is the famous sermon of
Jonathan Edwards, preached to a terrified congregation at
Enfield, Connecticut, in 1741, called "Sinners in the Hands
of an Angry God." For perceptive commentaries on Edwards'
rhetoric see Perry Miller, Jonathan Edwards, original edition, 1949 (New York: Delta Books, 1967), pp. 145-147; H.
R. Niebuhr, The Kingdom of God in America, original edition,
1937 (New York: Harper Torchbooks, 1959), pp. 137-139.

32. Cf. William McLoughlin, Modern Revivalism, p. 21:
". . . the generation of settlers to which Finney belonged,
attained manhood in a more settled, prosperous, and confident atmosphere than their parents had faced. Their faith
in man's ability to solve life's problems by himself, and
their growing optimism about the future, made the pessimis-
tic religion which their parents had found strangely satisfying seem singularly unattractive and unreasonable."

33. Quoted in Cross, The Burned-over District, pp.
22f. In general Cross tends to regard the theological
innovations of Finney, as well as those of Beecher and
Taylor, as afterthoughts, following the tumultuous success
of the revivals. My thesis is that Finney, at least, began
his career with a profound interest in order, not disrup-
tion, and that not only he, but the folks who responded to
his preaching, were seeking the security and direction of
regulation more than the anarchic ecstasy of enthusiasm.

34. The conflict was particularly sharp for Presbyterians, for their denomination was the most prominent, with
the strongest ties to traditional Calvinism. "Their membership and allied population having comprised from the start
the best educated, most prosperous, and socially most established class of Yankee emigrants, their assumption of super-
iority was strongly inbred . . . . Their doctrine was the
one historically orthodox in the parent section" (Cross, The
Burned-over District, p. 46).

35. "Growth and Crises of the Healthy Personality," Identity and the Life Cycle, Psychological Issues, I:1 (1959), pp. 50-100. A revised version of the now famous "stages" can be found in Childhood and Society, revised edition (New York: W. W. Norton, 1963), pp. 247-274.

36. Childhood and Society, p. 37: "A human being . . . is at all times an organism, an ego, and a member of a society and is involved in all three processes of organiza-tion . . . . We are speaking of three processes, the somatic process, the ego process, and the societal process."

37. Erik Erikson, Identity: Youth and Crisis (New York: W W. Norton, 1968), p. 188.

38. "Growth and Crises," p. 50.

39. See Young Man Luther: A Study in Psychoanalysis and History (New York: W. W. Norton, 1958).

40. Childhood and Society, p. 254.

41. Colton was a contemporary supporter of revivals who wrote that "the secret" of successful awakenings is the sensitive adaptation of preaching to "the character and temper of the community," that is, to "the exigencies of the public mind" [History and Character of American Revivals (London: Frederick Westley and W. H. Davis, 1832), p. 274]. Finney's career is a dramatic illustration of the truth of Colton's observation.

42. Cited by G. Frederick Wright, Charles Grandison Finney (Cambridge: The Riverside Press, 1891), pp. 59f., from P. H. Fowler, Historical Sketch of Presbyterianism (Utica, 1877).

43. "The American People: Their Space, Time and Relig-ion," p. 251.

44. The Rise of the Legal Profession in America, Volume 2: The Revolution and the Post-Revolutionary Era (Norman: University of Oklahoma Press, 1965), pp. 97f.

45. For representative anecdotes about the early courts, see Levi Beardsley, Reminiscences. Beardsley began his career as an apprentice in 1810, was licensed to prac-tice in the court of equity by the famous Chancellor James Kent, and rose to the presidency of the New York Senate.

46. Perry Miller provides a detailed account of what he calls "the amazing rise, within three or four decades, of

the legal profession from its chaotic condition of around
1870 to a position of political and intellectual domination"
(Life of the Mind in America, Book Two: The Legal Mentality, pp. 99-265).
   47. Annual Address before the State Bar Association
of New York, at Albany, September 20, 1881 (Cincinnati:
Robert Clarke and Co., 1881), pp. 23f.
   48. Charles Warren explained that the "popular odium"
of the legal profession in the early nineteenth century was
due to "the general feeling that the intricacies of special
pleading which made the law so mysterious and unintelligible
to laymen, the technicalities of the old Common Law, and the
jargon of Latin, French and unfamiliar terms in which it was
so often expressed, were all tricks of the trade, designed
and purposely kept in force by the Bar, in order to make
acquisition of a knowledge of the law difficult to the
public, and in order to constitute themselves a privileged
class and monopoly" [A History of the American Bar (Boston:
Little, Brown & Co., 1911), pp. 224f.].
   49. James Willard Hurst, Law and the Conditions of
Freedom in the Nineteenth-Century United States (Madison:
University of Wisconsin Press, 1956), p. 4. Emphasis added.
Stanley Matthews points to the most primitive settlements as
evidence that legal order is the formal expression of the
civilizing power latent even in uncouth social customs:
". . . see how rapidly and completely the unique local
customs of rough and illiterate miners establishing themselves without previous legislative authority upon public
lands became judicially recognized as giving rise to legal
rights and obligations, before they were confirmed by statu-
atory enactments" ("The Function of the Legal Profession in
the Progress of Civilization," p. 27).
   50. "The American People: Their Space, Time and Religion," p. 247.
   51. Roscoe Pound, The Formative Era of American Law
(Boston: Little, Brown, 1938), pp. 18f, 23. The interest
in promoting individual freedom can be found in Blackstone
himself: "that constitution or frame of government, that
system of laws, is alone calculated to maintain civil liberty, which leaves the subject entire master of his own

conduct, except in those points wherein the public good
requires some direction or restraint" [Gareth Jones, ed.,
The Sovereignty of the Law: Selections from Blackstone's
Commentaries on the Laws of England (University of Toronto
Press, 1973), p. 60].

52. Law and the Conditions of Freedom, p. 6.

53. Ibid., pp. 24, 28.

54. Ibid., pp. 36f.

55. Ibid., p. 70.

56. George Ritter, An Essay on the Lawyer and the Law
as a Profession (St. Louis: L. C. Lavat, 1880), p. 10.

57. James H. Fairchild, Oberlin: Its Origin, Progress
and Results. An Address, prepared for the alumni of Oberlin
College, assembled August 22, 1860 (Oberlin: Shankland and
Harmon, 1860), p. 18.

58. Charles C. Cole, The Social Ideas of the Northern
Evangelists, 1826-1860 (New York: Columbia University
Press, 1954), p. 11.

59. Cf. William G. McLoughlin, ed., "Introduction" to
The American Evangelicals, 1800-1900 (New York: Harper
Torchbook, 1968), p. 1.

60. Lee Benson has demonstrated in painstaking detail
that the major political parties in New York State both
"accepted egalitarianism as the ideology of the Good Society," and that it is, therefore, misleading to attribute the
promotion of individual liberty exclusively to the "Jackson
party" [The Concept of Jacksonian Democracy: New York as a
Test Case (New York: Atheneum Press, 1964), p. 336]. Consequently, even though the revivalists emphasized individual
freedom of choice, it is not satisfactory simply to identify
revivalism as the religious expression of "Jacksonian democracy," as William McLoughlin tends to do. Leonard Sweet
has stated the issue bluntly with respect to Finney. "The
long-standing attempt to make a man who refused to vote
Jacksonian a religious representative of Jacksonian democracy needs to be abandoned" ["The View of Man Inherent in
New Measures Revivalism," Church History 45:2 (June 1976),
221].

61. Edward Pessen notes that Finney attracts followers
among both the pragmatic and individualist "populace" of the

age of Jackson, and also the professional and commercial classes of the urban areas who were anti-Jacksonian in politics [Jacksonian America: Society, Personality and Politics (Homewood, Ill.: The Dorsey Press, 1969), pp. 75-84].

62. Paul E. Johnson, A Shopkeeper's Millennium: Society and Revivals in Rochester, New York, 1815-1837 (New York: Hill and Wang, 1978).

63. W. W. Sweet, Religion in the Development of American Culture, 1765-1840 (New York: Scribner's, 1952), chapter 5.

Chapter II

THE LEGAL VISION

From his twenty-sixth to his twenty-ninth year Charles Finney was a lawyer, and he never abandoned a primary identification with that vocation. In later years he described his
preaching as akin to the pleading of a counsellor, his
interpretation of the Bible as proceeding in the manner of a
legal brief, and his success in promoting revivals as based
on his correct understanding of the "laws of mind" that were
utilized by every persuasive attorney. It is clear that
Finney's abbreviated legal career made an impression on him
entirely out of proportion to the quantity and quality of
his apprenticeship. Indeed, besides his fondness for parallels between the style of the preacher and that of the
lawyer, Finney claims to draw the very organizing principles
of his theology from those "old authors" he read as a clerk
in the office of Judge Benjamin Wright.

It must be recognized that Finney exaggerated his independence from the Reformed theological tradition in which
law plays a central role. Some scholars seriously doubt his
claim that he had not even read the Westminster Confession
before his ordination; and it is certain that by the time he
published his theological lectures he had been considerably
influenced by colleagues at Oberlin who were thoroughly
familiar with the language of Reformed legalism. Nevertheless, the parallels in ideas and language between Finney's
written works and those of the major legal authors from
Justinian to Blackstone are clear and numerous.

What accounts for this remarkable obsession with law? There can be no doubt that Finney discovered in the law a resolution to those crises of personal consciousness and ideological loyalty that Erik Erikson has located at the center of the search for identity. In the law—in the grand principles and majestic authority and compelling system of law—Finney found what Erikson calls a "coherent world-image," which both defined the limits and possibilities of his own creative energies and also provided a rational scheme for unifying and directing the collective energies of society. The law both restrains and liberates; and it accomplishes both by canalizing energy according to the inherent structure of reality. That was at least the promise of natural law, as formulated by the medievalists and mediated to America by Grotius, Pufendorf, and Blackstone. As Harold Berman observed,

> In the centuries prior to World War I religion and law—especially in America—were the patrimony of our collective life. They embodied our sense of common purpose and our sense of social order and social justice—'the style of integrity' (in Erikson's words) 'developed by our civilization.'[1]

While some of Finney's contemporaries, who continued to wrestle with the increasing complexities of legal practice in America, became embroiled in the practical problems of codifying the Common Law, Finney steadfastly maintained the grand, visionary claim that the highest end of the individual and of society lay in obedience to the system of universal moral principles whose authority rests in the divine government of the universe, and that those principles are, like the principles of the Common Law, accessible to every person of good will and common sense.

The law, understood as the system of personal, social, and cosmic order, sanctions and enhances the personal identity which for Finney emerged in young adulthood. In the vocation of a lawyer Finney found a means of resolving the conflict between his own initiative and the demands of

social order. As a revivalist, he defined the provisions of
universal moral law by which the self-affirming impulses of
Yankee energy could be liberated from the self-denying
strictures of the Puritan conscience. Law made possible the
reconciliation of aggression and security, of confidence in
one's own judgment and respect for authorities. For the
religious mind, nourished on the theology of New England,
Finney's announcement that God governs human affairs by a
rational, consistent, and fully-revealed body of laws meant
that one could pursue vigorously both one's salvation and
one's fortune within intelligible guidelines; and, if one
were reasonable and resolute, the efforts could not fail to
win divine approval. In this way the hidden catch in the
so-called "Protestant ethic" is removed: one need not feel
guilty about seeking spiritual prosperity with the same
energy and forceful means that one employs in commercial
transactions, for there are divinely sanctioned rules for
seeking salvation, what Finney called "the main business of
life."

Apprenticeship

After graduating from the Oneida academy, Finney taught for
four years (1808-1812) in the district school near his
parents' home in Henderson, then struck out on his own for
the first time. This was no journey West, in romantic imi-
tation of his parents' example, but rather a return to his
home town in Connecticut for a more sophisticated secondary
education. He taught for a while in New Jersey, probably to
help finance his studies. At this point Finney was twenty-
four; he had been absent from home four years; he had tested
the vocation of teaching. Erikson argues that many youth
need, and take, a "moratorium" in late adolescence for
experimentation with different social roles, "a span of time
after they have ceased being children, but before their
deeds and works count toward a future identity."[2] This
period seems to have been Finney's moratorium, and it was
brought to an end by a critical decision.

Finney's preceptor in Connecticut offered to guide him through his undergraduate curriculum in half the time it would take him at Yale College. In return Finney was to assist him "in conducting an academy in one of the Southern States." Here was a promising opportunity and Finney later admits that "I was inclined to accept his proposal." But standing against this adventure were the values of order and continuity represented by the family, now "settled" in Jefferson county. Upon being informed of the "contemplated movement south," Finney's parents "both came immediately after me, and prevailed on me to go home with them." There is no deliberation recorded regarding either the decision to return or the decision not to resume the role which he had formerly filled in Henderson.[3] The vocational interest in the southern academy and the concern to attain a college education were abruptly dropped. The time for experimentation was over; the decision that seemed entirely unexpected, yet was supported by all the deeper springs of Finney's consciousness, was suddenly fixed: "After making a visit, I concluded to enter, as a student, the law office of Squire W--, in Adams, in that county. This was in 1818." (MF, p. 5).

Adams was only a few miles from Henderson,[4] but Finney mentions his parents only once more in the Memoirs; and then not until at least three years had elapsed, when he returned, triumphant in the cause of revival, to provide them with the faith they had not supplied him or themselves. The heart of this faith was a remarkable translation of the Christian gospel into the terms of that social institution in which the conflict of autonomy and order could be resolved: the law.

All that Finney says about his legal training is that in the study of "elementary law" he found the "old authors" referring to "the Mosaic Institutes, as authority for many of the great principles of common law" (MF, p. 7). In the interest of research, he purchased his first Bible and began reading in the Books of Moses. Apart from this reference, Finney provides no list of his legal reading. We can say

with confidence, however, that Finney would have been required, as were all apprentices, to work through those classic authors whose names recur in reading lists of trainees
for the bar, particularly what Perry Miller aptly called the
"implacable Blackstone."[5] Although public sentiment sustained an anti-British prejudice sufficient to resent the
use of English Common Law as the basis of American justice,
that highly adaptable body of traditional wisdom, organized
by William Blackstone's famed Commentaries, was the main
staple of the country lawyer.

In the circumstances of the western counties of New
York State in the 1820's, however, as in the frontier areas
further west, most cases did not require extensive legal
training. A-H. Chroust observes that "a knowledge of the
fundamental elements of the common law, often gleaned from
Blackstone, as well as an intuitive sense of natural justice
were chiefly relied upon . . . ."[6] Many judges ruled on the
basis of what one of Finney's contemporaries in the legal
profession called, "the common sense reasonable construction
of each transaction."[7] A New York paper, from August, 1852,
provides an example of the "common sense" approach to justice. The case is reported of a judge who

> personally laid hands on a convicted horse thief:
> 'Hold up your head, you d . . . d ornary pup!
> Look the court in the eye,' he commanded the
> trembling culprit and planted a horny judicial
> fist between [the man's] eyes.[8]

Such instances of due process convinced American jurists
that a more scientific approach to law was needed to secure
the blessings of a perfected social order. It was their
hope to organize the American judicial system on the basis
of British common law, following Blackstone's own dictum
that "Law is to be considered not only as a matter of practice, but also as a rational science."[9]

The haphazard character of the common law, however,
even in the elegant form of Blackstone's Commentaries, and

despite the lofty claims of their author, was viewed with
suspicion in the east.[10] To provide more precise standards
of judgment, and to relieve the embarrassing reliance on
British tradition, the American law book was created.[11]
Yet, while volumes of case reports had been issued in the
east and south since the first collection in 1789 by Ephraim
Kirby, a printer in Litchfield county, the first official
reports in New York were not issued until 1804. It is un-
likely that Finney's apprenticeship allowed much opportunity
for careful perusal of this growing bulk of case reports and
the accompanying doctrinal writings. Although New York was
one of the states which resisted the tendency to erode standards of admission to the bar in conformity with the egalitarian tendencies of the age, still an apprentice in a
country law office "received little formal instruction:
theory was hardly ever discussed. There were no definite
requirements or standards, nor was there a systematic program of study."[12] Although Finney had the advantages of a
mentor with some local standing,[13] his experience as an
apprentice was probably typical of those who pursued a legal
vocation in newly-settled areas.

> Western lawyers, as a rule, were the sons of poor
> or middle-class people, and seldom had a college
> education. They were the products of the law
> office and courtroom, and in some instances, of
> self-study (or no study at all). Most states and
> territorial statutes before 1820-30 required a
> student to spend at least two years, and sometimes
> three, studying under the supervision of a prac-
> ticing lawyer or judge . . . Upon application for
> a license he was, as a rule, subjected to a purely
> perfunctory examination as to his knowledge of the
> law by a disinterested and often ignorant judge or
> by a "board" of equally uninterested and ignorant
> lawyers.[14]

One of the limitations of the apprenticeship system
most lamented, especially by those with an interest in
transforming law into an academic discipline in the

foundling schools of New England, was the inability of the
trainee to concentrate on the great systematic principles
which underlie legal order and inform every other branch of
human endeavor. Blackstone himself had complained that
apprenticeship was a process of mechanical learning that
produced unimaginative formalists: "ita lex scriptura ist
is the utmost his knowledge will arrive at; he must never
aspire to form, and seldom expect to comprehend, any arguments drawn a priori, from the spirit of the laws and the
natural foundations of justice."[15] At the dedication of the
Dane Law College in 1832, Josiah Quincy, the President of
Harvard explained that when the common law is introduced
into the university curriculum, "it becomes liberalized and
refined." Whereas under apprenticeship, if it were the
"student's lot to be placed in the office of one of the
great lights of the bar . . . What copying of contracts!
What filing of writs! What preparing of pleas! How could
the mind concentrate itself on principles amid the perpetual
rotation of this machinery?" Much to be preferred is the
"systematic course of prescribed study," informed by the
liberal arts, through which "the foundation of a solid and
lofty structure of intellectual and moral action" can be
laid.[16] Finney did not benefit from a legal education
informed by the liberal arts; and, serving in the office of
a surrogate county judge, it is certain that he was occupied
in a great deal of clerical routine. Finney's training in
law, then, proceeded under an unregulated process that was
subject to increasing criticism within the profession, and
particularly in the state of New York.

As the law became the "science of justice," lawyers
came to regard themselves as stellar examples of erudition
and eloquence. The leaders of the profession were as unhappy to have unlearned bumpkins for colleagues, as they were
to acknowledge the unscrupulous "pettifoggers" in their
midst. In 1835 Benjamin Butler, then attorney general of
the United States, in a plan to organize the law faculty of
the University of the City of New York, traced the source of
embarrassment to the apprenticeship system, which, he
sniffed, "is necessarily quite imperfect."

. . . the progress of [clerks] in the principles
of legal science is usually tardy and laborious.
In many cases they are left to grope their way in
the dark, with little or no assistance from the
principals. And even where this disadvantage is
not experienced, the means of instruction in a law
office will yet be found too limited to meet the
needs of the student. The consequence is that
many of our attorneys and solicitors when licensed
are very ill-qualified for the duties of their
profession; and though they may afterward, by
proper exertions, acquire sufficient to guide them
in the performance of their duties, much of this
knowledge will have been gained by slow degrees,
and sometimes, it may be feared, at the expense of
their clients.[17]

When we describe Finney's theology as shaped decisively
by his legal training, then, it must be remembered that the
limitations of his apprenticeship, and the distractions of
his increasingly intense religious interests, prevent our
ascribing to him the full range of "intellectual elegance"
(Miller) that characterized the sophisticated product of
Harvard Law School in 1820. We might even suspect that,
given Finney's minimal secondary education and the short
tenure of his apprenticeship, his admission to the bar would
have been an occasion for more hand-wringing among the distinguished jurists of New York City.

Further, Finney had barely begun to practice law when
he abandoned the bar for the pulpit; consequently, he never
gained that practical knowledge of the law considered indispensable for those admitted on the basis of apprenticeship.[18] Nevertheless, he did gain a theoretical understanding of the law as "a rational science." Finney was
lastingly affected by the vision of the power and grandeur
of the law, as it slowly formed in his mind through the
reading he managed in the few slack moments in the day's
business, or during the long evenings in the village of
Adams.

Metaphysics of the Law

Legal authors of the nineteenth century were fond of pre-
facing their works with a quotation from Richard Hooker:

> Of Law, there can be no less acknowledged than
> that her seat is the bosom of God, her voice the
> harmony of the world. All things in heaven and
> earth do her homage--the very least as feeling her
> care, and the greatest as not exempted from her
> power.[19]

Law evokes the images of maternal love and discipline, whose
authority is identified with the divine father. It is
significant to note that the image of the law is not mascu-
line, as instrument of aggressive domination, but feminine,
providing the comfort of careful order which nourishes and
directs tentative human steps in an otherwise threateningly
chaotic world. Her power is universal and comprehensive;
she is everywhere respected; and she guarantees that the
government of the world is just. The origin of both the
feminine image and the notion of an eternal principle of
cosmic order may lie in Hooker's devout reading of the
biblical book of Proverbs, where Wisdom is praised as the
teacher of righteousness, by whose counsels princes reign.

The identification of divine Wisdom with the Torah, or
eternal law of God, was a natural development in Jewish
piety and passed, largely unnoticed, into the foundations of
Western civilization. There it combined with the Greco-
Roman respect for law to produce the belief in the transcendent authority of law which persists in the West, however
wanly, yet today. The transcendence of law as celebrated by
Hooker is also acknowledged with varying degrees of emphasis
and enthusiasm by all the classic authors whose names appear
on the reading lists of American jurists from colonial
times. Even a country apprentice could be expected to have
at least a glancing acquaintance with such standards as
Justinian, Montesquieu, Vattel, Pufendorf, Grotius, and
above all others, Sir William Blackstone.

The name of Blackstone is ubiquitous in all the accounts of legal education in the first century of America's
independence. Blackstone's work was known to John Adams as
early as 1759, ten years before the set of Commentaries was
completed; and several generations later, the most famous
figure in the history of the New York bar, James Kent,
commented "that he owed his reputation to the fact that,
when studying law he had but one book, Blackstone's Commentaries, but that one book he mastered."[20] In 1803 St.
George Tucker issued a five-volume edition of the Commentaries which "had widespread circulation, both as a textbook
and otherwise."[21]

Whatever else Finney may have read during a lull in his
routine of clerical duties, then, Blackstone remained for
him the model of legal reasoning by which the common law was
transformed into what American lawyers called "the science
of justice."[22] In the introductory lecture of the Commentaries, as we have seen, Blackstone insisted that "law is to
be considered not only as a matter of practice, but also as
a rational science." Specifically, criminal law "should be
founded upon principles that are permanent, uniform, and
universal; and always conformable to the dictates of truth
and justice, the feelings of humanity, and the indelible
rights of mankind."[23] This systematic interest accorded
well with the concerns of American society. Charles Warren
observes that

It was the advent of Blackstone which opened the
eyes of American scholars to the broader field of
learning in the law. He taught them, for the
first time, the continuity, the unity, and the
reason of the Common Law--and just at a time when
the need of a unified system both in law and
politics was beginning to be felt in the
Colonies.[24]

This concern to discover in Blackstone the rudiments of a
rational system can be illustrated from a jurist of the next
generation. W. G. Hammond, Chancellor of the Law department

of Iowa State University, in the introduction of the first
American edition of Thomas Sandars' translation of The
Institutes of Justinian, deplored the tendency to separate
the common and civil law, rather than "to patiently study
out the essential unity of plan hidden beneath these."[25]
This unity "has grown by continuous forces from the Twelve
Tables to the codes and statute books, and reports and
treatises of the present day," and forms the "foundation of
scientific jurisprudence" upon which Blackstone's Commentaries are built. According to Hammond, the Justinian Code
is one attempt to arrange statutory laws and judicial decisions according to some coherent pattern. Although "desti-
tute of scientific order," the Institutes bear testimony to
the true nature of law which "Blackstone and his system"
sought to clarify.

> . . . all law, properly studied, is one system,
> one science, and . . . no man has ever done any-
> thing of real value to the grand edifice unless,
> like Blackstone, he was willing to follow the
> plans of the Great Architect, revealed in history
> . . . .[26]

The conviction that natural law is the basis of organizing a
just society was predominant in the period between the
Revolution and the Civil War and "guided the creative process of applying reason to experience which has been the
life of the law."[27] The apprentice in Benjamin Wright's
office would have found assurance in the first book of the
Institutes that the quest for a system of universal meaning
can be satisfied in the law. "Jurisprudence is the knowledge of things divine and human," came the words from the
sixth century, "the science of the just and the unjust."[28]

Indeed, Blackstone went so far as to claim for law the
highest measure of both scientific clarity and moral efficacy. Law, he told the gentlemen of Oxford, is a science

> which distinguishes the criterions of right and
> wrong; which teaches to establish the one, and

> prevent, punish, or redress the other; which em-
> ploys in it's theory the noblest faculties of the
> soul, and exerts in it's practice the cardinal
> virtues of the heart: a science which is univer-
> sal in it's use and extent,accommodated to each
> individual, yet comprehending the whole community
> 29

The eminent lawyers and jurists of Finney's day, giants like
James Kent and Joseph Story, identified the best hope of
American civilization with the moral and intellectual excel-
lence of the legal profession. Justice Kent, for example,
informed his audience at Columbia in 1824, that the study of
law promoted all the nobler sentiments of human nature.

> No man can preserve in his own breast a constant
> and lively sense of justice, without being insen-
> sibly led to cherish the benevolent affections.
> Those affections sharpen the perceptions of the
> moral sense, and give energy and a proper direc-
> tion to all the noble powers of the under-
> standing.30

Law brought into harmonious exercise both the heart and the
mind, achieving a synthesis of human powers not unlike that
"moral sanity" which Finney claimed was the chief benefit of
obedience to the Christian gospel.

The notion that law is the fundamental principle of the
order of the universe has, of course, its origin in the
theological doctrine of natural law. In the opening sen-
tences of Montesquieu, for instance, Finney would have read
that

> Laws, in their most general signification, are the
> necessary relations arising from the nature of
> things. In this sense all beings have their laws;
> the Deity his laws, the material world its laws,
> the intelligences superior to man their laws, the
> beasts their laws, man his laws.31

All the positive laws made by God and human governments are specifications of the systematic "relations of justice" which underlie the universe and which are disclosed to human rationality. Montesquieu observed that because man is disposed to forget his Creator, God has "reminded him of duty by the laws of religion"; and because he is liable to "forget himself," philosophy has provided laws of morality; and because, although "formed to live in society, he might forget his fellow-creatures," legislators "by political and civil laws confined him to his duty."[32] "Law in general is human reason, inasmuch as it governs all the inhabitants of the earth; the political and civil laws of each nation ought to be only the particular cases in which human reason is applied."[33] As an illustration of a coherent system of legal reasoning, this "old author" claimed that "the laws of Moses were perfectly wise."[34]

The other classic authors also exhibit an interest in the systematic relation of natural law, witnessed by reason and conscience, to the laws of civil order. Emeric de Vattel (1714-1767) was a Swiss jurist, with an interest in the rationalist philosophy of Christian Wolff. The title of his major work, available in a Boston edition of 1802, is a statement of the grand ambition of the legal mind: Droit des gens, ou Principes de la loi naturelle appliques a la conduite et aux affaires des nations et des souverains (1758).

Samuel Pufendorf (1632-1694) appears on the reading lists of both John Adams and James Kent and is quoted frequently throughout Blackstone's Commentaries.[35] His eight-volume work, De jure naturae et gentium (1672), defines "the Law of Nature in General" as "that most General and Universal Rule of Human Actions, to which every Man is obligated to conform as he is a Reasonable Creature."[36] Pufendorf rejects the notion that humans and beasts share a common law of nature, for law refers to duties; therefore, it is an "abuse" of the term to apply it to irrational creatures. The distinguishing mark of human nature is the capacity for rational choice, and the basis of all human government is the recognition that moral responsibility can be assigned only if that capacity has been exercised. One can be judged for only those actions performed as a human being, that is, in full possession of one's reason and in unrestricted employment of one's will. This claim is the fundamental premise of all interpretations of human life as subject to legal order, from the milder provisions for crimes of ignorance in the books of Moses to the famous principle of Kantian ethics that obligation implies ability.

For Pufendorf the continuance of civilization depends upon the maintenance of universal law, and the principles of creation guarantee that continuity. Since God has made each of us as "a Being not possibly to be preserved without the Observation of the Law," we may be assured that God will not "either reverse or alter the Law of Nature so long as He brings no change on Human Nature itself," and as long as conformity to this law promotes "Society, in which is contain'd all the Temporal Happiness of Man."[37]

The discovery of natural law, then, proceeds from "the accurate Contemplation of our Natural Condition and Propensions," chief of which is "self-Love."[38] From an interest in promoting our own well-being, and an awareness of our "wonderful Impotency and Natural Indigence," we are drawn to seek the benefits of "peaceful Sociableness with others." To promote "Sociableness"--"the Disposition of one Man towards all others, as shall suppose him united to them by Benevolence, by Peace, by Charity, and so as it were, by a silent and a secret obligation"--is the chief duty of moral beings.[39] However, the obligatory force of natural law does not rest upon its social utility, but upon the fact that it is the means of fulfilling the will of "the Creator and Governour of the World" who has "so form'd and dispos'd the Nature of things and of Mankind, as to make a Sociable Life necessary to our Subsistence and Preservation . . . ."[40]

Pufendorf's analysis of moral agency is echoed in Blackstone's lecture on the three "natural foundations of sovereignty," rooted in the divine wisdom, power, and

goodness. Since law is "a rule of action dictated by some
superior being," it could be imposed by mere force; but God
is a being of infinite wisdom who regulates his creatures
according to "the eternal, immutable laws of good and evil,
to which the creator himself conforms; and which he has
enabled human reason to discover . . . ."[41] Further, to
make the obedience of these laws even more attractive than
the beauty of their rational order allows, God has benevolently "interwoven the laws of eternal justice with the
happiness of each individual, that the latter cannot be
attained but by observing the former." Thus the Creator has
"graciously reduced the role of obedience to this one pater-
nal precept, 'that man should pursue his own true and sub-
stantial happiness.'"[42] What Finney learned here about the
legal definition of moral responsibility, the rationality
and benevolence of natural law, and the means of true human
happiness through participation in a lawful society, exerted
a strong influence on his development of the theology of
moral government.

The chief work of Hugo Grotius (1583-1645), the famed
Dutch jurist, is an exposition of

> that Law, which is common to many Nations or
> Rulers of Nations, whether derived from Nature, or
> instituted by Divine commands, or introduced by
> Custom and tacit Consent, few have touched upon,
> and none hitherto treated of universally and me-
> thodically; tho' it is the Interest of Mankind
> that it should be done.[43]

As the other classic legal theorists, Grotius argued that
natural law is the basis of the order of the universe and is
disclosed to human reason.

> NATURAL RIGHT is the Rule and Dictate of Right
> Reason, showing the Moral Deformity or Moral
> Necessity there is in any Act, according to its
> Suitableness or Unsuitableness to a reasonable

Nature, and consequently, that such an Act is
either forbid or commanded by GOD, the Author of
Nature.[44]

The natural law, then, is prior to the exercise of "Voluntary Divine Right." Thus "the Law of Nature is so unalterable, that God himself cannot change it."[45] The claim for
the priority of the law over the divine will approaches
blasphemy for the religious mind trained in Calvinism. Even
Pufendorf, who follows Grotius' views in general, raised
devout objection to the notion that God is obligated to
observe natural law: "without doubt those Impious Terms,
God ought necessarily, are very unsuitable to the Majesty of
an Omnipotent Legislator."[46] Yet Finney was willing later
to argue that the majesty of God was displayed precisely in
his conformity to moral law, for God reveals his authority
in the faithfulness with which he upholds the principles of
moral government in the universe and in the harmony of those
principles with the intuitions of human reason and conscience. In his early lectures at Oberlin, for example,
Finney teaches that the Law of God is the "rule of universal
benevolence to which himself and all moral beings are under
immutable obligations, to conform their whole being."[47]
Further, all divine commands are obligatory only to the
extent they are consistent with rational order. "Neither
God nor any other being has the right to require any course
of conduct, without some good reason."[48] But having said
that, Finney proceeds on the assumption that God does always
act reasonably for he always acts to achieve the highest
welfare of the universe of moral beings. Once one has
grasped the foundational principle of divine law, one has
the key to the right application and proper authority of
human laws as well.

Thus, if Finney's apprenticeship in Adams followed the
general pattern of American legal education in this period,
he would have been taught that legal order emerges from the
systematic application of natural law to specific cases. It
was only a short step, taken by a professor at Columbia in

1810, to identify the law of nature, the system of civil legislation, and the divine government.

> The science of the Law is, of all others, the most
> sublime and comprehensive, and in its general
> signification, comprises all things, human and
> divine. The heavens, the earth, and all creation,
> are governed by laws, universal, eternal, immu-
> table, and fixed.[49]

The "science of law" discloses not merely the conventional arrangements of social order, but the very structure of reality. The lawyer is no mere technician, then, but a metaphysician of the first order whose vision finds its proper object in the flawless ordering of human life.[50] When Stanley Matthews addressed the State Bar Association of New York in 1881, he echoed the ambitions of two generations of American lawyers. The final end of the judicial system, Matthews declared, is the construction of "a perfect social order," in which each person

> will be able to perfect his individual being . . .
> when every right will be the most richly enjoyed,
> when every duty will be the most faithfully per-
> formed; where the perfect law of justice will be
> accomplished in every human relation, and cover
> with its invincible shield the weakest from every
> conceivable wrong.[51]

Thus Matthews was convinced that the legal profession ren- ders its "greatest indirect service" to society by educating people in the way of justice: "It makes common and intro- duces into the popular mind and speech the ideas and lan- guage of jurisprudence."[52] To the thoughtful apprentice in Benjamin Wright's office this grand conviction would serve as a bridge between two ways of life: in becoming a revival preacher, Finney believed himself to be following the intrinsic possibilities of the legal profession to their highest fulfillment.

The Law in the Millennium

While Finney was the only revivalist who was trained in the
law and consciously drew upon its principles in his theology, other evangelists had also perceived the crucial importance of translating the Christian gospel into the language
of legal order, in whose terms the highest hopes of their
generation were commonly expressed.

In the enthusiastic years following the opening of the
Erie Canal in 1825, the representatives of human and divine
government sought to realize the promise of millennial civilization in the villages and cities of America. The ambitions of the lawyers to create a "perfect social order"
through the systematic application of law as "a rational
science" were matched in both principle and passion by the
revivalists. For example, the Reverend Jonathan Blanchard
devoted his address entitled, "A Perfect State of Society,"
to a description of the endless necessity of legal regulation, enforced by public agreement.

> Society is perfect where what is right in theory
> exists in fact; where practice coincides with
> principle, and the law of God is the law of the
> land . . . the most striking feature of a perfect
> state of society is, a holy public sentiment,
> enforcing the law of God, so that, in it a bad man
> cannot be popular nor a good one despised.[53]

The time seemed ripe for the advent of such happy circumstances. The progress of the revivals in the 1830's and
1840's was so dramatic that the entire country seemed to be
awakening to its duty. The moment of cultural renewal for
which the revivalists had labored and prayed, the creation
of a Christian nation in which each individual would be
brought under the regulation of divine law, seemed at hand.

One of the most sophisticated expressions of the revivalists' vision was a work by Calvin Colton, written in 1832
to sympathetic, but critical, British observers of American

revivals. Colton explained that a revival is "the multiplied power of religion over a community of minds."[54] Raising a revival, then, is a matter of strenuous public activity "in which it is expected man will be a co-worker with
God. [Revivals] are made matters of human calculation, by
the arithmetic of faith in God's engagements."[55] For Colton
revivals are regulated by certain systematic principles
which can be learned and used by enterprising "promoters."

What is the end of all this calculated promotion?
Nothing less than "the universal amalgamation and purification of society."[56] At the height of his rhetoric Colton
excitedly announced that the present outpouring of the
Spirit of God, "by the experience of the Church, and the
necessary revolution of society," will prepare the way for
the rebirth of the nation.

> Everyone knows, or may know, that the design of
> Christianity is to bring back this apostate world
> to God--to reduce the kingdoms and the men of this
> world to the reign of Messiah--to recover mankind
> from a state of rebellion against their Maker, to
> the submissions of obedience . . . It is to reduce
> the world, and the whole world, by a system of
> moral means and agencies. This is certainly a
> stupendous scheme, a sublime enterprise, charac-
> teristic and worthy of that Almighty Being, who
> has devised and undertaken it.[57]

America has the distinction of being the first society to be
purified because its democratic form of government is most
amenable to the establishment of a national Christian community. Apologizing to his British audience for giving the
appearance of "undue national partialities," Colton claimed
that only in American society are the conditions present for
"a quick and thorough operation of the social and sympathetic influence of religion, through the entire community."
Such sympathetic communication is enhanced by "that mighty
engine of human improvement--the press," as well as by
"commercial and social intercourse" that is "open, and

constant, and generous."[58] Colton was convinced that American democracy was governed by those laws which most truly
reflected the divine law of the kingdom of God. At the
point that civil laws and the divine law exactly correspon-
ded, the kingdom of God would be established in America.

It follows that the type of preaching most effective in
promoting revivals is

> . . . a studious effort to combine the cardinal
> principles both of original and evangelical law,
> and a persevering application of those principles,
> in their various Scriptural forms, through the
> understanding and reason, to the consciences of
> sinners, until they come to repentance.[59]

Colton prefers the formulation, "original and evangelical
law," rather than the more common, "law and Gospel," because
the former more clearly expresses "the obligations of both
upon the conscience as law." The form of preaching in which
the sinner is confronted with the Gospel "clothed with all
the sanctions of law, as truly and as much as the institutes
of the Decalogue," is "more especially the reigning characteristic of those ministers in the United States, who are
more earnestly engaged in promoting revivals of religion."[60]
As his prime example of such a successful American revivalist, Colton probably had in mind Charles Finney, who "came
right forth from a law office to the pulpit, and talked to
the people as I would have talked to a jury" (MF, p. 89).
"For me," Finney declared,

> the Law and the Gospel have but one rule of life
> . . . I have long been satisfied that the higher
> forms of Christian experience are attained only as
> a result of a terribly searching application of
> God's law to the human conscience and heart [MF,
> p. 339].

It is significant that Colton located the secret of
successful revivals in America in the sensitive adaptation

of preaching to "the character and temper of the community."
The revivalists, as well as the lawyers, understood and respected the high regard for legal order wherever the ambitious "sons of the Pilgrims" sought their fortunes, in the
fields of the settlements or on the streets of the cities.
Finney and his fellow evangelicals constituted what R. W. B.
Lewis has called the party of Hope: a broad range of religious thinkers who believed that the achievement of the
perfectly righteous and happy society was a real possibility
for America.[61] One of the leading members of the party was
Lyman Beecher, who had been an advocate of revivals even
before Finney's successes in western New York. Following
the Reformed tradition, Beecher insisted on preaching from
"the Bible as a code of laws," as he entitled an ordination
sermon of 1817. In the address to the new pastor, Beecher
asserted, "Your duty is plain. It is to explain and enforce
the laws of the divine moral government contained in the
Bible." Those laws imply the free agency of the sinner and
all the other elements of the "new divinity" that undergirded revivalism. Thus, Beecher urged, let all other
attainments "be counted as loss in comparison with [the
people's] actual conversion to God. Set your heart upon the
great blessing of a revival of religion."[62]

Following his own advice, Beecher pursued the blessing
of revival in "the majestic West." He wrote his daughter in
1830,

> The moral destiny of our nation, and all our
> institutions and hopes, and the world's hopes,
> turns on the character of the West, and the compe-
> tition now is for that of preoccupancy in the
> education of the rising generation, in which Cath-
> olics and infidels have got the start of us . . .
> If we gain the West, all is safe; if we lose it,
> all is lost.[63]

For Beecher, his decision to accept the presidency of Lane
Seminary in Cincinnati settled "the question whether the
first and leading seminary of the West shall be one which

inculcates orthodoxy with or without revivals"—a question
"of as great importance as was ever permitted a single human
mind to decide."[64] For the destiny of America, and the
world, "the great battle is to be fought in the Valley of
the Mississippi," and the headquarters for the decisive
campaign of the evangelical crusade would be staffed by the
most loyal general in the ranks of New School revivalists.

The magnificent hope that the kingdom of God would come
to America through the agency of the revival, however, was
shared even by those who belonged to the Old School of
Calvinist theology. Heman Humphrey was a pastor in Pitts-
field, Massachusetts, and one of those who spoke against
Finney's "new measures" at the New Lebanon Convention of
1827. In his memoirs, Humphrey regrets the use of protracted meetings and the arrogance of itinerant evangelists.
He is, nevertheless, proud of the "very extensive and powerful" revival in New York State between 1820 and 1825; and he
makes bold to predict that

> as the millennium approaches, we may expect to see
> greater things than have yet been witnessed . . .
> It would certainly be very remarkable if God were
> to convert all in a great revival. But that he
> can, if he pleases, no praying person can doubt.[65]

Even though Humphrey does not mention Finney, he finds the
revivalists' vision of a national awakening alluring; and he
shares Finney's conviction that such revival would require
the subjection of each individual to the demands of moral
conscience.

> When the doctrines of the gospel are distinguish-
> ingly and faithfully preached, sinners are gener-
> ally slain by the law, before they find joy and
> peace in believing.[66]

That conviction spans the gulf between New School and Old
School and is part of their common inheritance from the
evangelical Calvinists of the preceding century for whom the

law played essential roles in both conversion and regeneration. "The Christian's goal was to make 'the glory of God
the end and the law of God the rule of all his actions.'"[67]
The consistent claim of the revivalists is that the redemptive rule of God in America can be exercised only through
promulgation of moral law. God "rules the universe," Finney
told his audience, "by righteous law and our race also on a
Gospel system which magnifies that law and makes it
honorable."[68]

By 1830, as Perry Miller wrote, "even the sprawling
frontier had been taught that in the wake of the Revival
came the Courts."[69] Both revivalists and lawyers were engaged in setting out the rules by which people could most
peaceably and profitably live together. They shared not
only a common means, namely, legal order, but also a common
end, nothing less than the perfectly just society. For the
revivalists this end was the fulfillment of the biblical
promises of the kingdom of God. The lawyers, though less
pious, were equally ambitious; they too claimed to be archi-
tects of a perfected national community.[70]

NOTES

1. Harold J. Berman, The Interaction of Law and Religion (Nashville, Tennessee: Abingdon Press, 1974), p. 23.
2. Erikson, Young Man Luther, p. 43. That the moratorium is not a period of frivolous meandering is clear in
Erikson's argument that Luther's time of moratorium was
spent in the monastery.
3. Wright records that "in view of his mother's ill-
health, he was led to remain within reach of her" (Finney,
p. 4).
4. Adams was fourteen miles south of the county seat at
Watertown. In 1836, while ranking tenth out of the nineteen
towns in Jefferson County in acreage, Adams is listed
seventh in improved acreage, sixth in assessed value of real
estate and third in value of personal property. From 1820
to 1835 the population increased from 2,467 to 2,970, a rate

of growth indicating a quite prosperous village, an ideal place for beginning a law career (Gordon, Gazetteer, pp. 493-494).

5. Cf. Roscoe Pound, The Formative Era of American Law (Boston: Little, Brown & Co., 1938), pp. 25-26: "Blackstone continued to be the student's first work in the law office and in most law schools until the end of the nineteenth century . . . and select chapters from Grotius and Pufendorf were in law school curricula until 1850."

6. Chroust, The Rise of the Legal Profession, p. 107.

7. Beardsley, Reminiscences, p. 72.

8. Chroust, The Rise of the Legal Profession, p. 95.

9. Jones, ed., Commentaries.

10. While Blackstone gave the appearance of a rational system to the common law, there were those who complained that it was mysterious and unintelligible to lay people who found themselves increasingly dependent upon professional lawyers. Robert Rantoul, a respected Democratic member of the Massachusetts bar, delivered the objection in an eloquent oration for the Fourth of July, 1836: "No man can tell what the Common Law is; therefore it is not Law: for law is a rule of action, but a rule which is unknown can govern no man's conduct. Notwithstanding this, it has been called the perfection of human reason. The Common Law is the perfection of human reason, just as alcohol is the perfection of sugar . . . No one knows what the [common] law is, before he [the judge] lays it down . . . No man knows what the [common] law is after the judge has decided it." Therefore, Rantoul concluded, "all American law must be statute law" (quoted in Chroust, The Rise of the Legal Profession, pp. 60-61).

Blackstone's own defense against complaints about the "intricacies of our legal system" was that the great refinements of "subdivisions" is necessary to gain "sufficient precision" in the application of law to specific cases. Thus any injured party can find in the elaborate system of common law "a remedial unit, conceived in such terms as are properly adapted to his own peculiar grievance" (Commentaries, ed. Jones, p. 168). In this way legal remedy is removed as far as possible from the arbitrary decision of

the individual judge. Daniel Boorstin argues that it was
Blackstone's intention to retain a certain degree of obscurity in the law lest human pride be tempted to conclude that
"reason was the sole test of legal institutions" and begin
to question existing social and political order (The Mysterious Science, p. 24).

11. Charles Warren, A History of the American Bar, p.
332: "The American law text book, like the American law
report, owed its origin largely to the demand for the creation of a native body of law, distinct from the English
law."

12. Chroust, The Rise of the Legal Profession, p. 175.

13. Benjamin Wright is listed as the surrogate judge of
Jefferson County for the years 1820-1821, and 1823-1840.
See Alden Chester, Courts and Lawyers of New York: A History, 1609-1925, three volumes (New York: The American
Historical Society, 1925). In the State of New York, the
surrogate county judge "has jurisdiction over the probate of
wills and testaments and the settlements of estates, and
often has power to appoint and supervise guardians of infants and other incompetent persons" (Webster's International Dictionary, 1927). Since Adams boasted of only
four lawyers as late as 1836 (Gazetteer, p. 487), we may
conclude that "Squire" Wright was a man of considerable
business, with little time for the conscientious instruction
of apprentices.

14. Chroust, The Rise of the Legal Profession, p. 106.
In New York State "prior to 1871 . . . no specified length
of time for study of the law existed, nor was there a pre-
legal requirement to make candidates eligible for admission
to practice" (Chester, Courts and Lawyers of New York, vol.
2, p. 888).

15. Jones, ed., Commentaries, p. 22.

16. Chroust, The Rise of the Legal Profession, pp. 221-
222.

17. David McAdam, et al., History of the Bench and Bar
of New York, two volumes (New York History Co., 1897), vol.
1, pp. 183-184.

18. In an address to the Law School of Columbia in 1867,
Benjamin D. Silliman lamented the fact that, under

apprenticeship, the novice "was at once engaged in the practice of that of which he had not learned the principles. . .
the proper order of his instruction was inverted. Blackstone's Commentaries . . . were placed in his hands for
perusal in the intervals of office business; but there was
perceptible to him little relation between their contents
and the daily routine of his clerical duties . . . he could
rarely feel at home in his profession until he had acquired,
by subsequent laborious and anxious practice, a knowledge of
very much that he should have obtained at the outset."
(Quoted in McAdam, History of the Bench and Bar of New York,
vol. 1, pp. 180f.)

    19. Laws of Ecclesiastical Polity (1594), Book I.

    20. Warren, History of the American Bar, p. 187.

    21. Warren, History of the American Bar, p. 336. The
first American edition of Blackstone was issued in 1771-72.
Not even Jefferson's assessment that the Commentaries contained a mere "smattering of everything," including clear
anti-republican sentiments, could discourage their use
(Jones, ed., Commentaries, p. lii).

    22. A typical statement can be found in Stanley Mat-
thews, The Function of the Legal Profession in the Progress
of Civilization, pp. 13-15: " . . . the law, springing from
the reason and conscience of mankind, becomes the science of
human rights and obligations, the science of justice . . .
grounded in the indestructible and immutable nature and
constitution of the universe."

    23. Jones, ed., Commentaries, p. 188.

    24. History of the American Bar, p. 177.

    25. The Institutes of Justinian (Chicago: Collagham &
Co., 1876), p. viii.

    26. Institutes, p. lxi. Berman attributes the rise of
secular bodies of law, along with the formulation of canon
law as the "first modern legal system of the West," to the
rediscovery of Justinian about 1100 (The Interaction of Law
and Religion, p. 58).

    27. Pound, The Formative Era of American Law, p. 13.

    28. Institutes, p. 68.

    29. Jones, ed., Commentaries, p. 19.

    30. Quoted in Miller, Life of the Mind in America, p.
189. Miller summarized the patriotic intention of these

learned and disciplined guardians of legal affections: "they were saving civilization in America by creating a rationality for the law" (p. 119).

31. Charles Louis de Secondat Montesquieu, _The Spirit of Laws_, tr. Thomas Nugent, two volumes (Cincinnati: Robert Clarke & Co., 1873), vol. 1, p. 1.

32. _Ibid._, vol. 1, pp. 3-4.

33. _Ibid._, vol. 1, p. 7.

34. _Ibid._, vol. 2, p. 143. To his credit, however, Montesquieu does find the Hebrew treatment of slaves as if they were their master's money to be "extremely severe," indeed, a "strange" relaxation of "the law of nature" (vol. 1, p. 284).

35. See Warren, _History of the American Bar_, "A Colonial Lawyer's Education," pp. 157-187, and "Early American Law Books," pp. 325-340. Chroust notes that as early as 1756 "the College of Philadelphia, now the University of Pennsylvania, gave a course which also included the 'civil laws'; and Grotius' _De jure belle et pacis_ (of 1625) as well as Pufendorf's _De jure naturae et gentium_ (of 1672) became permanent 'reading assignments'" (_The Rise of the Legal Profession_, p. 176).

36. Samuel Pufendorf, _Of the Law of Nature and Nations_, in Eight Books, tr. Basil Kennett (London, 1710), Book II, Ch. II, p. 95.

37. _Ibid._, p. 98.

38. _Ibid._, pp. 109-110.

39. _Ibid._, p. 111.

40. _Ibid._, p. 116.

41. Jones, ed., _Commentaries_, p. 28.

42. _Ibid._, p. 29.

43. Hugo Grotius, _The Rights of War and Peace, in Three Books, wherein are explained, the Law of Nature and Nations, and the Principal Points relating to Government_ (London, 1738), p. xiii.

44. _Ibid._, p. 9.

45. _Ibid._, p. 11.

46. _Of the Law of Nature and Nations_, Book II, Ch. III, p. 100.

47. <u>Skeletons of a Course of Theological Lectures</u> (Oberlin: James Steele, 1840), p. 174.
48. <u>Skeletons</u>, p. 201.
49. D. T. Blake, quoted in Miller, <u>Life of the Mind in
America</u>, p. 165.
50. H. J. Berman argues that the consistent elements of
modern democratic societies including "individualism,
rationalism, nationalism--the Triune Deity of Democracy,"
are drawn from "principles of legal rationality." Further,
"these 'jural postulates' (as Roscoe Pound would have called
them) were considered to be not only useful but also just,
and not only just but also part of the natural order of the
universe. Life itself was thought to derive its meaning and
purpose" from them (<u>Interaction of Law and Religion</u>, p. 69).
51. Matthews, <u>op. cit.</u>, p. 17.
52. <u>Ibid.</u>, p. 30.
53. "A Perfect State of Society," address before the
"Society of Inquiry," at Oberlin Collegiate Institute,
September 3, 1839 (Oberlin: James Steele, 1839), pp. 9, 12.
54. Colton <u>History and Character of American Revivals</u>,
p. 1.
55. <u>Ibid.</u>, p. 6.
56. <u>Ibid.</u>, p. 34.
57. <u>Ibid.</u>, p. 28.
58. <u>Ibid.</u>, pp. 170-172.
59. <u>Ibid.</u>, p. 256.
60. <u>Ibid.</u>, p. 257. Colton's enthusiasm for revivalism
waned considerably in the next few years; and by the time of
his return to America in 1835 he was so disturbed by the
disorder among the Presbyterians that he "took orders" in
the Episcopal Church. [See Alfred A. Cave, "Calvin Colton:
An Antebellum Disaffection with the Presbyterian Church,"
<u>Journal of Presbyterian History</u> 50 (1972), 39-53.] It is
significant, however, that all of Colton's objections--to
the increased power of the laity, particularly in the criticism of their social betters; to emotional sensationalism in
the raising of revivals; to various reform movements, especially abolition, which threatened existing laws and insti-
tutions--rested on the conviction that law is the foundation
of true religion. In 1836 Colton published his <u>Thoughts on</u>

the Religious State of the Country: With Reasons for Preferring Episcopacy, in which he wrote, "Religion without
government runs into fanaticism --into chaos--in the same
manner, as the ordinary state of society would be dissolved
into anarchy without civil order" (quoted by Cave, op. cit.,
p. 46). Charles Finney would have agreed heartily with
Colton's statement; the crucial difference between them is
that Finney believes every person can understand and partic-
ipate directly in the government of both Church and State.
Colton is an "aristocrat"; for him the law orders society
into ranks of relative rights and authority. Finney is a
"democrat"; for him the law is a set of divine precepts to
which all persons have equal access and equal responsibility. To juxtapose the two is to dramatize the ambivalence
toward law in the nineteenth century: is the law designed
to restrain and conserve, or is the law an instrument for
activity and change? Both the promoters and opponents of
Finney's revivals could appeal to law as the foundation of
their views.

    61. The American Adam: Innocence, Tragedy, and Tradi-
tion in the Nineteenth Century (Chicago: University of
Chicago Press, 1955), pp. 67-68.
    62. Barbara M. Cross, ed., The Autobiography of Lyman
Beecher (Cambridge, Mass.: The Belknap Press, 1961), vol. 1,
pp. 258-260.
    63. Ibid., vol. 2, p. 167.
    64. Ibid., vol. 2, p. 204.
    65. Revival Sketches and Manual. In Two Parts (New
York: The American Tract Society, 1859), p. 333.
    66. Ibid., p. 472.
    67. Glenn T. Miller, "God's Light and Man's Enlighten-
ment: Evangelical Theology of Colonial Presbyterianism,"
Journal of Presbyterian History 51:2 (1973), 106. Miller
here quotes Ebenezer Pemberton, Practical Discourses
(Boston, 1741).
    68. "On Trusting in the Mercy of God," Sermons on Gospel
Themes, ed. Henry Cowles (Oberlin: E. J. Goodrich, 1876),
p. 26. The sermons in this collection were preached at
Oberlin from 1845 to 1861. Cowles took the sermons down in

shorthand and Finney corrected the transcripts for publication, with a minimum of changes.

69. Life of the Mind in America, p. 103.

70. In subsequent years the revivalists, suffering a
massive failure of nerve, turned to premillennialism and the
hope of Christus ex machina as the solution of national
unrighteousness; the lawyers discovered politics as "the art
of the possible" and abandoned the vision of a "perfect
social order." For an analysis of the reasons for the wreck
of their common hope, see David L. Weddle, "The Law and the
Revival: A New Divinity for the Settlements," Church
History 47:2 (June, 1978), 212-214.

Chapter III

THE CALLING OF A PREACHER

Autobiography

Erik Erikson speaks of the last stage in the development of a healthy personality as the establishment of "ego integrity" against the alternative of "despair." This is the point in the life cycle at which one is able to affirm one's personal history as a pattern of events which discloses one's true identity. Thus a person is willing to defend the meaningfulness of that particular pattern against all threats, including death,

> . . . for he knows that an individual life is the accidental coincidence of but one life cycle with but one segment of history; and that for him all human integrity stands or falls with the one style of integrity of which he partakes.[1]

The writing of religious autobiography may be seen as the act of achieving and declaring what Erikson goes on to call "the ego's accrued assurance of its proclivity for order and meaning." For Finney this cumulative stage of the mature mind finds expression in his Memoirs.

Written in his seventy-fifth year, the Memoirs contain Finney's reflection on his nearly completed personal history, a reflection unified by Finney's perception of himself as a revival preacher and "winner of souls." That the Memoirs are governed by this perception is clear from the

careful way he excises from the account those activities not
directly related to the promotion of revivals, most notably
his early life and his later theological teaching and writing at Oberlin College. Nevertheless, he does attribute
elaborate theological views to himself at points considerably earlier than the time of their actual formulation.
Such anachronisms are consistent with his purpose to defend
"the doctrines that were preached . . . the measures used,
and . . . the results of preaching those doctrines and the
use of those measures" (MF, p. 2)--although they also limit
the usefulness of the Memoirs as a historical source.[2]

In the last paragraphs Finney refers to the Memoirs as
"my revival narrative" and in the opening pages he explicitly denies any interest in the interior life except as his
private experiences relate to his public role.

I am not about to write an autobiography, let it
be remembered; and shall enter no farther into a
relation of the events of my own private life than
shall seem necessary to give an intelligible
account of the manner in which I was led, in relation to these great movements of the Church [MF,
p. 4].

What is more telling about Finney's state of mind than this
disavowal is the fact that he thought an account of his own
actions the most appropriate form for a history and defense
of the revival movement. Finney wrote his story as the
interpretative key to the larger pattern of God's movement
in history. By defending that pattern, Finney defended that
"one style of integrity" by which he believed all human
integrity, including his own, stands or falls.

The act of fixing the contours of one's identity in the
language of autobiography is itself an essential part of the
process of coming to clear consciousness of "oneself." As
Roy Pascal notes, "the life is represented in autobiography
not as something established but as a process; it is not
simply the narrative of the voyage, but also the voyage

itself."[3] Through the exercise of autobiographical imagination, to borrow a phrase from Samuel Taylor Coleridge, "a
subject becomes a subject by the act of constructing itself
objectively to itself."[4] By acknowledging a definite image
of the self, one assumes responsibility for a defined pattern of moral response to other subjects. In religious
autobiography moral action is interpreted as a response to
the formative action of God; the subject becomes conscious
of itself as an object of divine attention and care.[5] Thus
religious autobiography, from St. Augustine onward, is
grounded in the confession that the ultimate ground of one's
identity is the shaping power of divine providence: a
confession of the belief in a unifying pattern in history
which affirms not only the integrity and value of the self,
but also the being and goodness of God. For Finney his
Memoirs constitute a form of theological argument that human
and divine action are unified and regulated by moral law.

The problem, of course, is how to discern the pattern
of divine action in the present since pattern in history can
be recognized only in retrospect. In light of this problem,
Wilhelm Dilthey, the nineteenth-century pioneer in the study
of interpretation, insisted that it is only to the past that
the category of "meaning" properly belongs. The autobiographer seeks "meaning" by organizing the events of his or her
life according to some interpretive pattern. By means of
this pattern memory can reconstruct the past as an intelligible "history."[6] Thus, Dilthey concluded that the relation of part to whole in a given life, that is, its meaning,
can be ascertained only when the course of that life has
been completed. Prior to that point, "our conception of the
meaning of a life is constantly changing,"[7] since new experiences in the present cause us to re-evaluate the meaning of
the events of the past and to set new purposes for the
future. Autobiographical accounts focusing on conversion
illustrate this point inasmuch as the conversion becomes the
central development of the author's life which determines
the meaning he or she assigns to its subsequent course.
What cannot be related to that criterion of significance is
lost to the memory as irrelevant. What Erikson has

described as the ultimate stage of a mature personality,
then, Dilthey has expressed as the primary end of philosophy: to discover the pattern and meaning of history.

Inasmuch as the writing of autobiography is the declaration, as well as the achievement, of personal integrity,
personal narrative has an implicit instructional function.
As an "edifying example," the autobiographer's story stands
in continuity with that history in which God effects salvation in human life. It is one's contribution to the confes-
sional task of one's religious community. By telling one's
own story the autobiographer "re-presents" his or her experiences as an exemplification of personal alignment with the
divine intention in history that is revealed to all people.
That representation gains in validity as the community's
acknowledgement of its saving power confirms one's own
"style of human integrity." Out of this reciprocity of
witness and response a new understanding of personal and
social identity emerges. As Erikson points out, ideological
leaders "are able, out of the deepest personal conflicts, to
derive the energy which meets their period's specific need
for a resynthesis of the prevalent world image."[8]

James Olney, in a recent study of autobiography, has
described the process of finding such an image as the search
for a "metaphor" of the self.

> The focus through which an intensity of self-
> awareness becomes a coherent vision of all real-
> ity, the point through which the individual suc-
> ceeds in making the universe take on his own
> order, is metaphor: the formal conjunction of
> single subject and various objects.[9]

The metaphor chosen as the key to self and cosmos may be a
single figure which organizes all one's thought and action,
as "light" pervades the autobiographical reflections of
George Fox. Or, the autobiographer may use a "double," or
reflexive, metaphor which regulates recollection, while
allowing for some degree of criticism, as in Augustine's

"awareness of his own awareness" in the Confessions. In Finney's Memoirs, however, there is no principle of critical reflection on the process of his own memory. He is a man with only one metaphor to establish the conjunction between himself and the various objects which constitute his field of action, as he recognizes only one "style of human integrity" and only one "pattern and meaning in history." That metaphor is, as we have seen, legal order.

Conversion

We have already pointed to the conflict of constructive energy with an ideology of submission to authority and order which was a central ingredient in Finney's decision to study for the law. In the account of his conversion in the Memoirs, the same dynamic tension is present, now expressed in theological terms, and a parallel resolution is reached. By a determined exercise of will Finney affirms his fidelity to a higher, more inclusive, order of law than that which attracted him into apprenticeship with Benjamin Wright.

Further, by turning to religion for the resources to understand the meaning to his life in the context of a universal order, Finney is addressing that primary crisis in the development of personality which Erikson calls "basic trust versus mistrust." However, the religious ideology available to him--the theology of traditional Calvinism--did not adequately resolve this crisis. For, while the Westminster Confession gave assurance that the world was ordered by a faithful God, whose covenantal promises could be trusted, it failed to nurture in people themselves a concomitant sense of their own trustworthiness. The ancient saying of the prophet Jeremiah, "The heart is deceitful above all things, and desperately wicked: who can know it?" (Jeremiah 17:9), was a motto for such preaching as Finney heard from the Presbyterian ministry. This doctrine, however, did not accord with the robust confidence in his own judgment which Finney's sense of identity and choice of vocation demanded. Further, in the process of his conversion Finney discovered in himself a natural capacity to do what is right. While a struggle was required, in the end he found that he could trust himself to repent, and to conform his will to the divine law: "all that was necessary on my part, was to get my own consent to give up my sins, and accept Christ" (MF, p. 14).

The story of Finney's conversion is well known in evangelical circles, and the chapter from his Memoirs in which the conversion is recorded is often reprinted in inspirational volumes to stir the flagging spirits of the faithful.[10] It was a practice which Finney would have approved, for he frequently drew from the story himself to illustrate sermonic points. The account is ordered according to the "plan of salvation" as he worked it out through fifty years of preaching, beginning with his first "relation" before the startled townspeople of Adams (MF, pp. 27f.). In the village Finney had distinguished himself as bright, confident, and aggressive--just the type of man to represent one's interests in the rough-and-tumble of the early courts. He was noted for his physical stature and intellectual resources. Competent in social graces, endowed with musical gifts, he was a man of action with no known mystical tendencies.

Further, Finney enjoyed baiting the local Presbyterian minister, a severe young man from Princeton, the Rev. George Gale. Gale attempted to defend the theology he had learned in the great New Jersey bastion of orthodoxy, but Finney beleaguered him with questions. The minister was caught in a painful bind: he realized that his congregation was not a center of evangelical zeal; but he could not accept the diagnosis offered by this apprentice lawyer, viz., that the reason the congregation did nothing was because their theology taught them that there was nothing they could do, except pray and wait for God's Spirit to move the unbelievers to faith. Finney was unimpressed with this kind of religion. When he was asked if he desired them to pray for his salvation, he testily declined.

You have prayed enough since I have attended these
meetings to have prayed the devil out of Adams, if
there is any virtue in your prayers. But here you
are praying on, and complaining still [MF, p.
10].[11]

To make matters worse, Finney was leading the church choir
and having what the minister suspected was an unhealthy
influence on the young people.

In the meanwhile, however, that Bible Finney had looked
into for the first principles of legal theory began to weigh
heavily on his mind. He found himself hiding it under a
pile of law books for fear that someone might see him reading it and conclude that he took religion seriously after
all. That conclusion, as it turned out, would have been
entirely justified. After several "restless" days, on Octo-
ber 7, 1821, a Sunday evening, Finney resolved to settle the
question of religious commitment, alone. He was agitated by
the fact that in Adams he was "brought so continually face
to face with religious truth; which was a new state of
things to me" (MF, p. 10). But he felt a deep sense of
shame about his religious concerns; he was reluctant to
appear before the townspeople as an "inquirer." He withdrew
from conversation about religion and avoided the minister
and elders of the Presbyterian Church which was next door to
his law office. So complete was his withdrawal from the
usual resources of spiritual counsel that he could say, "I
felt myself shut up to the Bible" (MF, p. 13.).

It had taken "two or three years" for his mind to
become "quite settled that whatever mystification there
might be either in my own or in my pastor's mind, or in the
mind of the church, the Bible was, nevertheless, the true
word of God" (MF p. 11). Once having accepted the authority
of the Bible, the matter seemed simple enough: "I was
brought face to face with the question whether I would
accept Christ as presented in the Gospel, or pursue a world-
ly course of life" (MF, p. 11). The issue is conceived in
moral terms; what is required is a responsible decision.

Therefore, "I made up my mind that I would settle the question of my soul's salvation at once," even to the extent of
neglecting business in order "to give myself wholly to the
work of securing the salvation of my soul" (MF, p. 12).

Finney is motivated in his quest by the recognition
that he was "by no means in a state of mind to go to heaven
if I should die." It is not guilt that sets him on the way,
but a desire to secure "happiness in heaven" (MF, p. 9).
The motive accords with his later view that obedience to the
gospel is not only right but also fulfills the condition for
human happiness.[12] Conversion is the means of properly
fulfilling a natural desire which Finney regards as the
divinely given conatus of human nature. He is prepared to
accept the gospel, then, not as a repudiation of his own
being as "corrupt," but as an extension of his mature powers
of reason and will to their proper end. As he reflects upon
the event, conversion appears as a process by which he
willingly submitted himself to the moral law wherein he
recognized his true happiness.

During Monday and Tuesday of the decisive week, he
reports, "my convictions increased; but still it seemed as
if my heart grew harder. I could not shed a tear; I could
not pray" (MF, p. 13). However, these convictions crystal-
lized not first in a sense of guilt, but in fear.

> Tuesday night I had become very nervous; and in
> the night a strange feeling came over me as if I
> was about to die. I knew that if I did I should
> sink down to hell; but I quieted myself as best I
> could until morning [MF, p. 13].

The terror of hell is one of the agencies later used by
Finney himself to persuade people of their need to accept
the gospel; and Finney refers to his own experience in one
dramatic sermonic appeal:

> Said a young man, "I am afraid to go to sleep
> at night, lest I should awake in hell." . . . I

> recollect having this thought once impressed upon
> my mind, and so much agonized was I, that I almost
> thought myself to be dying on the spot! O, I can
> never express the terror and agony of my soul in
> that hour![13]

The relation between such fear and guilt comes clear to the
mind in the conviction of "the guilt and hell-desert of
unbelief."[14] For Finney his past actions are irrelevant to
his salvation, but not in themselves necessarily evil. What
is evil is present unbelief, the refusal to accept whole-
heartedly the demands of Christianity.

But how is unbelief to be overcome? Finney refers to
the quieting of his early skepticism in odd terms.

> In my early life, when I was tempted to skepti-
> cism, I can well recollect that I said to myself--
> It is much more probably that ministers and multi-
> tudes of good men who believe that Bible are
> right, than that I am. They have examined the
> subject, but I have not. It is, therefore, en-
> tirely unreasonable for me to doubt.[15]

In the context of this sermon Finney's point is to underscore the reasonableness of accepting the gospel since it is
so perfectly adapted to the human situation; however, this
example has an instructive inner tension. On the one hand,
the gospel is commended for its inherent rationality; on the
other, what constitutes the standard of reasonableness is
the authority of "ministers and good men." Certainly in the
Memoirs there is no indication that Finney is aided in his
acceptance of the Bible by established religious authorities. If anything, the Memoirs are an argument against the
spiritual efficacy of orthodoxy and its representatives.
When Finney decides to seek salvation, the means he employed
were Bible reading and private prayer, not pastoral counsel.
The spiritual resources of the Presbyterian Church had prov-
en fruitless to him. As he would preach repeatedly, piety
can be nourished only from the Bible; traditional teaching,

including the Westminster Confession, and educated clergy must be critically evaluated in the light of a prayerful lay reading of Scripture and the moral results of "heart religion."

This tension between reason and "experience" is present throughout Finney's preaching. The gospel appeals through the reason to the will, yet its final evidence of truth lies in its "efficiency" in producing "good men." On this basis orthodoxy is scored for being "cold, lifeless theory"[16] and is rejected along with Unitarianism and Universalism for failing to meet "this one plain simple principle: That and only that which saves from sin is true; all else is false and ruinous."[17] Moral productivity constitutes the first characteristic by which the truth is recognized. In the final analysis rationality is a function of moral experience; what is reasonable is what promotes sanctity. In this light, Finney's reference to "good men" in the quotation above is clarified. The Bible deserves a hearing because it produces virtuous character; thus his later insistence on judging truth by its moral fruit has a clear basis in the process of his own conversion.

Wednesday morning, on the way to his office, he was halted on the street by "an inward voice," urging him to proceed at once to "give [his] heart to God." At this point Finney realized that the promise of salvation in the Christian gospel was "an offer of something to be accepted; and that it was full and complete; and all that was necessary on my part, was to get my own consent to give up my sins, and accept Christ" (MF, p. 14). He responded with a bold vow: "Yes, I will accept it to-day, or I will die in the attempt." Secluding himself deep in the woods, "so far out of sight that no one from the village could see me," he struggled to pray, but found that pride still blocked his confession of sin.

The problem foremost in Finney's mind was a sense of shame and uncertainty about these new attempts to intrude into the unfamiliar space of religious experience; he feared

premature "exposure." Thus, even when he determined to seek
salvation in earnest, he found that his "inward soul hung
back," reluctant to appear before the townsfolk of Adams,
among whom he was held in considerable repute, in a "broken
down" condition. It was only when he overcame the sense of
shame by the conviction that his efforts to gain salvation
were legitimated by divine promise that he was free to pray.
And the fact that Finney was secluded a quarter-mile into
the timber does not alter the significance of his decision
to pray aloud for forgiveness.

> Just at this moment I again thought I heard some
> one approach me, and I opened by eyes to see
> whether it were so. But right there the revela-
> tion of my pride of heart, as the great difficulty
> that stood in the way, was distinctly shown to me.
> An overwhelming sense of my wickedness in being
> ashamed to have a human being see me on my knees
> before God, took such powerful possession of me,
> that I cried at the top of my voice, and exclaimed
> that I would not leave that place if all the men
> on earth and all the devils in hell surrounded me
> [MF, p. 16].

At that point of moral decision, Finney realized that
God could be trusted to fulfill his promises and to provide
salvation. This time Jeremiah again came to mind, but with
a more hopeful message:

> Then shall ye call upon me, and ye shall go and
> pray unto me, and I will hearken unto you. And ye
> shall seek me, and find me, when ye shall search
> for me with all your heart [Jeremiah 29: 12-13].

Finney recalls that he "instantly seized" this text, as a
disclosure of the fact that "faith was a voluntary trust"
(MF, p. 16). We might say, following Erikson's suggestion,
that faith is the "basic trust" that the terms of the world-
order are trustworthy. Faith, for Finney, is the affirma-
tion that both God and he himself are responsible agents

whose actions conform to a lawful order. God can be
trusted--not to fulfill his own mysterious, and at times
terrifying, purposes, but--to uphold the moral law.

What Finney discovered was that such trust was immediately and unconditionally open to him. There was no need
for prolonged penitence or any other form of "preparation"
for grace. In a sermon on the "conditions of being saved,"
Finney proclaims that his own hesitancy was entirely unnecessary.

> In my early experience I thought I could not
> expect to be converted at once, but must be bowed
> down a long time. I said to myself--"God will not
> pity me till I feel worse than I do now . . . ."
> The fact is, God does not ask of you that you
> should suffer.[18]

Rather, God asks for the sinner to submit his "stubborn will
to Him." Just as a child's tantrum of crying is not an
adequate substitute for obedience to parental demands, so
the sinner's contrition cannot replace actual repentance.
To those who resist the gospel because, as Finney sarcastic-
ally phrases the objection, "my case is not yet desperate
enough," he replies that if one "is a sinner and knows it,
this constitutes his preparation and fitness for coming to
Jesus."[19]

The central issue of the gospel is obedience to the
divine will as one's "supreme law"; salvation requires only
understanding the conditions of the "contract into which you
are to enter with your God and Savior" and consenting "at
once." As Finney looked back upon his own "case," he discovered that his own conversion exemplified the nature of
faith.

> Now, said I to myself--"This is the word of the
> everlasting God. My God, I take Thee at Thy word.
> Thou sayest I shall find Thee when I search for
> Thee with all my heart, and now, Lord, I do search

for Thee, I know, with all my heart." And true
enough, I did find the Lord. Never in all my life
was I more certain of anything than I was then
that I had found the Lord.[20]

Turning to his auditors, Finney closed with an exhortation
that dramatizes the extent to which salvation depends on
human initiative: "Sinner, the infinite God waits for your
consent!"

William James cites Finney's conversion narrative as a
prime example of what he calls "the volitional type," as
distinguished from "the type of self-surrender." As he
quickly points out, however, "even in the most voluntarily
built-up sort of regeneration there are passages of partial
self-surrender interposed . . . ."[21] That is, the penitent
reaches a point of "temporary exhaustion" in the struggle to
acknowledge guilt and abandon personal sin. Such a reprieve
from conviction is necessary for "so long as the egoistic
worry of the sick soul guards the door, the expansive confidence of the soul of faith gains no presence."[22] Finney
reaches that stage in the process on his way back from the
crisis in the woods, and he begins to worry that he has been
abandoned as hopeless by the Holy Spirit: "I tried to
recall my convictions, to get back again the load of sin
under which I had been laboring . . . I was so quiet and
peaceful . . . ." (MF, p. 18). The fact, as he soon real-
izes, is that his transformation has begun to take place:
the conflict between his will and the ultimate law of the
universe is over; and he is free to move joyously into the
world, as into a "clean, well-lighted place," ordered and
illumined by moral law.

The crisis of conversion was followed by a strange
calm: " so perfectly quiet was my mind that it seemed as if
all nature listened" (MF, p. 18). In words that are remi-
niscent of the eloquent Personal Narrative in which Jonathan
Edwards records his conversion, Finney describes "the most
profound spiritual tranquility" and "a great sweetness and
tenderness" in his thoughts and feelings. Both also record

the common testimony of converts that the spiritual release from sin and guilt found its physical expression in a flood of tears. Finney seems entirely reconciled to God--"all consciousness of present sin and guilt, had departed from me"--and to his world.

Finney was not among those religious converts who are driven by a sense of alienation from the world, but his conversion is accompanied by a heightened appreciation for natural phenomena as the vehicle of divine revelation. The next morning, for example, he is awakened by the sun, "pouring a clear light" into his room, and triggering a fresh experience of the Spirit of God (MF, pp. 22f). One is reminded of Edwards' testimony that, following his conversion, "scarce anything, among all the works of nature, was so sweet to me as thunder and lightning; formerly, nothing had been so terrible to me."[23] Conversion restores Edwards to communion with the natural order, opening his eyes to the "emblems" of spiritual truths therein, and increases his delight in contemplation as he walked through the fields of his father's farm. Finney is not given to wondering enjoyment of contemplation, and his main business in the fields is shooting quail; but he is affected by the vision of the world of nature ordered by divine providence, for it confirms his trust that the correlative moral order of human action is also under divine governance.

The fundamental difference between the conversion accounts of Edwards and Finney provides the key to the difference between the forms of spirituality in the "awakenings" each promoted in his own century. Edwards is given a vision of divine beauty which reconciles him to the "horrible doctrine" of unconditional predestination,[24] while Finney receives a summons to action which encourages him to take the matter of his eternal destiny into his own hands. Edwards is "wrapt up" in the beauty of holiness and rejoices in the harmony of mercy and justice which is revealed to him. Finney is challenged by the judgment of holiness and must take responsibility for bringing his own will into conformity with the moral government of the universe. His

acceptance of the gospel is so far from being conditioned
upon his assenting to the "horrible doctrine" of predestination that it in fact entails his rejecting the notion as an
obstacle to conversion. What Finney discovers is that faith
is "within the voluntary powers of my mind". It is not God,
but Finney himself who decides whether he will be saved.
The peace which follows immediately his "seizing upon" the
promise of salvation confirms the truth of his discovery,
being the fulfillment of St. Paul's statement, "Being justified by faith, we have peace with God through our Lord Jesus
Christ" (Romans 5:1). "In this state," Finney writes, "I was
taught the doctrine of justification by faith, as a present
experience" (MF, p. 23).

Returning to his office, he discovered that all sense
of guilt was gone and that the very act of playing some
hymns on his bass viol was enough to bring tears to his
eyes. That night, after Judge Wright left, Finney went to
the back room to pray.

> There was no fire, and no light, in the room;
> nevertheless it appeared to me as if it were
> perfectly light. As I went in and shut the door
> after me, it seemed as if I met the Lord Jesus
> Christ face to face [MF, p. 19].

On reflection Finney realized that the vision was "wholly a
mental state"; yet, he added with some understatement, "I
have always since regarded this as a most remarkable state
of mind" (MF, p. 20). But there was more to come.
Returning to the front office, Finney recalls,

> . . . the Holy Spirit descended upon me in a
> manner that seemed to go through me, body and
> soul. I could feel the impression, like a wave of
> electricity, going through and through me. Indeed
> it seemed to come in waves and waves of liquid
> love; for I could not express it in any other way.
> It seemed like the very breath of God. I can
> recollect distinctly that it seemed to fan me,
> like immense wings [MF, p. 20].

This "mighty baptism of the Holy Spirit" was repeated the next morning and convinced Finney beyond all doubt that "the Spirit of God had taken possession of my soul" (MF, p. 23). So powerful was the impression that Finney adds, "so far as I could see, I was in a state in which I could not sin." Although it would be twenty years before Finney was again seized by the baptism of the Spirit, and began to preach the possibility of living without sin, the seeds of his perfectionist teachings were sown in his conversion.

What is remarkable is that the dynamics of the baptism seem quite different from those of the repentance in the woods. There is no persuasion involved; the Spirit takes "possession" unexpectedly, without Finney's prior consent. The Spirit acts as power, or energy, coursing through Finney's being, while he is the passive object of its operation. The discrepancy is sharpened in light of Finney's criticism of Old School views of the Spirit's work in regeneration:

> . . . some persons speak of a change in heart as something miraculous--something in which the sinner is to be entirely passive, and for which he is to wait in the use of means, as he would wait for a surgical operation or an electrical shock.[25]

Finney's own experience of sanctification, then, seems to transgress those "laws of mind" by which he claimed all relations between God and moral agents were regulated. In fact, however, this is an example of the relative roles of reason and experience in Finney's more developed understanding of "moral suasion." The purpose of the repeated baptisms that night and the following morning is to overcome Finney's doubts about his own salvation. The experience itself is a mode of persuasion to which Finney must respond with voluntary trust. Given the experience of the baptism of the Spirit, it is no longer "reasonable" to doubt that one has been regenerated. The Spirit presents to the mind incontrovertible "evidence" that one is forgiven and filled with the love of God.

The morning following these extraordinary events, a
client came by the office to confirm Finney's appearance in
court as his attorney. In his famous reply Finney announces
his new commission in terms of his old profession: "Deacon
B--, I have a retainer from the Lord Jesus Christ to plead
his cause, and I cannot plead yours" (MF, p. 24). The
astonished deacon found himself pre-empted: "I had enlisted
in the cause of Christ." Charles Finney was embarked on the
campaign trail.

Prophet

For Finney conversion to Christianity was at the same time a
private transformation and public commission. He began at
once to persuade others also to make professions of faith
and his example was a great inducement. In a pattern often
followed in revivals, the winning over of the chief skeptic
in the village set off a wave of conversions. Finney began
an early-morning prayer meeting and went around the town
with the indignant zeal of a new convert to rouse the lag-
gards from their sleep. He sadly notes that "the brethren,
I found, attended with more and more reluctance; which fact
greatly tried me" (MF, p. 34). One morning, returning to
the meetinghouse where only a few had gathered, Finney was
arrested in his tracks by "a light perfectly ineffable"
which "shone in my soul. . . . In this light it seemed as if
I could see that all nature praised and worshiped God except
man" (MF, p. 34). The spectacle of humanity, refusing to
acknowledge the praiseworthiness of God and thus violating
the very purpose of which it was created, brought forth a
"flood of tears," releasing at least the frustration built
up during his pre-dawn rounds. If the brethren did not
attend to the prayerful praise of God, how could the unbelievers be brought to see their duty?

A task of such magnitude called for no ordinary messen-
ger. "I think I knew something then, by actual experience,
of that light that prostrated Paul on his way to Damascus

I saw the glory of God; and . . . I could not endure to think of the manner in which he was treated by men" (MF, p. 34). Like St. Paul of old, Finney knew himself to be designated by God to carry the message of salvation--a message that was at variance with the dominant Protestant tradition, but whose authority was grounded in "divine manifestations" (MF, p. 35). As Paul challenged the appropriateness of applying traditional Jewish practices of the Palestinian church to his Gentile converts by setting the authority of his own gospel over against those "who seemed to be pillars" (Galatians 2:9), so Finney breaks free from the theological and pastoral heritage of New England Calvinism to establish a new language for the "sons of the Pilgrims," with the accent on spiritual freedom. Perhaps it does not strain the parallel over much to suggest that, as Paul found it necessary to develop a new vocabulary (in fact, several new vocabularies) in order to communicate the Christian message to his Hellenistic audiences in Asia Minor, so Finney was constrained to develop a "new divinity" to make the gospel intelligible to the self-reliant Yorkers, whose sensibilities in religious matters he so intimately shared.

Other notices in the Memoirs encourage the conclusion that Finney saw his own career, like that of St. Paul, directed by prophetic visions.[26] Early in his revivals in western New York, while pressed into preaching at a town called Brownville, Finney received a "direct revelation from God" to proceed to Gouverneur--even though there was a great opposition to revival in that town and the only church member from Gouverneur Finney met before embarking was "cold as an iceberg" (MF, p. 114). With the help of Brother Daniel Nash, however, sent ahead to scout out the spiritual terrain and engage in that mighty exercise of prayer for which the older man was famous in the region, Finney held a spectacular revival at Gouverneur.

Again, at a crucial point in his early career, when Finney was at Auburn and tides of resistance were beginning to rise from other New School ministers, he received another vision. Asa Nettleton had announced that "all the New

England churches especially were closed to me," and a letter
from Lyman Beecher, in support of Nettleton's opposition,
had surfaced. Finney, "much impressed with the extensive
working of that system of espionage," prayed "to be directed" (MF, pp. 192f). What happened was not at all expected,
and Finney's account resonates with Rudolph Otto's well-
known description of the mysterium tremendum et fascinans.[27]
Finney was overpowered by a vision of the divine majesty of
the Lawgiver, he felt the fragility of his creatureliness,
and at the end a beatific peace assured him that no obsta-
cles could hinder the progress of his work.

> The Lord showed me in a vision what was before me.
> He drew so near to me, while I was engaged in
> prayer, that my flesh literally trembled on my
> bones. I shook from head to foot, under a full
> sense of the presence of God. At first, and for
> some time, it seemed more like being on the top of
> Sinai, amidst its full thunderings, than in the
> presence of the cross of Christ. Never in my
> life, that I recollect, was I so awed and humbled
> before God as then. Nevertheless, instead of
> feeling like fleeing, I seemed drawn nearer to
> that Presence that filled me with such unutterable
> awe and trembling. After a season of great humil-
> iation before him, there came a great lifting up.
> God assured me that he would be with me and uphold
> me; that no opposition should prevail against me;
> that I had nothing to do, in regard to all this
> matter, but to keep about my work, and wait for
> the salvation of God. The sense of God's presence
> . . . led me to be perfectly trustful, perfectly
> calm, and to have nothing but the most perfectly
> kind feelings toward all the brethren that were
> misled, and were arraying themselves against me
> [MF, pp. 193f].[28]

This testimony is followed by a quotation from the prophet
Jeremiah, whose words precipitated the critical moment in
Finney's conversion. Here he copies out a long passage in

which Jeremiah proclaims his trust in the Lord's protection, even though he is "in derision daily." While Finney admits that the parallel is not exact, "there was so much similarity in the case, that this passage was often a support to my soul" (MF, p. 195). The prophet, like the apostle, finds that God compensates his suffering servants with occasional private audiences, re-affirming their call in the face of discouraging circumstances. Finney makes it clear in the Memoirs that he has known that strange comfort which often leads God's messengers ever more deeply into conflict.[29]

There are other marks of a prophet which Finney also bears. He is ruled by a single controlling vision, formed during his years of legal study and expanded to the horizon of the universe in his conversion: the vision of all reality governed by a single coherent system of moral government. This vision was not burned into his brain by the desert sun, the blazing catalyst of ancient monotheistic conviction, but imprinted gradually on his imagination by the metaphysical speculations of the "old legal authors." But it is no less demanding than the visions of other prophets, for every statement Finney utters and every action he performs he intends to be regulated strictly by the provisions of that image of reality.

Because of his complete devotion to his own vision, like most prophets, he finds himself alienated from the established clergy and their investment in the status quo. Finney plays the prophet to the Old School ministers' role as priests, guardians of tradition, custodians of continuity with the past. As many prophets, Finney sees himself primarily as a reformer, who does not wish to supplant the institution which the priests preserve, but to recall it to its original mission which has been increasingly neglected by those very guardians. Thus Finney claims that it is precisely the Old School which has obscured the true meaning of the Bible by overlaying the text with a deterministic philosophy, while he interprets the Bible by a reasonable, "common sense" construction, the way good judges interpret

the law. Further, the prophet is alienated not only from
the established religious institutions, but also from other
sectarians. Prophets are notoriously bad team-players.
Thus, while Finney seeks to cooperate with all ministers who
share his views regarding revivals, he rejects all sects,
from Adventists and Mormons to Universalists and Masons.

Finally, the prophet bears an ambivalent relationship
to the general populace. On the one hand, he eventually
must find his largest following among the common people; and
unless his vision and message correspond to their secret
needs and desires, his voice will not be heard in his own
generation, and his mission will have failed. Finney's
message, resonating with the widespread interest in legal
order, finds such a correspondence. On the other hand,
however, the prophet is often searchingly critical of the
prevailing morals and manners of his hearers. The only way
to the prophet's mountaintop is, for most common folk,
through the humiliating pass of denunciation. John the
Baptizer greeted those who came to hear his message with the
words, "O generation of vipers, who hath warned you to flee
from the wrath to come?" (Matthew 3:7). Finney's Memoirs
contain many examples of the same sort of prophetic hospi-
tality to the very people he is inviting into the kingdom of
God. Strong drink, Sabbath frivolity, the poison of tobacco, dishonest business dealings, and vain fashions are among
the features of the popular culture against which Finney
thunders loudly. His success depends on finding in his
hearers a trace of vestigial Puritan conscience about personal indulgences or, as in the case of promoting temperance, a certain alliance with the temporal interest of major
groups within his audience.[30]

The relationship between the prophet and the group he
wishes to reform, then, is complex and multifaceted. A
series of seemingly slight changes in that web of motives,
interests, hopes, and fears that hold together any large
religious movement can bring the whole enterprise to a
grinding halt. Finney's career demonstrates a consuming

attention to making whatever adjustments are possible, within the limits of his controlling vision, to sustain the forward momentum of revivals. To do so required an entirely new conception of the ministerial calling.

Vocation

The counties of western New York were accustomed to preachers: some dignified and dull, others ignorant and amusing. But they had never seen one like Finney before.

> I was from the very first aware that . . . there was this wide gulf in our views, and would be in practice, between myself and other ministers. I seldom felt that I was one of them, or that they regarded me as really belonging to their fraternity. I was bred a lawyer. I came right forth from a law office to the pulpit, and talked to the people as I would have talked to a jury. [MF, p. 89].

For Finney the gospel is a case to be won. What is required of a preacher is that he learn the laws of the court in which he pleads, that he learn to interpret the Bible according to "the close and logical reasonings of judges, as I found them reported in our law works" (MF, p. 53), and that he understand the laws of the mind so that he becomes skillful in persuasion. Finney preached in order to move his auditors to action; he appealed for a verdict. He recalled with pride that the members of the Oneida presbytery "used to complain that I let down the dignity of the pulpit; and I was a disgrace to the ministerial profession; that I talked like a lawyer at the bar . . . that I said 'you' instead of preaching about sin and sinners, and saying 'they'; that I said 'hell,' and with such an emphasis as often to shock the people . . ." (MF, p. 83).

Finney's new measures first encountered such criticism when he began attracting wider attention in the Western

Revivals. On reflection, he claims that his innovations
grew out of his belief that the influence of the Spirit in
conversion was "moral, that is persuasive," and that "the
Holy Spirit operates in the preacher" through the proper use
of means "calculated to convert" the people (MF, pp. 154f).
Since human depravity is "a voluntary attitude of mind," it
can be corrected by voluntary action. To elicit such consent, the divine Spirit uses the preacher as the medium
through whom the truth is presented to the mind of the
sinner. The object of the Spirit's work "is always the
same--namely, to produce voluntary action in conformity to
His law." Finney pictures the "striving of the Spirit" in
terms that express the strength and integrity of the human
will in the process as strongly as possible:

> [The striving of the Spirit] is an energy of God,
> applied to the mind of man, setting truth before
> his mind, debating, reasoning, convincing, and
> persuading. The sinner resists God's claims,
> cavils and argues against them; and then God, by
> His Spirit, meets the sinner and debates with him,
> somewhat as two men might debate and argue with
> each other.[31]

The image is drawn explicitly from the courtroom. Consistent with his exegetical method, Finney interprets the biblical description of the work of the Holy Spirit "to reprove
the world of sin" (John 16:8) as referring to "judicial
proceedings." The Holy Spirit, speaking in whispers to "the
inner ear of the soul," seeks to persuade accused sinners of
the justice of the charges brought against them.

> When the judge has heard all the testimony and the
> arguments of counsel, he sums up the whole case
> and lays it before the jury, bringing out all the
> strong points and making them bear with all their
> condensed and accumulated power upon the condemna-
> tion of the criminal. . . . Thus does the Spirit
> convince or convict the sinner by testimony, by
> argument, by arraying all the strong points of the

case against him under circumstances of affecting
solemnity and power.[32]

For the many sinners who have been deafened in varying
degrees to the Spirit's earnest whispers, the accusation is
amplified through the shouts of the preacher. If the will
cannot be roused by gentle inner promptings, then let it be
startled and moved by public urgings--but the will must
somehow be excited to action, or the soul is lost. Because
Finney interprets the responsibility of a minister as analogous to the responsibility of a lawyer, preaching for him
must be effective advocacy. The tragedy of the ministry is
that most preachers are not as intensive in the pursuit of
cases with eternal consequences, as attorneys are in the
defense of temporal interests. Finney once commented to
George Gale, "If advocates at the bar should pursue the same
course in pleading the cause of their clients, that ministers do in pleading the cause of Christ with sinners, they
would not gain a single case" (MF, p. 155).

Finney preached to gain cases, and no one could deny
his record. He remembers with satisfaction that one of his
most prestigious critics, Lyman Beecher, was astounded that
Finney's revival in Rochester resulted in 100,000 people
"having connected themselves with churches" in one year (MF,
p. 301). Finney's aggressive style was unquestionably
effective, drawing crowds both large and anxious. Henry
O'Reilly noted that the First Presbyterian Church of Rochester was remarkable for its many buttresses, "added to
strengthen the walls, after an alarm occasioned by some
imaginary insecurity of the building, owing to the large
concourse who thronged to hear the Rev. Mr. Finney during a
revival."[33] These results, Finney insisted, were directly
attributable to his forceful appeal to the individual's
moral ability to obey the law of God. One minister who
heard Finney preach in Rochester testified to his forceful-
ness: "for two hours it rained hailstones."[34] Another
member of the audience reported that "it did not sound like
preaching, but like a lawyer arguing a case before a court
and jury."[35] Finney proudly recorded that the revival

affected "the highest classes of society" in Rochester, and
that "very soon the work took effect, extensively, among the
lawyers in that city" (MF, p. 289). And not in that city
alone. He is pleased to report that his critics among the
established clergy "found that, under my preaching, judges,
and lawyers, and educated men were converted by scores,
whereas, under their methods, such a thing seldom occurred"
(MF, p. 84). Finney's pride is understandable, for his
success among the lawyers is proof of the skill with which
he adapted their own techniques of courtroom advocacy to his
new vocation as the chief counsel for the divine government.

Some modification of traditional methods of preaching
was inevitable since, according to his recollections, Finney's crisis of conversion was in considerable part a crisis
of vocational choice. Upon emerging from the woods, on the
afternoon of his conversion, "brushing through leaves and
bushes, I recollect saying with great emphasis, 'If I am
ever converted, I will preach the Gospel'" (MF, p. 17). He
admits, however, that the prospect was troubling.

> When I was first convicted, the thought had occur-
> red to my mind that if I was ever converted I
> should be obliged to leave my profession, of which
> I was very fond, and go to preaching the Gospel.
> This at first stumbled me [MF, p. 25].

While exhorting the students at Oberlin to enter the work of
evangelism, and threatening them with hell if they did not,
Finney testified that his conversion hinged on accepting the
unattractive call to become a minister.

> A long time I had a secret conviction that I
> should be a minister, though my heart repelled it.
> In fact, my conversion turned very much upon my
> giving up this contest with God, and subduing this
> repellency of feeling against God's call.[36]

Even taking into account the probable exaggeration, for
homiletical purposes, of this factor in the decision,

Finney's confession here underscores the fact that his conversion included a conscious commitment to a vocation which
repelled him.

Part of this "repellency" was an aversion to the pulpit
styles of both the learned clergy of the Presbyterian persuasion and the unlettered exhorters of various denomina-
tions he had encountered so far. While growing up in Oneida
County, Finney remembers his neighbors laughing at itinerant
preachers for "the strange mistakes which had been made and
the absurdities which had been advanced" (MF, pp. 4f).[37]
The minister in Connecticut, whose church Finney attended
occasionally during his secondary education, droned on mono-
tonously from passages systematically marked by his fingers:
"when his fingers were all read out, he was near the close
of the sermon" (MF, p. 6). Even when Finney sat under the
educated ministry of George Gale in Adams, he found the
preaching singularly uninspired. It was understandably
difficult for the aggressive young lawyer to consider seriously a career as a minister. To Finney's mind the choice
was between the intellectually sophisticated, but practically ineffective, sermons of established ministers; and the
rousing, but often illogical and melodramatic, performances
of intinerants.

To reduce the available models to these alternatives
was manifestly unfair, of course, to the polished pulpiteers
of the New School, such as Beecher and Taylor; but at this
point Finney was entirely unacquainted with revival preaching in New England. His experience indicated that he could
accept the divine call only if he fashioned his own prophet's mantle out of a lawyer's robe, spun in western New
York. Thus Finney did not so much assume the ministerial
role as transform it, creating a new model for the "man of
God," patterned after the practice of the learned and eloquent members of the legal profession and supported by the
principles of their tradition.

Finney entered the Christian faith with a vision of God
focused through the lens of Grotius and Blackstone, rather

than Calvin and Edwards: the vision of a God who rules the
universe by laws, that is, intelligible principles of operation by which people may manage their affairs in a way to
insure the fulfillment of the divine purpose which is won-
derfully coincidental with the increase of human happiness.
Finney's decision to enter the ministry was not a repudiation of the legal vision of reality, but a translation of it
into evangelical Christian terms. His conversion represented his resolution of the tension between the conviction
that reality is intelligible and receptive to the individual's informed efforts at self-improvement, and the devout
claim that God's ways are mysterious and that grace (whether
in this life or the next) is an arbitrary act whose ultimate
ground the human mind cannot penetrate.

Finney's earlier decision to practice law indicated a
sense of individuality defined over against an articulated
pattern of authority. As a lawyer, his vocation was to
mediate that order to the confusions and alienations of the
young society. This sense of mission was carried over in
his view of the ministry as "pleading the case of the gospel," of revival as the application of courtroom techniques,
and of theology as the exposition of the "moral government"
of God--all for the purpose of restoring perfect and universal order. Finney's religious consciousness, as we have
seen, is informed by the "metaphor" of legal order: God and
his human subjects are moral agents whose relationship is
mediated by a legal code. God is known only inasmuch as he
discloses his nature in the principles of moral government
which in turn organize and direct the energies of his subjects. For Finney the Gospel presents to the sinner a
rational system of laws, which one is capable of understanding and obeying without the assistance of supernatural illumination. The task of the preacher, therefore, is to provide the occasion for his hearers to understand the demands
of God and to decide whether or not to submit to them.

Finney soon realized, however, that to answer the call
to represent the interests of divine government in his
generation required more than "new measures." There must

also be a "new divinity" which allows for that exercise of
initiative in religious life which the prophet, "who was
bred a lawyer," seeks to elicit. According to his own
account, Finney did not expect to receive any more help in
his theological education at the seminaries of New England
than what he had already gathered from his conversations
with George Gale. Thus, in 1822 when he put himself under
the care of the Oneida Presbytery as a candidate for the
ministry, he spurned their offer to support his theological
studies at Princeton.

> . . . I plainly told them that I would not put
> myself under such an influence as they had been
> under; that I was confident they had been wrongly
> educated, and they were not ministers that met my
> ideal of what a minister should be. I told them
> this reluctantly, but I could not honestly with-
> hold it. They appointed my pastor to superintend
> my studies. . . . But my studies, so far as he was
> concerned as my teacher, were little else than
> controversy [MF, pp. 45f.].

The Reverend Gale claims in his autobiography, however, that
he tried but failed to obtain scholarships for Finney at
Princeton, Andover, and Auburn, and that in fact Finney
developed his "peculiar views" much later.[38]

Finney's recollection not surprisingly emphasizes his
own independence; but it is ironic that he does so in the
terms of the Scottish school of "Common Sense Realism" which
were common place in the moral philosophy of his time: "I
had no where to go but directly to the Bible, and to the
philosophy or workings of my own mind, as revealed in consciousness" (MF, p. 54). What he found there was precisely
what all the legal theorists insisted was an unmistakable
fact, viz., the power to determine one's own actions.
Finney read the Bible with a mind "used to the close and
logical reasonings of the judges, as I found them reported
in our law works." Thus, "when I went to Mr. Gale's old
school library, I found almost nothing proved to my

satisfaction" (MF, p. 53). This uneasiness extended to the
venerable Westminster Confession itself, which was the
source of "the theological fiction of imputation" of Adam's
sin to all and of Christ's righteousness to the elect. "As
soon as I learned what were the unambiguous teachings of the
confession of faith upon these points, I did not hesitate on
all suitable occasions to declare my dissent from them" (MF,
p. 59).[39]   Indeed, he claims to have been "totally ashamed"
of the Confession.

> I could not feel any respect for a document that
> would undertake to impose on mankind such dogmas
> as those, sustained, for the most part, by
> passages of Scripture that were totally
> irrelevant; and not in a single instance sustained
> by passages which, in a court of law, would have
> been considered at all conclusive [MF, p. 60].

Nevertheless, the presbytery could hardly deny the
practical results of Finney's unorthodox preaching. The
spiritual harvest he had already begun to reap was indisput-
able evidence to his own mind, at least, that he was right.

> The more experience I had, the more I saw the
> results of my method of preaching, the more I
> conversed with all classes, high and low, educated
> and uneducated, the more was I confirmed in the
> fact that God had led me, had taught me, had given
> me the right conceptions in regard to the best
> manner of winning souls [MF, p. 87].

His sense of alienation from his "brother ministers" on the
matter of both what to preach and how to preach it
established yet another parallel to the first great
apostolic theologian:

> I say that God taught me; and I know it must have
> been so; for surely I never had obtained these
> notions from man. And I have often thought that I
> could say with perfect truth, as Paul said, that I

was not taught the Gospel by man, but by the
Spirit of Christ himself [MF, pp. 87f].

While commissioned directly from heaven, Finney takes
his instruction in preaching from those who are most effective as persuaders on earth. He begins the chapter in the
Memoirs on ministerial education with an extended account of
advice he received from "a judge of the supreme court" to
keep his language simple, his illustrations direct, and his
repetitions forceful. Speaking of the jury, the judge emphasized, "We mean to convince them; and if they have doubts
as to the law, we make them understand it, and rivet it in
their minds. In short, we expect to get a verdict, and to
get it upon the spot . . . (MF, p. 86). Finney concludes
that the finely honed paragraphs of a written sermon can
hardly provide a suitable vehicle for such earnest pleading.

This is the reason why, formerly, the ignorant
Methodist preachers, and the earnest Baptist
preachers produced so much more effect than our
most learned theologians and divines. They do so
now. The impassioned utterance of a common
exhorter will often move a congregation far beyond anything that those splendid exhibitions of
rhetoric can effect [MF, pp. 90f.].

It follows that "our theological schools would be of much
greater value than they are, if they were much more
practical" (MF, p. 91).[40]

In accepting the call to preach, then, Finney also took
on the challenge of creating a new style of rhetoric and a
new theology appropriate to the calling. But he constructs
neither out of whole cloth. Underlying many other influences, including those of his colleagues at Oberlin, were
the principles of law Finney learned as an apprentice,
during the only period of his life in which he engaged in
sustained reading and study. It is consistent with those
principles that his theological views should emerge--as do
verdicts in a court of law--through the "adversary process"

of debate. Under Gale's tutelage, as Finney admits, he was
"no theologian, [so] my attitude in respect to his peculiar
views was rather that of negation or denial, than that of
opposing any positive view to his" (MF, p. 53). Thus the
initial points of what would later become his "systematic
theology" were established as counterpoints to traditional
Calvinism. But, as he quickly learned, they served also as
effective weapons against other enemies of moral government
as well. As a theologian, Finney was made in the crucible
of fiery polemics; and like steel, his mind became both
tempered and unbending in the heat.

NOTES

1. Erik Erikson, Childhood and Society (New York: W.W.
Norton, 1963), p. 268.
2. Cf. George F. Wright, Charles Grandison Finney (Cambridge: The Riverside Press, 1891), p. 6: " . . . Finney
has accompanied his narrative by numerous doctrinal disqui-
sitions, in which those familiar with the controversies of
the time readily detect the result of subsequent years of
reflection interjecting their later theology in the narrative of early experience."
Wright was a professor at Oberlin in the generation
following Finney; his biography remains the standard work on
Finney's life and theology. More recent, and less comprehensive, works reveal a marked dependence on Wright. F. G.
Beardsley, in A Mighty Winner of Souls: A Study in Evangelism (American Tract Society, 1937), supplies a simplified
summary of the Memoirs, making the same observations as
Wright, but without the elegance of Wright's prose. Basil
Miller's work Charles G. Finney: He Prayed Down Revivals
was the official biography for the Finney Sesqui-Centennial
Conference, Chicago, 1942 (Grand Rapids, Mich.: Zondervan
Publishing House, 1941). It is a popularized summary of the
Memoirs, supplemented by Wright and the recollections of A.
M. Hill, a student at Oberlin during Finney's last years.
Miller's intention, like all the evangelical authors who
have produced biographies of Finney, is hortatory: "We are

reaching back to him to enkindle the dying embers of evan-
gelism that now smoulder among Christ's followers" (p. 137).
R. E. Day offers a highly simplified account of Finney's
revival successes; the study, Man of Like Passions: A
Dramatic Biography of Charles G. Finney (Grand Rapids,
Mich.: Zondervan Publishing House, 1942), offers no significant analysis of Finney's theology.   William Henry Harding,
Finney's Life and Lectures. Selected Lectures by Charles
Grandison Finney, Edited with original notes and sketch of
the Author's Life (London: Oliphants Ltd., 1943), consists
of annotated excerpts from Lectures on Revivals of Religion.
Most of the notes are homiletical expansions, significant as
evidence of the enduring utility of Finney's "measures" in
evangelical circles. These titles constitute a sample of
many similar studies in which Finney is presented as a man
of exemplary devotion to the cause of evangelism. This type
of biography would have pleased Finney for it is an appropriation of his life consistent with his own self-under-
standing. There has been neither a complete biography nor a
full-scale review of Finney's theology published recently,
although James E. Johnson devoted his Ph.D. dissertation to
the subject ["The Life of Charles Grandison Finney" (Syra-
cuse University, 1959)], and has since published several
articles on Finney's theology. The most helpful work on
Finney as a revivalist has been done by William G. McLoughlin, Jr., in Modern Revivalism: Charles G. Finney to Billy
Graham (New York: The Ronald Press Co., 1959), pp. 11-153.
Bernard A. Weisberger has also provided a critical account
of the revival period in They Gathered at the River: The
Story of the Great Revivalists and Their Impact upon Religion in America, orig. ed., 1958 (Chicago: Quadrangle Books,
1966), pp. 87-126. Perry Miller set Finney's work in its
broad cultural context in The Life of the Mind in America
from the Revolution to the Civil War (New York: Harcourt,
Brace & World, Inc., 1965), Book One, "The Evangelical
Basis." The classic study of the area from which Finney
emerged is Whitney R. Cross, The Burned-over District: The
Social and Intellectual History of Enthusiastic Religion in
Western New York, 1800-1850 (Ithaca, N.Y.: Cornell University Press, 1950), especially pp. 151-251. Cross details

the relation between various forms of social and religious "ultraism" and revival measures and doctrines.

3. Roy Pascal, Design and Truth in Autobiography (Cambridge, Mass., Harvard University Press, 1960), p. 182.

4. Samuel Taylor Coleridge, Biographia Literaria, ed. J. Shawcross (Oxford University Press, 1907), vol. 1, p. 183.

5. H. Richard Niebuhr was one of the first modern theologians to recognize the significance of the unifying power of the imagination in religious experience in The Meaning of Revelation (New York: Macmillan, 1941).

6. William Dilthey, Pattern and Meaning in History: Thoughts on History and Society, tr. H. P. Rickman (New York: Harper Torchbooks, 1962), pp. 104-105: "As history is memory and as the category of meaning belongs to memory, this is the category which belongs most intimately to historical thinking . . . . Memory is the comprehensive category through which life becomes comprehensible." Finney notes that his account is based entirely on memory, since he "kept no diary" (MF, p. 2). While he admits that this procedure leads to some discrepancy with the accounts of these same events by others, "Of course, I must state the facts as I remember them" (MF, p. 3).

7. Ibid., p. 106.

8. Erik Erikson, Identity: Youth and Crisis (New York: W. W. Norton, 1968), p. 224.

9. James Olney, Metaphors of Self: The Meaning of Autobiography (Princeton, N.J.: University Press, 1972), p. 30.

10. For example, the collection of testimonies by evangelical leaders edited by V. Raymond Edman, then President of Wheaton College (Illinois), They Found the Secret: Twenty Transformed Lives That Reveal a Touch of Eternity (Grand Rapids, Mich.: Zondervan, 1960).

11. The town of Adams "was settled, in 1801, by New England emigrants" (Barber and Howe, Historical Collections, p. 200); and its people had been instructed to wait for divine grace. Nevertheless, Finney protests overmuch, for elsewhere he recalls that his own conversion occurred during

a revival in Adams, which must at least have been supported by the local congregation (MF. pp. 296, 304).

12. In the sermon, "On the Atonement," for example, Finney claims that God's purpose in the death of Christ was to demonstrate "that He is no tyrant, and that He seeks only the highest obedience and consequent happiness of His creatures" (Gospel Themes, p. 208).

13. "The Spirit Not Striving Always," Gospel Themes, pp. 271f.

14. Ibid. Emphasis added.

15. "The Inner and the Outer Revelation, " Gospel Themes, p. 244.

16. "Victory over the World Through Faith," Gospel Themes, p. 378.

17. "On Refuge of Lies," Gospel Themes, p. 125.

18. "Conditions of Being Saved," Gospel Themes, p. 177.

19. "The Saviour Lifted Up, and the Look of Faith," Gospel Themes, p. 64. The practice of preparing oneself to receive grace was brought by the Puritan divines from England, but had already been criticized by Edwards in the Great Awakening, although for reasons opposite from those of Finney. See Norman Pettit, The Heart Prepared: Grace and Conversion in Puritan Spiritual Life (New Haven, Conn.: Yale University Press, 1966). Finney is particularly hard on those who seek salvation through tortuous introspection—"spiritual quack remedies," he calls them—rather than "simple faith."

20. "Conditions of Being Saved," Gospel Themes, p. 190.

21. William James, Varieties of Religious Experience (New York: Longmans, 1886), p. 208.

22. Ibid., p. 212.

23. "Personal Narrative," Selected Writings of Jonathan Edwards, ed. Harold Simonson (New York: Ungar, 1970), p. 31.

24. Ibid., pp. 28f.

25. "Sinners Bound to Change Their Own Hearts," quoted by McLoughlin, Modern Revivalism, p. 69.

26. It is a curious coincidence that St. Paul alludes to Jeremiah in the account of his call to preach Christ "among the Gentiles" (Galatians 1:15-16. Cf. Jeremiah 1:5),

since Finney also feels a close identification with Jeremiah. See below.

27. Rudolph Otto, The Idea of the Holy, tr. John Harvey
original ed., 1917 (New York: Galaxy Books, 1971). Otto
offers a neo-Kantian analysis of religious experience which
emphasizes the ambivalence toward the divine. In the holy
presence, one feels ontologically inferior, as it were, the
proper sense of "creatureliness." Further, the holy evokes
a trembling sense of overpoweringness, and an urgency to
respond to the energy of the divine will. The human mind is
overwhelmed in such experience with a stupor; the holy
appears as the fathomless abyss. Finally, despite the awe-
fulness of the divine, the worshiper is filled with bliss,
not wishing ever again to leave the enthralling presence.

28. While Finney's account of the vision contains many
of the elements of Otto's analysis, it is important to note
the emphasis Finney places upon the moral character of God.
For Otto moral attributes are later "schematizations" of the
primal experience constructed in order to give intelligible
form to the immediate intuition of awe. For Finney the
primary intuition of God, the image in which God appears
most impressive to him, is as the "Lawgiver." All his ideas
about God are, in Otto's sense, "schematizations" of that
image.

29. Additional examples are the decision to go west
from Utica in 1830 to Rochester, rather than east to the
beckoning fields of Philadelphia and New York City (MF, pp.
284-286); and the resolution of "unspeakable wrestling and
agony in my soul" over the decline of revivals during his
voyage to recuperate from cholera in 1834. On that occasion, an extraordinary season of prayer issued in the assurance of providential guidance: "The Spirit led me to believe that all would come out right, and that God had yet a
work for me to do . . ." (MF, p. 329). (The parallels in
St. Paul's experience can be found in Acts 9:1-18, 13:1-4,
16:6-10.) Of Finney's second baptism by the Holy Spirit in
Boston, in 1843, we shall have more to say later.

30. Paul E. Johnson offers evidence that in Rochester
most of Finney's converts were among the landed gentry:
"millers, merchants, master craftsmen, and county-seat

lawyers who had filled the churches since the beginning of settlement." These people had a vested interest in regulating the disruptive influence of liquor as the economic pressures for greater productivity among workers increased. "Temperance propaganda promised masters social peace, a disciplined and docile labor force, and an opportunity to assert moral authority over their men" [A Shopkeeper's Millennium: Society and Revivals in Rochester, New York, 1815-1837 (New York: Hill and Wang, 1978), pp. 36, 81].

31. "The Spirit Not Striving Always," Gospel Themes, p. 265.

32. Ibid., p. 266.

33. Settlement in the West. Sketches of Rochester: With Incidental Notices of Western New-York (Rochester: William Alling, 1838), p. 279.

34. Arthur Leon Shumway and Charles DeWolf Brower, Oberliniana, A Jubilee Volume of Semi-Historical Anecdotes Connected with the Past and Present of Oberlin College, 1833-1883 (Cleveland: Home Publishing Company, 1883), p. 71. The minister was C. C. Foote, who was also deeply impressed by Finney during his college days: "When I came to Oberlin, I could not endure his eyes, but when I became acquainted with him, I liked nothing better."

35. Cited by McLoughlin, Modern Revivalism, pp. 55f.

36. "Prayer and Labor for the Gathering of the Great Harvest," Gospel Themes, p. 332.

37. Levi Beardsley describes an intinerant Baptist preacher, one Elder Pray, who owned a fine farm and "a poor tavern, where he sold most villainous New England brew." "His education was so defective that he could hardly read his bible intelligently . . . . He used the most unsavory similes . . . to show how inadequate human means were, to promote the new birth, he illustrated his views, by introducing as a simile, a carved basswood woman, and then went on with his comparison, altogether too indecent to repeat" (Reminiscences, p. 71).

38. Cross, Burned-over District, p. 158. Cross regards Gale's memory as more reliable than Finney's and concludes that "not only was his doctrine at this time by no means distinctive or original, but it is fair to question whether

he had at the beginning anything whatsoever which deserves
the title of a theology." This is an overstatement to the
extent that Finney had absorbed the implicit and explicit
theological claims in the classic legal authors.

39. Similar dissent was, of course, rising in New Haven
also at the time; but Finney is unaware of its voice. Foster is close to the mark when he says of Finney, "Influenced
by legal analogies, and early adopting the doctrine of the
freedom of the will, he had struck into the path which all
New England theology was following, and had arrived at its
main results before he left the seclusion of his home and
became the most famous revivalist in his time" (New England
Theology, p. 453).

40. While Finney insists that he does not intend to
denigrate formal schooling, his views strongly supported
what Sidney Mead describes as "the rise of the evangelical
conception of the ministry" as the "charismatic" instrument
of unceasing revival. Since winning souls was the primary
measure of one's worth as a pastor and the primary contribution one made to the perfecting of society, there were
growing doubts about the utility of formal education. See
H. Richard Niebuhr and Daniel Day Williams, eds., The Ministry in Historical Perspectives (New York: Harper and Row,
1956), pp. 219-230.

Chapter IV

THE MAKING OF A THEOLOGIAN

Finney's system of theology is not built in the traditional manner as a logical sequence of doctrines, beginning with creation and running to eschatology. His theology is not comprehensive; his lectures do not touch on all the classic topics. Rather, he calls himself an "innovator," who restates certain doctrines whose formulations by the Old School Calvinists had, in his opinion, obstructed the progress of revivals. Finney is pre-eminently a practical theologian and is, therefore, concerned with the correct statement of doctrine only as a means of persuading sinners that they are "bound to change their own hearts."

Finney's theology is not, however, merely an ad hoc collection of eccentric objections to the Westminster Confession, but a consistently developed set of revisions. It is true that the bulk of Finney's theological reflection was occasioned by particular controversies with his opponents in the field, most notably the Old School Calvinists and the Universalists. Nevertheless, Finney's conclusions in each case are based on the same conviction: that God rules by the rational principles of moral law; therefore, any theological statement must satisfy the demands of reason and conscience.

The most appropriate image of Finney's theology is the wheel: the hub is his commitment to moral law as the center of the universe; the spokes are the separate doctrines related to each other through their junction at the center; the rim is the ceaseless movement of the revival, supported

by doctrines whose soundness is measured by the strength of
their connection with the center. Finney was convinced
that, thus equipped, the engine of revival would move steadily in one direction: ever forward.

Finney's theology proceeds along each doctrinal radius,
revising the traditional statement according to the requirements of the legal notion of moral agency, until the doctrine itself has become another means by which the wise
minister can promote revivals. Then he returns to the
center and repeats the process with another doctrine. Thus,
Finney's theology moves between the theoretical principles
of legal order and the practical requirements of the
revival. The result is a powerful and imaginative system,
which compensates for its lack of literary elegance and
philosophical sophistication by its rigorous consistency and
dramatic polemics.

Opponents

The polemics begin as soon as Finney accepts the retainer to
plead the case of Jesus Christ. According to the Memoirs,
after his conversion, he emerges from the woods and steps
directly into theological debate with a representative of
Universalism, a heresy that plagued him throughout his career. In that first encounter Finney is triumphant: "in a
moment I was enabled to blow his argument to the wind" (MF,
p. 26). The logic of what he understood as Old School
Calvinism played into the hands of the Universalists; therefore, his defense entailed the reformulation of the traditional Presbyterian teaching that George Gale had labored to
establish in Adams. In this early incident, he prevents the
Universalist from persuading members of Gale's church by
abandoning Gale's own position. The Universalist was
routed, one young woman converted, and Gale was dumbfounded,
"for the evidence was that the Spirit of God had blessed my
views . . . " (MF, p. 51). In this story all the elements
of the "revival narrative" to follow are present--with the
exception that not all of the Old School Calvinists were as

impressed as George Gale with Finney's results. The anecdote is appropriately placed at the beginning of Finney's
account because he early identified Universalism and Old
School Calvinism as his chief ideological opponents, flank-
ing him on the left and on the right. Both denied basic
principles of moral agency, and so both were enemies of the
revival.

Cross notes that by 1823 there were ninety congregations of Universalists in western New York, whose views were
publicized in no less than four periodicals. Even more than
the Catholics, the Universalists were a highly visible and
vocal dissenting minority within the Protestant domain.
They provided a "kind of foil for the evangelists, stimulat-
ing them to ever more-heroic efforts."[1] Universalism is
regarded by Finney with special antipathy because there can
be no impetus for evangelism in a position which assumes
that everyone will ultimately be saved. Further, by their
insistence that punishment for sin could not _justly_ be
eternal in duration, Universalists charged revival theology
with impugning divine morality. Such a criticism struck at
the heart of Finney's position, forcing him to argue for the
eternal misery of the wicked dead from the principles of
God's moral government. As developed in the revival sermons, this defense rested upon the infinite guilt of all
sinners and the integrity of their "moral relation" to God.

If through temporal suffering one could repay whatever
debts one owed divine justice, Finney exclaimed, "I don't
wonder that Universalists pray but little; what have they to
pray for? . . . the mercy of God they need not on their
scheme for they suffer all they deserve."[2] The notion that
one could claim entrance into heaven on the basis of justice
is absurd to Finney since the obligation of any sinner is
"infinite." His argument proceeds from a consideration of
what is involved in moral choice. Guilt "is to be measured
by the mind's knowledge or perception of the value of that
end which the law required to be chosen. This end is the
highest well-being of God and of the universe."[3] Because

sinners have intuitive knowledge of the infinite value of divine interests, they become infinitely culpable when they deliberately prefer their own interests to God's. "In other words the guilt consists in rejecting the infinitely valuable well-being of God and of the universe for the sake of selfish gratification." Every sin, therefore, merits endless punishment, although the degree of suffering is relative to the clarity of one's perception of this infinite responsibility. Thus the nominal churchgoer bears greater guilt for unbelief and faces "<u>direr</u> and <u>deeper</u> <u>damnation</u> <u>than</u> <u>all</u> <u>the</u> Heathen <u>world</u>." What is central to Finney's defense of endless punishment is the claim that humans are responsible moral agents with the capacity to understand their obligations before God. The refusal to heed the warnings of conscience is a willed act of defiance against the highest good. The sinner intends infinite evil inasmuch as one consciously refuses to pursue infinite value in one's actions. If one is to be forgiven, then, it cannot be on the basis of justice, for on that basis no one could ever merit forgiveness.[4]

Finney insists that the Universalist scheme undercuts the moral structure of God's relations with persons by denying that God consistently deals with them as responsible beings. If the love of God guarantees salvation to all, even those who refuse the divine appeal in Christ, then God is failing to take human moral agency with complete seriousness. If God is to govern according to the laws of moral relation, he can grant salvation only to those who accept it; and he must send to hell those who refuse it out of respect for the integrity of their choice. "It is only by moral power that God saves, and this can save no man unless he consents to be saved." If God should act upon the mind in the way he coerces the physical universe, "we certainly know there could be neither moral action nor moral character in such beings as we are." It follows from the nature of persuasion that it can be rejected: " . . . a moral agent must be able, in the proper sense of this term, to resist every degree of moral influence."[6] By the nature of his governance God cannot deliver sinners from the consequences of their own willing. "God is a great public magistrate, sustaining infinitely responsible relations to the moral universe."[7] For God to dispense with those relations would be to "upset His throne, convulse the moral universe, and kindle another hell in His own bosom."[8]

Sin is a conscious refusal to submit to God's moral government, and it must be taken with complete seriousness as an act of rebellion which God cannot ignore. Thus the sinner must be urged to cease resisting the Spirit's influence, for the character of God's moral government requires that, as one makes a bed in time, one shall lie in it for eternity.[9]

Finally, Universalism fails the ultimate test of promoting moral growth.[10] In the Memoirs Finney relates the sad case of a New York legislator who had brushed off "the question of submission to God." "He remained in his sins, finally fell into decay, and died at last, as I have been told, a dilapidated man, and in the full faith of his Universalism" (MF, p. 41). Significantly, the campaign against the alleged antinomianism of the Universalists reached beyond the confines of theological debate to bring into question their civic respectability.

> The religious press constantly labeled criminals prominent in the news as Universalists, suggesting that without the fear of eternal punishment one could not remain moral. School houses, court houses, and other public places were usually closed to Universalist and Unitarian meetings alike, and in some places the appropriateness of allowing Universalist testimony in court was debated.[11]

While maintaining ferocious controversies among themselves, then, both Old School and New School Calvinists were united against their common enemy, whose doctrine threatened the foundation of both divine and human government.

The criticism was particularly galling to the Universalists, who tended to be among the more educated and better
situated members of the village societies. The editor of
the leading Universalist periodical, the Gospel Advocate,
followed the old advice that the best defense is an offense
in his reply, published in 1835:

> It is not for want of information that the people
> here reject the wicked dogmas of Calvin . . . but
> the reverse:--they are generally too well informed
> . . . to swallow the disgraceful absurdities of
> Andover Seminary. . . . The moral condition of
> this section . . . is not a whit behind that of
> other places . . . .[12]

The Old School theologians, however, received such outraged
protestations with knowing smiles. They knew that no mere
outward observance of moral law, what Calvin called "civic
righteousness," could save one from the condemnation which
sinful human nature so richly deserved. If all people are
the fallen children of Adam, then all their actions are
fundamentally evil, issuing from a sinful disposition. For
Finney, who was as opposed to the doctrine of inherent moral
depravity as the Universalists themselves, such a reply
would never do. Besides, if Universalists conduct themselves with moral discipline, as many demonstrably did, the
basis of their restraint must be more exalted than the mere
fear of punishment. If so, according to the principles of
moral action, their motive for virtue is of a higher order
than that of the orthodox!

Therefore, while following the standard line of attack
on the Universalists, Finney begins from a position which,
in the language of later ethical discussion, we may call
"psychological egoism." While no one is incapable of acting
from true benevolence, he insisted, all people choose to act
from selfish motives, even in the performance of moral duty.
Thus, the most commendable citizen of the republic is, in
his or her unconverted heart, a rebel against divine government. The argument is subtle and, as we shall see later,

not quite satisfactory. But neither is it decisive in Finney's rejection of Universalism. Finally, what is most important to him is the consideration that the Universalists' guarantee of eventual salvation for all contradicts the sovereignty of human moral choice, and thus denies the rationale of revival preaching. Indeed, on the basis of that error many postpone conversion until they fall, like the hapless legislator, "delapidated," into the eternal flames.

Finney's encounters with Universalists in the Memoirs often have happier endings, but they are always conditioned upon the heretics' accepting the strict discipline of moral law and abandoning the fatal illusion that the court of divine justice will excuse the slanderous notion that the sinner will receive less than the full penalty of the law.[13]

Throughout his career, Finney waged a running battle also with Old School Calvinism. It follows from the principles of moral government that Finney would have to challenge the tradition of Presbyterian theology, as set out in the Westminster Confession and taught with particular vigor at Princeton. In his revival preaching and theological lectures Finney thoroughly refuted each of the so-called Five Points of Calvinism, popularly referred to by the acronym, TULIP: Total depravity because of original sin; Unconditional election by which God alone determines who is to be saved and who is not; Limited atonement inasmuch as Christ died only to forgive the sins of the elect; Irresistible grace by which God draws those he has sovereignly chosen into his kingdom; Perseverance of the saints which guarantees that those who are elect will remain steadfast in the faith. Finney was convinced that this set of ideas was entirely mistaken and resulted in a disastrous neglect of the task of building the kingdom of God. "To a great extent," he announced in the preface to his theological lectures, "the truths of the blessed gospel have been hidden under a false philosophy."[14]

In his Memoirs Finney identified these ideas with Samuel Hopkins; and in the Lectures he associates "physical," as opposed to "moral," notions of divine government with "the Edwardean school" in general, charging Jonathan Edwards in particular with confusing the will with the sensibility, and thereby replacing the active center of human responsibility with a passive faculty of the mind (LST, p. 320). In both cases it must be admitted that Finney read neither Hopkins nor Edwards with a discerning mind or a generous spirit. We shall examine his criticism of Edwards in the next chapter, since it is Edwards' view of sinful "affections" to which Finney specifically objects.

Throughout his career, Finney regarded Hopkins' system of doctrines as representative of Old School Calvinism. He never appreciated the ways in which Hopkins anticipated some of the developments in the New School, particularly in emphasizing moral responsibility and in adopting the governmental theory of the atonement.[15] Finney is impressed only with the practical consequences of those features of the older Calvinism with which Hopkins' name was associated, such as the doctrine that God decreed some persons to be eternally damned (the decree of reprobation, included in the belief in "double predestination"), and the claim that sin is somehow necessary to achieve the highest good.[16] Finney found that "Hopkinsianism" allowed sinners to evade responsibility for their own transgressions. "Indeed, I felt it my duty to expose all the hiding-places of sinners, and to hunt them out from under those peculiar views of orthodoxy, in which I found them entrenched" (MF, p. 242). While Hopkins himself had prepared the way for the belief that conversion was a result of the sinner's own act of repentance and faith, the popular impression of his system of doctrine was that it allowed little room for human initiative. Finney was fond of reciting a well-known jingle to make the point:

> You can and you can't;
> You will and you won't;
> You're damned if you do;
> And damned if you don't.[17]

Finney's account of "Hopkinsianism," although hardly fair to
Hopkins, was at least a fair representation of what was in
the mind of most pastors and educated church members at the
time.

A merchant in the village of Gouvernor, whose conversion Finney recounts in the Memoirs, is an example of the
sort of person who was "stumbled" by the views of "old
school Presbyterians." A "reading, reflecting man," he
objected to the teachings of "the catechism," such as inherited guilt from Adam, as "a direct contradiction of my
irresistible convictions of right and justice" (MF, p. 125).
Finney astounded him by heartily agreeing that whatever
contravenes the "innate sense of justice," including the
notion that Christ died only for the elect, ought to be
rejected. Intrigued, the businessman listened closely while
Finney explained his "views of both the law and the gospel."
These proved so satisfying that soon "he warmly espoused the
cause of Christ, and enlisted heartily in the promotion of
the revival" (MF, p. 127). It is important to emphasize in
light of the many episodes like this one in the Memoirs that
Finney engages the ideas of the Old School as they appear in
opposition to the revival. He is not as interested in their
scholarly pedigree as in their practical consequences in the
lives of the people to whom he directed his preaching. As
Calvin Colton had observed about revivalists in general,
Finney was finely attuned to "the character and temper of
the community."[18]

In general, Finney's criticism of the Old School invites comparison with the acknowledged academic leader of
the New School, Nathaniel W. Taylor, professor of theology
at Yale Divinity School at the time Finney's lectures were
published.[19] George Wright notes that Finney was especially
impressed with Taylor's exposition of "the self-determining
power of the human will,"[20] and it is obvious that Finney
would have agreed that "moral government" (the title of
Taylor's course of theological lectures) is the proper context for discussing the doctrines of sin and regeneration.[21]
The voluntary nature of sin and holiness, subtly deduced by

Taylor and Lyman Beecher in arguments designed at least to
leave the impression of an evolutionary development from
Calvinist belief, was to Finney a blunt fact of "moral
consciousness" which Calvinism had ignored or suppressed.
Finney adamantly opposed all compromises with Calvinism
because its views of sin and conversion undercut the revival. His lifelong commitment to the cause was matched in
principle by Taylor, but not in active, untiring participation in "crusades." As professor at Yale, Taylor remained a
preacher; as president of Oberlin, Finney remained an evangelist. His theology knows no loyalties except to the
maintenance and promotion of revivals. Indeed, in order to
establish his converts in holiness he became willing to
embrace the Methodist doctrine of entire sanctification
(howbeit with characteristic modifications) in defiance of
every shade of Calvinism.

Thus, while Finney's formulations are not as original
as the meager references to other theologians in his lectures would make them appear,[22] underlying his appropriation
of all these influences is a uniquely "practical" stand-
point, arising from what George Wright justly calls "the
marvellous experiences through which he was passing at the
time,"[23] and giving to his reflections a direction and
intensity not found in other New School theologians. Frank
H. Foster dismisses Finney's theological system "in the one
word 'Taylorism,' independent as it was and vigorously as
its author had impressed upon it the marks of his own pronounced individuality."[24] Foster's dismissal is premature
for it is just those "marks of his own pronounced individuality" that give Finney's system its remarkable power as an
expression of theological anthropology. The uniqueness of
Finney's work lies in his exclusive reference to the field
of legal relations as the sphere in which freedom under law
can be most intelligibly understood, and by his consistent
demand for the utility of theology, when translated into
sermonic language, for promoting revivals.

Stated in the broadest terms possible, Finney's indictment of the Old School is that its teachings provide a

built-in excuse for people who are seeking to evade responsibility for their actions. Moral failure becomes Adam's
fault, or more darkly, the result of a mysterious divine
decree. Righteousness is an equally mysterious gift, having
no causal relation to one's attempts at virtue, but entirely
a result of perfect goodness being credited to one's account
because of an arbitrary identification with Christ. In his
early debates with George Gale the central issue was Finney's rejection of "that theological fiction of imputation"
(MF, p. 56) in both its applications, in the doctrine of
original sin by which people are held responsible for Adam's
transgression and in the doctrine of Christ's imputed righteousness by which the elect could demand their pardon as the
"just" reward of their unearned merit. In the first case
one is accounted guilty for an act one did not commit, and
in the second one is acquitted on grounds independent of
one's own actions of repentance and reformation. In both
cases human moral agency is subverted.

On the theoretical level, then, according to Finney's
analysis, Old School Calvinism denies that God honors the
first principle of moral government, viz., individual responsibility. For Finney, however, even "God has no right
to give up the moral law."[25] On the practical level, Old
School doctrines effectively narrow the field of spiritual
cultivation to the garden of one's own soul and leave the
harvest of the world to God's unaided action. Finney once
commented to George Gale, "if advocates at the bar should
pursue the same course in pleading the cause of their
clients, that ministers do in pleading the cause of Christ
with sinners, they would not gain a single case" (MF, p.
155). Lawyers must at least assume that the jury is capable
of making a decision on the basis of the evidence, a moral
ability which the Old School does not admit in the sinner.

Thus, when Finney was invited to join the Rev. Mr.
Gilbert in Wilmington, Delaware, in 1827, he found that his
first task was to challenge those "oldest of old-school
views of doctrine," viz., that "God would convert sinners in
his own time; and that therefore to urge them to immediate

repentance, and in short to attempt to promote a revival, was to attempt to make men Christians by human agency, and human strength, and thus to dishonor God by taking the work out of his hands" (MF, p. 234). On the evening he chose to begin the work of public correction, Finney felt a "strange excitement" in the church as he proceeded to expose "with irresistible clearness the peculiar dogmas of old-schoolism" (MF, p. 236). The excitement was the stirring of a new revival coming to life; many "broke down, and became thoroughly changed in [their] views and religious experience" (MF, p. 238).

Finney gives many examples of "the influence of that old school teaching of which I have complained," but one of the most striking involves a lawyer, who was trained at Princeton. While a student, he and some companions sought advice from the president of the college about salvation and were counselled to be devout and "pray God to give them a new heart." Their efforts went unrewarded. The other two were in "drunkards' graves," and the lawyer, "being a man that made too free use of ardent spirits" himself was in despair. Finney convinced him that the role of the Spirit is not to create new hearts, but to persuade the sinner to renounce sin and accept "the plan of salvation." Seizing this new possibility, the lawyer submitted immediately, "and to all human appearances, became a thorough convert right upon the spot" (MF, p. 265).

Finney was convinced that both his opponents, for different reasons, menaced the entire "sublime enterprise" of winning souls. The problem, as he explained to his British host during a tour of London, is that "ministers talk about sinners; and do not make the impression that God commands them, now to repent; and thus they throw their ministry away" (MF, p. 410). Finney is determined that such spiritual profligacy shall never be charged to his account, and the intensity with which he attacks Universalism and Old School Calvinism is the measure of his loyalty to the cause of revival. It is not surprising, then, that his revival theology is significantly shaped by his desire to avoid any

theory that would conflict with the practice of his revivalist vocation.

Skeletons

The primary sources for the study of Finney's theology are
the outlines, or "skeletons," of his early lectures at
Oberlin; several volumes of sermons, transcribed by atten-
tive auditors and approved for publication by Finney himself, including Lectures on Revivals of Religion (1835) and
Lectures to Professing Christians (originally given in 1837-
38); the instructive digressions and illustrative anecdotes
in his Memoirs; and most definitively, at least to his own
mind, the elaborated version of his mature lectures on
systematic theology, first published in 1846, then expanded
for a British edition in 1851, and finally edited to manageable size in 1878 by James H. Fairchild, Finney's successor
to the presidency of Oberlin.[26]

The Skeletons were prepared as an aid for the students
who braved the suspicion and calumny surrounding the Oberlin
Collegiate Institute in its early days to join the forces of
revival and reform which were gathering there. Fairchild's
account of the frenetic activities of the students in evangelism, temperance meetings, and anti-slavery campaigns
leaves little wonder that they did not patiently copy down
Finney's arguments in the minute detail he required. In
1835, when disaffected students from Lane Seminary and Western Reserve College acceded to Oberlin, "within the circle
of the forest which bounded the vision, all was life and
animation."[27] In the midst of a "sort of spiritual elec-
tricity"[28] Finney conducted the systematic questioning of
his students, requiring each in turn to present his views
whereupon his "statements are then made the subject of
thorough examination and discussion by the class, and by the
Instructor."[29]

The ominous capitalization in the last phrase conveys
something of the intimidating effect Finney had on even as

lively and as independent young thinkers as made their way
to the new college in the wilderness of Ohio. His penetrating gaze was legendary. An incoming student in 1836 reported that, when he presented his credentials to Finney, "he
looked through my letters and then he looked through me
until I felt it . . . His eyes were his greatest force."[30]
A tall, imposing figure, Finney's personal presence was a
forceful inducement to agreement among his students. The
line between moral and physical agency, however, is difficult to keep clear under such circumstances. Once Finney
responded to students' complaints about the many preaching
services they were required to attend with a thundering
reminder that their primary duty was to be devoted to God,
and that the purpose of Oberlin was to assist them in that
duty. "The appeal was overwhelming," Fairchild cooly observed, "and silenced if it did not satisfy."[31] There are
other accounts, of course, of Finney's humility, compassion,
and even humor, but "the Instructor" did not take the study
of theology lightly and his students were no doubt greatly
relieved to have a reliable copy of his "reasonings."

At the end of the Skeletons the publisher promises the
speedy release of subsequent volumes. The limitations of
the format, however, were soon apparent. At places the
outline is too sketchy for even a careful student to fill in
the lacunae in the arguments; the mere listing of "remarks"
designed to show practical applications of the spiritual
truths could hardly suggest the hortatory power of such
sections as given in the classroom; and the care which
Finney was learning to take in theological discourse, thanks
to educative conversations with colleagues at Oberlin, demanded a more controlled form of expression than an outline
could provide. Such considerations must have weighed in the
decision to bring out the later edition of his lectures in
the more standard form of detailed systematic exposition.
As usual with Finney, when the pendulum swung, it did not
stop mid-way through the arc: the 1851 edition of the
lectures reached nearly a thousand pages.

The Skeletons, nevertheless, provide an instructive
look at Finney's theological method in its early stages.

Fresh from the successes of the revival circuit that carried him from the obscurity of rural villages to a newly flourishing town like Rochester and finally to New York City itself, Finney strode into the classroom with the enthusiastic momentum of a man unacquainted with personal failure. Appointed professor of theology, without benefit of seminary training himself, Finney came to Oberlin to provide a new generation of revivalists with the doctrinal "innovations" required to interpret and justify the "new measures" of evangelistic persuasion of which he was the recognized master. In the Memoirs he describes his theological education as largely a result of his own reading in the Bible, informed by those principles of interpretation he found in law books. Not surprisingly, the influence of that legal training is evident in both the form and content of the arguments outlined in his early lectures.

If the mark of a modern theologian or philosopher is to begin with the question of how we know, rather than with what we know--epistemology rather than ontology, then Finney must be regarded as thoroughly modern. Furthermore, he follows the familiar line of nineteenth-century thought on such matters directly into the self-authenticating awareness of one's own mental "states."

> I am conscious of thought, emotion, volition, and consciousness is to my own mind the highest possible evidence . . . no objection can set aside the direct testimony of consciousness.[32]

On the basis of that testimony, Finney accepts the standard terms of Cartesian dualism: "Man, therefore, is a compound being, uniting in one person two distinct natures, called Body and Mind."[33] The "natural attributes" of mind include intellect, will, reason, conscience. As one is "directly conscious" of possessing such attributes, so one is aware also of having the power and responsibility of moral agency, which leads in turn to the remarkable claim that "as man is capable of endless improvement, economy demands his immortality."[34] The sentence suggests Kant's argument for

immortality as a postulate of practical reason, but there is
no evidence that Finney had read any of Kant's works.

He certainly did not allow the line of modern critical
philosophy that extended from Hume and Kant to shake his
confidence in the traditional "proofs for the existence of
God." He offers quite unsophisticated versions of St.
Thomas' arguments from causality, design, and contingency;
Descartes' argument from self-consciousness (but with none
of the subtle self-criticism which informs the Meditations);
and a very convoluted argument for the "necessary idea" of
God's existence which seems to bear some distant kinship to
the ontological argument in the Prosologion of St. Anselm.
In each case the "proof" appears to be Finney's restatement
of a second- or third-hand account of the original. It is
evident that while he naively concludes that "the argument
for the existence of God amounts to a demonstration,"[35] he
did not have sufficient interest in the "proofs" to study
either their original statements or the extensive criticism
that had been developed against them in the circles of
modern philosophy.

Such neglect is, of course, a large part of the reason
Finney has been regarded as unimportant in the history of
theology. In his own day the lions of Princeton growled
about the rough imperfection of his education; F. H. Foster,
at the beginning of the next century, as we have seen,
called his system of thought "warmed-over Taylorism"; and
Leonard Sweet maintains the complaint today with the unqualified judgment that Finney was a "simplistic derivative
thinker," which means, apparently, that even when he borrowed ideas he could handle only the easy ones.[36] The
harshness of his critics may reflect in part the fury of
academics scorned by a man who preferred to educate himself.
The learned criticism of Finney is the typical expression of
frustration by academic theologians when they are forced to
recognize the presence and work of an influential maverick.
Finney chooses to give only cursory attention to the ideas
and problems which occupied their time and energy, and to
concentrate on the religious issues of immediate and

practical import for most people of his generation. As
Sweet rightly says, howbeit with an unmistakable tone of
condescension, Finney is a "pulpit theologian." Finney
would have been happy to accept that title for he believed
that theology which did not serve the call of preaching was
empty speculation. He chooses, consequently, to concentrate
on theological questions that are raised by and in the grand
enterprise of declaring the gospel.

We have already traced the peculiar power of Finney's
preaching to the appeal of a well-ordered life to both the
rural settlers and the urban capitalists of his day. Finney
perceives human life as formed by a cosmic system of moral
law--a perception shared by the lawyers, the revivalists,
and the populace whose values they both shared and shaped.
What is paramount to Finney are questions of the nature of
universal moral government and the demands and liberties it
offers to human conduct. The existence of God as moral
governor is, therefore, a corollary to the claim that human
life is governed. One's own sense of moral obligation
provides direct evidence that human life is governed by law.

In a sermon on "The Inner and the Outer Revelation"
Finney claims that "we possess an intellectual and moral
nature which as truly reveals great truths concerning God
and our relations to Him and to law, as the material world
reveals His eternal power and Godhead."[37] The contents of
natural revelation include the intuition of the ideas of God
as moral governor and of duty to moral law, along with a
sense of transgression. "Indeed, if your nature spoke out
unbiased, it would not let you believe yourself really
forgiven, so long as you are doing violence to conscience."[38] The awareness of the divine determination to
maintain legal order brings the realization that one's sins
make forgiveness impossible. In this way the sinner is
brought to acknowledge the need for a "double salvation--
from condemnation and from sinning; first from the curse,
and secondly from the heart to sin--from the tendency and
disposition to commit sin." Thus, "your own moral nature
shows that you need an atoning Saviour and a renewing

Spirit."[39] Once one has come to look within, "to read
carefully the volume God has put on record there," one can
no longer deny the truth of the Bible. The scheme of redemption is perfectly adapted to the needs of the human
condition; no person of common sense could decline its
appeal.

For Finney, furthermore, it is precisely the capacity
to respond freely to rational appeal that constitutes the
creative spark in human nature: the persistent image of the
Creator himself, imparted to the dust of the earth to create
a living spirit. In words which echo the opening lines of
Calvin's Institutes, Finney writes that

> many of our notions of God are derived from our
> knowledge of ourselves. We are conscious of pos-
> sessing the powers of moral agency . . . . We are
> moral beings, and God is our Creator . . . . But
> if he possessed sufficient knowledge of what con-
> stitutes a moral being, to enable him to create
> moral beings . . . he must be himself a moral
> being.[40]

"The powers of moral agency" are "intellect, reason, will,
conscience. A susceptibility to pleasure and pain, with
some degree of knowledge on moral subjects. Man is conscious of possessing these."[41]

Apart from the appeal to immediate consciousness, Finney lists a number of "considerations" to prove his claim,
each of which represents a class of evidence he often employs. First, he argues from the necessary conditions of
moral order that 1) "all government is founded upon the
universal recognition of this truth"; and 2) assignments of
praise and blame, the entire process of moral judgment, is
rendered nugatory unless the subjects are free agents. Second, Finney appeals to the consensus of traditional wisdom:
"It cannot be and never was seriously disbelieved."[42] The
authority of tradition does not reside in itself, but in
that "common sense" which, in countless ordinary decisions

through the centuries, provides reliable insight and guidance. Just as Blackstone found a "common law," grounded in
immutable principles, running like a strong life line
through the shifting sea of English customs, so Finney
claimed that the principles of moral government were clearly
discernible in the maze of diverse forms of human ruling.
With regard to moral responsibility, Finney was confident
that most people could not deny the evidence of their own
conscience--even if a few theologians in New England sacri-
ficed their common sense in order to save their theories.
Third, and in many cases most decisive, Finney appeals to
the moral efficacy of an idea to establish its validity:
"the actual influence of moral considerations upon men,
demonstrates their moral agency."[43] That people universally
respond to persuasive arguments, examples, and appeals to
motives is the practical evidence that it is natural for
humans to act from reasons and not from physical causes
only.

The foundation of moral agency, then, lies in the fact
that "the soul wills to do or not to do, and thus is a moral
sovereign over its own activities." Such sovereignty is
enjoyed each time one is "a voluntary actor," rather than "a
recipient of influences and of actions exerted upon himself."[44] In a sermon calculated to impress upon his hearers
their awful responsibility to obey moral law, Finney declares that the difference between impressions and volitions
is self-evident even to the sinner, and that volitions are
"products of an original power in himself, for the exercise
of which he is compelled to hold himself primarily responsible."[45] While there is tragic abuse of this "natural
power" due to "moral weakness," liberty stands as an internal witness to the character of the Creator and his claims
upon the subjects of his moral rule.

> Only when reason and conscience control the will
> is a man free--for God made men intelligent and
> moral beings to act normally, under the influence
> of their own enlightened conscience and reason.
> This is such freedom as God exercises and enjoys;
> none can be higher or nobler.[46]

There is no possibility of excusing oneself from the right
use of freedom.

From that primary fact Finney draws the conclusion that
"accountability implies a rightful ruler. This ruler is
God"; therefore, "the existence of God is a dictate of my
moral nature."[47]

> Upon this argument the common convictions of men
> in regard to the Divine existence seem to be
> based, as this truth is admitted previous to a
> knowledge of any theoretic argument whatever . . .
> This argument always has insured, and always will
> insure the conviction of the great mass of men.[48]

The awareness of moral responsibility is prior to the consciousness of such finite attributes as contingency and
design or the understanding of the logic of necessary ideas
upon which the other "theoretic argument[s]" depend. Finney
argues that the defining characteristic of human existence
is the consciousness of moral agency. This conviction is
rooted in his legal training and controls both the content
and method of his theology.

Accordingly, the third introductory lecture of the
Skeletons outlines the "laws of evidence," distinguishing
"kinds and degrees of evidence to be expected" in "theological inquiry."[49] The most significant feature of the section
is Finney's recognition that theological arguments cannot
conclusively demonstrate the truth of their claims. This
limitation is not due, however, to the elusiveness of the
object, but to the conditions of the subject, viz., in "a
state of probation under a moral government."[50] The existence of God cannot be established with such certainty as to
make doubt impossible because in that case the proof would
be so overwhelming as to constitute coercion rather than
persuasion. Since persuasive means are the only legitimate
means of administering moral government, the proof must be
capable of being resisted, and therefore short of full
demonstration.

With the groundwork thus laid Finney proceeds to build a defense of "the divine authority of the Bible," reminding the reader that "such evidence only is to be expected that the nature of the case admits."[51] The terms of his defense are framed in the language of the courtroom: he cites the testimony of the apostles, argues for their credibility as witnesses, and rests his case on the moral efficacy of their teachings. He adds two points of what he considers "incontrovertible evidence": the miraculous powers of the apostles and the fulfillment of biblical prophecies. It does not seem to occur to him, in the heat of apologetic exertions, that both appeals are glaring examples of petitio principii. The argument for the authenticity of the New Testament based on its having been written by Palestinian Jews, using "hebraistic Greek," indicates that his modesty regarding his education in the language of the New Testament was appropriate. The boast that none of the "jarring Christian sects" contested the authority of the canonical books is, of course, empty, and demonstrates that Finney's program of self-education in theology had some gaping holes, especially in early Church history. The point in mentioning these sections, which Finney was wise enough to eliminate from the later editions of the Lectures, is to underscore the form of his arguments. He concludes the section on the authenticity of the Pentateuch with the claim: "what has been adduced then is good proof, and sufficient to establish such a fact in a court of law."[52] As a theologian, Finney follows the method of argument he had early come to respect as a lawyer.

He was not the first to employ such arguments, of course, since the "evidences" he offers were standard apologetic fare. Finney is distinguished from most other defenders of the faith, however, by his insistence that the evidence pass the test of courtroom advocacy. Further, while many of his arguments echo those of contemporary apologists, they also have clear parallels in the legal theorists he read as an apprentice. His defense of the harmony of science and the Bible may serve as an example.

> . . . if Geology really deserves the name of a
> science, and can really be depended upon as truth,
> its developments rather confirm than discredit the
> Mosaic account of creation, when that account is
> properly understood.[53]

The sentence is a profession of faith in the unity of truth,
grounded in the claims of natural law as expounded by the
"old legal authors." Blackstone, for example, outlines in
the introductory lectures to the Commentaries the hierarchy
of beings, from original inchoate matter through vegetables
and animals to moral beings, guided throughout "by unerring
rules laid down by the great creator."[54] As natural law
establishes a harmonious system of government, the study of
creaturely processes could not yield valid results which
contradict the revelation of the Creator in Scripture.   To
entertain such an idea questions the perfection of divine
rule and is thus not merely intellectual folly but what
Finney called "moral insanity."

    The influence of his reading in Blackstone is also
evident in the claim that certain Christian ideas are universally acknowledged. He quotes at length from the collections of testimonies gathered by Timothy Dwight from the
"heathen nations" and the "ancient Jews" to the ideas of
trinity and atonement; and in the section on the Fourth
Commandment he relies on another apologist for evidence that
the Sabbath is observed by nations other than the Jewish.[55]
The point of citing this borrowed research is to establish
the status of the commandment as "common law."

> As the law of the Sabbath is founded in the nature
> and relations of moral beings, and they exist in
> this world, it is common law, and of course uni-
> versally and perpetually obligatory.[56]

Finney's argument here clearly echoes Blackstone's defense
of the common law, "that ancient collection of unwritten
maxims and customs," as superior to statutory regulations
because it is everywhere acknowledged as binding.[57]

>This law of nature, being coeval with mankind and
>dictated by God himself, is of course superior in
>obligation to any other. It is binding over all
>the globe in all countries, and at all times: no
>human laws are of any validity, if contrary to
>this, and such of them as are valid derive all
>their force and all their authority, mediately or
>immediately, from the original.[58]

In the Skeletons, then, we see a trained mind beginning
the task of applying the forms of argument and principles of
evidence from one discipline to another. In his Commentaries Blackstone had cited the medieval maxim, "Nullus
clericus nisi causidicus" ("No clergyman is considered to be
such without a knowledge of law"), and Finney's theological
work demonstrates its truth. His revision of the lectures
for formal publication omits much that is amateurish or
superficial in the Skeletons, but the commitment to legal
principles as the key to understanding the ways of God with
humankind remains firm and impels his criticism of established Calvinist orthodoxy as well as the formulation of his
own theology. Compelling personal drama called Charles
Finney to be a preacher, but it was his training in the law
and his own acute sense of moral power that made him a
theologian.

First Principles

Finney's theological work achieves mature form in the closely packed lines of the Lectures on Systematic Theology. The
reader today feels some sympathy with the reviewer from
Princeton who wrote of the 1846 edition that "it is as hard
to read as Euclid. Nothing can be omitted; nothing passed
over lightly. The unhappy reader once committed to a perusal is obliged to go on, sentence by sentence, through the
long concatenation." Finney, however, is pleased to repub-
lish these words in his reply because, at the end of a
protracted complaint, the reviewer is forced to admit that
"we do not see that there is a break or defective link in

the whole chain. If you grant his principles, you have
already granted his conclusions."[59] Fair enough, and precisely the assessment of Finney's work that most gratified
the author. For the theologian who "was bred a lawyer" the
most successful argument was one which carried the persuasive force of reason and conscience. Since the body of the
lectures stood the test of logical consistency, all that
remained to convince his hostile critic was that those first
principles are grounded in the undeniable witness of moral
consciousness. What were the basis premises of Finney's
theology, which, if they could be established as true, would
convey even a stalwart of the Old School "forward to
Oberlin?"[60]

Following the Skeletons, Finney's printed lectures
begin, as do the classic works on law which he read in Judge
Wright's office, with an analysis of moral agency, drawn
from the direct evidence of "consciousness." He then proceeds to define moral law, listing its attributes, describing its proper administration, and identifying its ultimate
end and the basis of its universal obligatoriness. Finally,
he argues from the simplicity of moral action as a necessary
condition of moral responsibility. From these first principles he launches his attack on "Old Schoolism."

As we have seen, the organizing principles of Finney's
thought are derived from natural theology, specifically from
analysis of the laws of "consciousness." Finney uses the
term to designate the immediate awareness of one's mental
states and their primary "attributes."

Consciousness is the faculty or function of self-
knowledge. It is the faculty that recognizes our
own existence, mental actions, and states, together with the attributes of liberty or necessity,
belonging to those actions or states [LST, p. 13].

Moral agency is defined solely in terms of conscious operations of the mind; and it is Finney's claim that when one
reflects upon one's own actions, the primary features of

Finney's interpretation of moral responsibility are self-evident, especially the claim that being subject to moral obligation requires that one be free to comply with the law or to rebel. "By a necessity of his nature, every agent knows himself to be free" (LST, p. 19).

In describing moral consciousness Finney uses the classic tripartite division of mental faculties, "intellect, sensibility and free-will," sharply distinguishing the first two as "passive" functions of mind, determined by a "law of necessity" to receive what is given to them by external impressions, from the "voluntary" character of will. The intellect is composed of reason, conscience, and self-consciousness. In all three functions it is "a receptivity as distinguished from a voluntary power" (LST, p. 14). The will can direct the intellect in the selection of objects to which the mind attends, but what is known is what is given by those objects in themselves. Finney assigns no creative, or determinative, function to the mode of perception itself. The sensibility is likewise a passive faculty. "All its phenomena are under the law of necessity. I am conscious that I cannot, by any direct effort, feel what and as I will" (LST, p. 14). Sensibility is subject to the indirect control of the will in that the will is capable of directing the attention of the mind to certain objects with which corresponding feelings are associated. However, because the sensibility cannot control what it receives, a person is not responsible for feelings as such. Although one may be tempted by the sensibility to seek self-gratification, so long as the person does not incline his or her will toward pleasure, he or she remains guiltless. The responsibility of the will in such cases is to distract the attention of the mind from the object of temptation: the mental equivalent of a cold shower. Thus, people are not responsible for what or how they feel, but they are responsible for the influence which their feelings exert upon their individual wills.

It follows that the will of the individual determines his or her entire moral identity.

> Free-will implies the power of originating and
> deciding our own choices, and of exercising our
> own sovereignty, in every instance of choice upon
> moral questions . . . . That man cannot be under
> a moral obligation to perform an absolute impossi-
> bility, is a first truth of reason. But man's
> causality, his whole power of causality to perform
> or do anything, lies in his will. If he cannot
> will, he can do nothing. His whole liberty or
> freedom must consist in his power to will . . . if
> he has no freedom he is not a moral agent, that
> is, he is incapable of moral action and also of
> moral character [LST, p. 15].

The total independence of the will is asserted later to be
one of the "facts in mental philosophy as they are revealed
in consciousness."

> The will is not influenced by either the intellect
> or the sensibility, by the law of necessity or
> force; so that the will can always resist either
> the demands of the intelligence, or the impulses
> of the sensibility [LST, p. 136].

While Finney acknowledges some "indirect" relation among the
three faculties insofar as the intellect presents the possibilities of choice to the will, and the sensibility is
shaped by the ways in which one willfully focuses the attention of the mind, yet he denies any integral relation among
the faculties such that the will is determined in its choice
by the "passive" elements of consciousness. The unity of
the self, then, is a direct result of conscious acts of will
whereby the given impressions of intellect and sensibility
are organized around a freely chosen intention either to
obey or reject the moral law.

Consequently, it is Finney's intention to "urge to
their logical consequences, the two admissions that the will
is free, and that sin and holiness are voluntary acts of
mind" (LST, p. x). In his theology, as in his revival

preaching, the basis of Finney's understanding of human
nature was that "a sinner is, essentially, a moral agent."[61]
As a legal apprentice, Finney had already learned that the
principle of free choice was basic to legal order. Samuel
Pufendorf, for example, declared that if one denied that the
will exercises "Freedom of Determination" and that "the
chief Affection of the Will . . . is an <u>Intrinsical</u> <u>Indif-
ference</u>," then "all the Morality of Human Action is over-
thrown."[62] On the basis of the principle of moral responsibility, Finney argued that Old School teachings contradicted
the direct testimony of moral consciousness and threatened
the very foundation of God's rule over human life.

Finney's theological discourses are organized around
the central claim that people are responsible agents whose
relationship to God is ordered in every respect according to
rational principles of moral government. The ideas of freedom and order are juxtaposed throughout his work: liberty
is the condition of moral responsibility, and the law is the
structure within which both God and moral beings exercise
their freedom. Finney's theology thus sought to resolve the
same tension between autonomy and order that was the central
crisis of conscience for his generation. Both in theology
and in religious experience this tension was resolved by
drawing on the resources of law as the means of regulating
human action within the order of the universe.

Finney is a rigorously systematic theologian who prides
himself on the logical sequence of premises and conclusions.
He does not at all expect, in the exposition of theological
truth, to be surprised. For if truth is to be appropriated
responsibly, it must be thoroughly intelligible. In the
revival Finney had appealed to the will of sinners through
"reasoned" preaching; accordingly, the first page of his
lectures defines moral law as "an idea of reason developed
in the mind of the subject" (LST, p. 1). Finney was too
much a man of common sense to appreciate the delightful
wonder of Calvinist theologians in the face of divine
mystery.[63] If God's dealings with people are mysterious,
Finney argues, it follows that they are "arbitrary," that

is, without good reasons. But "if God has no good and wise
reasons for what he commands, why should we obey him?" An
appeal to "arbitrary sovereignty" reduces religion to either
"sheer superstition or gross fanaticism" making "intelligent
piety" impossible. Rather, God always acts "for reasons
that will, when universally known, compel the respect and
even the admiration of every intelligent being in the universe" (LST, pp. 80-85).

Finney follows the maxim that whatever is unintelligible cannot carry moral responsibility, and whatever does
not involve moral agency cannot be determinative of human
character. This is the maxim by which guilt and pardon are
assigned in human courts and which provided the framework
within which Finney himself, and those under his preaching,
approached the bar of divine justice.[64] Accordingly, the
lectures on theology begin with a description of moral law
as

>   the rule for the government of free and intelli-
>   gent action, as opposed to necessary and unintel-
>   ligent action . . . . Moral law is primarily a
>   rule for the direction of the action of free will,
>   and strictly of free will only . . . moral law
>   controls involuntary mental states and outward
>   action only by securing conformity of the actions
>   of free will to its precept [LST, p. 1].

It follows that the "essential attributes" of moral law
correspond to its function as the governing rule of free
moral agents (LST, pp. 1-6). These attributes are intelli-
gibility; practicality, in the sense that the agent is free
to obey its precepts ("To talk of inability to obey moral
law is to talk nonsense"); appropriateness to the "nature
and relations of moral beings;" universality; impartiality;
independence (because the moral law is the "eternal, self-
existent rule of divine conduct . . . which the intelligence
of God prescribes to himself," it is "obligatory also upon
every moral agent, entirely independent of the will of God";
thus the moral law is a "first truth" of reason which

reveals the nature of being and not merely the desire of God); immutability ("It is the unalterable demand of the reason, that the whole being, whatever there is of it at any time, shall be entirely consecrated to the highest good of universal being"); simplicity, inasmuch as all demands of the moral law are comprehended in the one requirement to have benevolence as one's ultimate intention; expediency (because obedience to the moral law necessarily contributes to the well-being of moral agents and promotes universal happiness Finney can say, "that which is upon the whole most expedient is right, and that which is right is upon the whole expedient"); exclusiveness inasmuch as there can be only one ultimate rule of moral character. To employ a medieval analogy, the remainder of the lectures represents a "gloss" on these definitions. (It seems appropriate to the analogy that the original glossarists were commentators on canon law.)

Given this exposition of the meaning of moral law, it follows that the only appropriate means of administering that law is moral government.

> Moral government presides over and controls, or seeks to control the actions of free will; it presides over intelligent and voluntary states and changes of mind. It is a government of motive, as opposed to a government of force--control exercised, or sought to be exercised, in accordance with the law of liberty, as opposed to the law of necessity [LST, p. 6].

This distinction had become a commonplace in New England theology by Finney's time, but perhaps no other thinker since Hugo Grotius had brought as thorough an understanding of law to its formulation.[65] On the basis of that understanding, Finney was convinced that the true meaning of moral government, as well as "the truths of the blessed gospel," have been "hidden under a false philosophy," viz., "the assumptions that all government was physical, as opposed to moral, and that sin and holiness are rather natural attributes, than moral, voluntary acts" (LST, p. ix). The assumptions of Old School Calvinism, as Finney understood them, contradicted the first principle of legal order, that human beings are free moral agents capable of rational choice. By denying human responsibility, specifically the capacity to respond without coercion to the law of God, the theologians of the Westminster Confession allowed "the true idea of moral government . . . no place in the theology of the Church" (LST, p. ix.).

Such a statement supports Finney's claim that he had not studied the Westminster Confession, for the section on "free will" states explicitly that "God hath endued the will of man with that natural liberty, that is neither forced nor by any absolute necessity of nature determined to do good or evil."[66] Unfortunately, however, "natural liberty" did not survive the expulsion from Eden, as the assembled divines declare later in the same section: "Man, by his fall into a state of sin, hath wholly lost all ability of will to any spiritual good accompanying salvation . . . ." Therefore, for all practical purposes--and Finney knew no other--the Confession teaches that every person is unable to will "spiritual good." It follows that fallen humanity cannot be governed by moral suasion, but only by coercive power. If "Old Schoolism" were true, Finney concluded, there would be no difference between the way God rules over clouds and boulders and the way he governs human conduct.

> But mind cannot be moved as God moves the planets
> . . . . If [physical force] should act upon mind
> as it does upon matter, we certainly know there
> could be neither moral action nor moral character
> in such beings as we are.[67]

But it is not only human nature that requires persuasive means of government, but also the supreme end of the moral law itself. That end is the highest well-being of the universe, the intrinsic value of which Finney regards as "essentially self-evident," and which provides the ultimate "foundation of moral obligation."

> The well-being of God, and of the universe of
> sentient existences, and especially of moral
> agents, is intrinsically important, or valuable,
> and all moral agents are under obligation to
> choose it for its own sake. Entire, universal,
> uninterrupted consecration to this end, or disin-
> terested benevolence is the duty of all moral
> agents [LST, p. 28].

As God is obliged to acknowledge the moral law as the
supreme rule of will, so also "his relation to the universe,
and our relations to him and to each other, render it obligatory upon him to establish and administer a moral government over the universe" (LST, p. 8). God's right to govern
is not founded on his "ownership" of the universe, but on
the fact that moral government by an infinitely wise Governor is the means best adapted to attain the well-being of
moral agents.

Inasmuch as moral government is the best means of
securing the highest good aimed at by the moral law, it is
incumbent upon God to rule accordingly. For the moral law
is not subject to revocation, even by the divine will, and
would be binding even if God forbade it (LST, p. 29). Thus
even God derives moral identity from compliance with law.

> God has moral character, and is virtuous. This
> implies that he is the subject of moral obliga-
> tion, for virtue is nothing else than compliance
> with obligation. If God is the subject of moral
> obligation, there is some reason independent of
> his own will, why he wills as he does; some rea-
> son, that imposes obligation upon him to will as
> he does. His will, then, respecting the conduct
> of moral agents, is not the fundamental reason of
> their obligation; but the foundation of their
> obligation must be the reason which induces God,
> or makes it obligatory on him, to will in respect
> to the conduct of moral agents, just what he does
> [LST, p. 31].

That is, God and humans are constituted moral agents on the
same basis, viz., loyalty to the moral law as the best means
of achieving universal happiness. They share the understanding of the moral law and its basis, and both are obligated to conform to that law.

The final principle of Finney's system to be discussed
here is the unity (or simplicity) of moral action.[68] In the
exposition of his theory of moral obligation Finney taught
that "a single eye to the highest good of God and the universe, is the whole of morality, strictly considered . . . "
(LST, p. 94). Right willing, then, consists in right intentions; consequently, "upon this theory, no one who is truly
honest in pursuing the highest good of being, ever did or
can mistake his duty in any such sense as to commit sin"
(LST, p. 94). If virtue consists in having as one's supreme
intention the well-being of the universe, it is impossible
that one could simultaneously have the supreme intention to
gratify oneself. Further, as the mind can entertain only
one ultimate end at a time, so it is "shut up to the necessity of willing the means to accomplish that end" and no
other (LST, p. 97). Holiness then is primarily a function
of the inner person: pursuing the proper intention by the
appropriate means, including the degree of enthusiasm that
accords with any specific duty (one ought not to exhaust his
or her emotional resources in every action). "The Bible
everywhere assumes that sincerity or honesty of intention is
moral perfection; that it is obedience to the law" (LST, p.
99).

Finney's psychology is a description of conscious mental processes; by definition the mind can attend with "all
its strength" to only one ultimate end at a time (LST, p.
98). In these terms there is no possibility of "complex"
motives or of two motives entertained with different degrees
of intensity. It is true that there may coexist with holy
intention a sensible attraction toward self-gratification;
however, as we have seen, the feelings do not have moral
status for they arise by natural necessity. If the emotions
are directed in a way antagonistic to holy intention, the

will must divert the mind to objects that produce appropriate feelings. A failure to do so simply proves that one has not maintained a righteous intention. Finney has no sympathy with the "weak-willed." One's will is directed toward either self-love or benevolence; if one falls into sin, it is not because the will was "weak," but because it was evil. The only remedy is repentance, a conscious determination to will benevolence. Such determination lies within one's "natural" power; it is the basis of moral consciousness. Both sin and holiness are functions of conscious decision by which the individual determines his or her own moral character in each successive moment. The presence of sin in the world, as Finney tirelessly preached, is due not to lack of resolution, but to deliberate "stubbornness of will."[69]

These principles of moral agency constitute the hub from which the various spokes of Finney's theology radiate. By and large, his views are phrased in the familiar terms of nineteenth-century American moral philosophy, much of which Finney learned from colleagues like Asa Mahan. Yet Finney's mind had been well-prepared for such ideas by his reading in classic legal theory; also, he possessed the energy and imagination to appropriate their practical power for the cause of religious advocacy on a scale unprecedented in the history of Christian evangelism to that time. Finney regarded the world as his jury and theological doctrines as points of evidence in the brief he was commissioned to present. The first item which Finney wished to clarify is the nature and severity of the indictment against humankind, which task required a revision of the doctrine of sin.

NOTES

1. Cross, Burned-over District, p. 17.
2. "On Trusting in the Mercy of God," Gospel Themes, p. 31.
3. Quotations in this paragraph are from "The Guilt of Sin," The Guilt of Sin, pp. 11-36. For another example of the same argument, see "On the Wages of Sin," Gospel Themes, pp. 37-56.

4. Finney claims that this line of reasoning occurred
to him even before his conversion, while listening to a
Universalist preacher. "I was no Christian then, but I saw
at a glance that he might far better infer from the goodness
of God that He would forgive none than that He would forgive
all" ("The Inner and the Outer Revelation," Gospel Themes,
p. 236).

5. "Where Sin Occurs God Cannot Wisely Prevent It,"
Gospel Themes, p. 228.

6. "Salvation Difficulties," So Great Salvation, p. 14.
Cf. "Quenching the Spirit," Gospel Themes, p. 261: "The
solemn truth is that the Spirit is most easily quenched.
There is no moral work of His that can not be resisted."

7. "On Trusting in the Mercy of God," Gospel Themes,
pp. 22-23.

8. Ibid., p. 30.

9. Finney is at pains to show that the sinner chooses
hell; one is not assigned to eternal punishment by divine
decree without reference to his or her own consent. Election is based upon foreknowledge. "The simple and plain
view of it is, that God, foreseeing all . . . determined to
deal with you according to your voluntary choice . . .
("Salvation of Sinners Impossible," So Great Salvation, p.
41).

10. Sidney Mead claims that Nathaniel Taylor and Lyman
Beecher were the first to grasp the significance of the
argument from "moral tendency" which heretofore the Unitarians had used effectively to enlist public sentiment against
Calvinism. Taylor and Beecher sought to make the "doctrines
of the Reformation" more appealing to the people, while at
the same time charging Unitarians with moral laxity. This
form of ad hominem was regarded as an important "advertising
technique" in the "campaign" against Unitarianism [S. Mead,
Nathaniel William Taylor, 1786-1858, A Connecticut Liberal,
original edition, 1942 (Chicago: Archon Books, 1967), pp.
177-187]. Finney utilized the technique with particular
relish.

11. Cross, Burned-over District, p. 44.

12. Quoted by Cross, Burned-over District, p. 45.

13. See MF, pp. 68-70, 106, 134, 196-199, 369.

14. Charles G. Finney, Lectures on Systematic Theology, ed. J. H. Fairchild (Oberlin: E. J. Goodrich, 1878). Reprinted edition (Grand Rapids, Mich.: Wm. B. Eerdmans, 1964), p. ix. This edition is a condensation of the 1851 edition, made by omitting repetitious material and "paragraphs of a hortatory nature." Hereinafter referred to as LST.

15. F. H. Foster, New England Theology, pp. 167-170, 177-182.

16. Finney took every occasion to denounce "Hopkinsianism, the two great points of which were understood to be, that man ought to be willing to be damned for the glory of God, and that God was the author of sin" (MF, p. 241).

17. Cited by McLoughlin, Modern Revivalism, p. 21.

18. Calvin Colton, History and Character of American Revivals, p. 274.

19. The standard work on Taylor is Sidney Mead, Nathaniel William Taylor, 1786-1858, A Connecticut Liberal, (see note 10 above). Mead argues that the views of Taylor and his colleagues at New Haven were more closely allied with pre-Revolutionary Calvinism than with the self-styled "consistent Calvinism" of the Edwardeans--especially in Taylor's emphasis on "means" to elicit a saving response from sinners and the correlative claim that the unregenerate person has the ability and obligation "to make himself a new heart" (N. W. Taylor, Practical Sermons, quoted by Mead, p. 120). William McLoughlin interprets Taylor (as well as other exponents of the "new divinity," including Lyman Beecher) as preparing the way theologically for the acceptance of Finney's "new measures" in the promotion of revivals (Modern Revivalism, pp. 44-46). The succinct outline of Taylor's views by George P. Fisher emphasizes the almost total coincidence with Finney's position [Schaff-Herzog Encyclopedia of Religious Knowledge (New York: Funk & Wagnalls, Pub., 1882), III, 2306-2307]. Joseph Haroutunian carefully details the central role Taylor played in the development of "liberal Calvinism" (Piety Versus Moralism, pp. 252-254, 266-280). For an earlier account of Taylor's role in the history of New England theology see Foster, New England Theology, pp. 369-400.

20. <u>Finney</u>, p. 179.

21. Cf. Sidney Mead's comment on New Haven theology:
". . . the foundation of the whole structure was Taylor's
enlargement of the 'whosoever will' of the revivalists into
a genuine theory of free agency in humanity. All the rest
of 'Taylorism' or 'Beecherism' was built upon that rock and,
taking on the complexion of a prevailing interest of the
day, was stated in terms of government. God was convinced
to be the great ruler of a 'moral government,' not the
irresponsible monarch of abject and helpless creatures, and
he ruled through the medium of established laws" (<u>Taylor</u>, p.
125).

22. Finney does not cite Taylor in the <u>Lectures on
Systematic Theology</u>, although there is evidence that the two
men met prior to 1836 (Wright, <u>Finney</u>, p. 179) by which time
Taylor had worked out distinctive departures from Edwardean
views of moral agency—departures corresponding almost exactly with Finney's own. While the story of Finney's intellectual development awaits telling in full, Wright mentions
parallels to Nathanael Emmons (1745-1840) on the "simplicity
of moral action"; and to the younger Jonathan Edwards (1745-
1801) on the notion of "public justice." Many of Finney's
ideas have parallels in the later "Hopkinsians," but in
order to establish lines of influence a careful study of
Finney's correspondence would be required since his published writings contain few explicit acknowledgments. Indeed, one of the stated purposes of his lectures is to
provide pupils with matters "which have not, to my knowledge, been discussed in any system of theological instruction extant" (LST, p. x). Finney's exaggerated sense of
isolation was due in part to the strenuous criticism of his
early revivals by people whose theology was similar to his
own. For example, in his meetings with Asa Nettleton, a
staunch opponent of the "new measures," Finney found that he
and Nettleton agreed on "all points of theology upon which
we conversed" (MF, pp. 202-203); yet the next year Nettleton
maintained resistance to Finney's "measures" at the New
Lebanon Convention (1827). At Oberlin Finney found colleagues who supported both his theory and practice. Wright
observes that Finney was "aided in the formulation of the

New School position both by his associate teachers and by his pupils" (Finney, p. 181).

23. Finney, p. 25.

24. New England Theology, p. 467.

25. "Law and the Gospel," Victory over the World, p. 64.

26. A surprisingly large proportion of this material is still available in print, although not always in the same order as the original editions. For example, Kregel Publications has reissued several of the sermons and lectures in a series of seven volumes, comprising the "Charles G. Finney Memorial Library." Bethany Fellowship has reprinted paperback editions of both the Skeletons (titled, The Heart of Truth) and the Lectures on Systematic Theology. Eerdmans had earlier issued a serviceable hard cover reprint of the Lectures. The only work by Finney to receive the attention of modern textual criticism, and the grace of a lengthy introduction in a prestigious edition, is the Lectures on Revivals of Religion (edited by William G. McLoughlin and published by Harvard University Press, 1960). Although Finney's description of the techniques for raising a revival became the indispensable handbook for evangelists in America and the British Isles, the lectures do not contain much explicit theological reflection and do not, therefore, much clarify the distinctive principles in which Finney considered his revivalistic methods to be grounded.

27. J. H. Fairchild, Oberlin: Its Origin, Progress and Results. An address, prepared for the alumni of Oberlin College, assembled August 22, 1860. (Oberlin: Shankland and Harmon, 1860), p. 25.

28. Ibid., p. 67.

29. Charles G. Finney, Skeletons of a Course of Theological Lectures (Oberlin: James Steele, 1840), p. 3.

30. Arthur Leon Shumway and Charles DeWolf Brower, Oberliniana, A Jubilee Volume of Semi-Historical Anecdotes Connected with the Past and Present of Oberlin College, 1833-1883 (Cleveland: Home Publishing Co., 1883), p. 73.

31. James H. Fairchild, Oberlin: The Colony and the College, 1833-1883 (Oberlin: E. J. Goodrich, 1883), p. 95.

32. <u>Skeletons</u>, pp. 16, 22. In general, the American development of natural theology based on human "consciousness" was influenced by the Scottish philosophy of "Common Sense Realism." See William McLoughlin, introduction to <u>The American Evangelicals, 1800-1900</u> (New York: Harper Torchbooks, 1968), pp. 2-4, for a summary of the position. Sydney Ahlstrom provides a survey of the origins of this school of theology, beginning with Thomas Reid, in "The Scottish Philosophy and the American Theology," <u>Church History</u> 24 (September, 1955), 257-272.

33. <u>Skeletons</u>, p. 17.

34. <u>Skeletons</u>, p. 19.

35. <u>Skeletons</u>, p. 27.

36. Leonard I. Sweet, "The View of Man Inherent in New Measures Revivalism," <u>Church History</u> 45 (June, 1976), 213.

37. <u>Gospel Themes</u>, p. 232.

38. <u>Ibid.</u>, 235.

39. <u>Ibid.</u>, 238-239.

40. <u>Skeletons</u>, p. 167.

41. <u>Skeletons</u>, p. 18.

42. <u>Skeletons</u>, p. 18.

43. <u>Skeletons</u>, p. 18.

44. "The Sinner's Natural Power and Moral Weakness," <u>Gospel Themes</u>, p. 193.

45. <u>Ibid.</u>, p. 194.

46. <u>Ibid.</u>, p. 197.

47. <u>Skeletons</u>, p. 23.

48. <u>Skeletons</u>, pp. 23-24.

49. <u>Skeletons</u>, p. 19.

50. <u>Skeletons</u>, p. 21.

51. <u>Skeletons</u>, p. 40.

52. <u>Skeletons</u>, p. 46.

53. <u>Skeletons</u>, p. 60.

54. Jones, ed., <u>Commentaries</u>, p. 27.

55. <u>Skeletons</u>, pp. 114-122.

56. <u>Skeletons</u>, p. 183.

57. Jones, ed., <u>Commentaries</u>, p. 12.

58. <u>Ibid.</u>, p. 29.

59. Charles G. Finney, <u>The Reviewer Reviewed: or Finney's Theology and the Princeton Review</u> (Oberlin: James

M. Fitch, 1847), p. 4. Finney originally wrote his response
for The Oberlin Quarterly Review.

60. Ibid., p. 6.

61. "Converting Sinners a Christian Duty," Gospel
Themes, p. 335.

62. Of the Law of Nature and of Nations, p. 28.

63. Nathaniel Taylor also argued against the Edwardean
appeal to the "mystery" of sovereignty and free will as
revealed in Scripture by holding that God "demands only a
rational faith of rational beings" and that even the Bible
must be interpreted according to the dictates of "common
sense and sound reason" [Essays, Lectures, . . . (1859),
quoted by Mead, Taylor, pp. 108-109].

64. Finney understood what Martin Luther had insisted:
that reason and law are inseparable. The difference is that
Luther regarded the combination as the supreme threat to the
gospel whereas Finney perceived submission to the rational
order of moral law as the only process by which authentic
Christian identity could be formed.

65. Joseph Haroutunian notes the influence of Hugo
Grotius on Joseph Bellamy (Piety Versus Moralism, pp. 160-
166) and on the younger Jonathan Edwards (pp. 169-172). F.
H. Foster traces the growing importance of the idea of
"moral government" in New England theology from Bellamy to
Nathaniel Taylor (New England Theology, pp. 393f).

66. Philip Schaff, ed., The Creeds of Christendom,
Vol. III (New York: Harper and Brothers, Pub., 1877), p.
623.

67. "Salvation Difficulties," So Great Salvation, p.
13.

68. George Wright notes the parallel with Nathanael
Emmons (Finney, pp. 221-225). F. H. Foster traces the idea
to Hopkins (New England Theology, p. 463 n. 17), and notes
that it was introduced at Oberlin by one of the graduates,
William Cochran, in an address of 1841 (ibid., pp. 458-463).
The doctrine provided ground for Finney's views of perfection and his rejection of any conflict of consciousness in
the saint.

69. "The Excuses of Sinners Condemn God," Gospel
Themes, p. 85.

Chapter V

THE HUMAN CONDITION

The doctrine of sin functions in Christian theology as a means of defining the person, both as an individual and as a member of the race. The familiar distinction between sin as a responsible action of disobedience and as a condition of human nature points to both aspects of personal existence. The dialectical relationship between the two underlies St. Paul's discussion of "sin" and "sins" in Romans 3-8, and is explicitly acknowledged by modern theologians, such as Paul Tillich.

> As an individual act, sin is a matter of freedom, responsibility, and personal guilt. But this freedom is imbedded in the universal destiny of estrangement in such a way that in every free act the destiny of estrangement is involved and, vice versa, that the destiny of estrangement is actualized by all free acts.[1]

The classic stand-off in the nineteenth century between Old School and New School Calvinists was over the question of which aspect of personal existence should be emphasized in formulating the doctrine of sin. Clearly, the Old School stressed "the destiny of estrangement," the tragic drama of human history. The New School, to which Nathaniel Taylor and Charles Finney belonged, tended to see in the human story the epic grandeur of "free acts." The first group of thinkers understand the self as a participant in the common substance or history of mankind, deriving value from that participation. The second locate the value of the person precisely in the unique configuration of actions by which one is differentiated from others within that common substance or history. The question both must address is, "How is the moral identity of a free agent affected by membership in a sinful race?"

For Finney, the individual derives moral identity from the shape into which one molds generic nature by specific actions. Adamic nature is potential, the plastic material of self-actualization. It is essential, furthermore, that the generic nature have no irresistible disposition to sin in itself; rather, each individual is responsible to form a unique design from the material common to all persons. Each person is commissioned by the Creator to determine the personal history of the race. While that history exerts certain influences, e.g., by setting cultural and geographical limits or providing compelling examples, those influences are always "moral," i.e., persuasive, never "physical," i.e., coercive. Finney's understanding of human nature rests on the conviction that one is capable of setting oneself against the entire social history of which one is a member and establishing a new identity through a disciplined act of will. Failure to do so is a culpable neglect of responsibility, allowing "moral weakness" to overcome "natural ability."

The Inner Revelation

For Finney, the phrase "human nature" points to the unique capacity of moral agents to originate acts of willing independently of external determination. "Free-will implies the power of originating and deciding our own choices and of exercising our own sovereignty in every instance of choice upon moral questions" (LST, p. 15). Thus by "natural ability" Finney means the power to determine one's own moral character through the free exercise of will, what Pufendorf called the "Internal Directress" of human actions.[2] Natural ability is a necessary condition of being human, which cannot be lost without forfeiting human nature itself.

Thus Finney protested to the view that fallen humans
have no ability to choose "spiritual good" on the ground
that people "cannot exist as moral agents without
choice . . . . They are free to choose in either direction, but they are not free to abstain from choice altogether" (LST, p. 180). Further, Finney argued that if sin
is ingredient in human nature, then the sinner is held
morally responsible for a natural defect with which one is
necessarily afflicted. His argument rests on the claim that
inasmuch as a disposition to sin is "natural," it cannot be
regarded as an action for which the individual is responsible. "Disobedience to moral law cannot consist in the
constitution of soul and body. The law does not command us
to have a certain constitution, nor forbid us to have the
constitution with which we came into being" (LST, p. 180).
But the law does hold people responsible for whatever moral
commands lie within their ability to know and to fulfill.

Since moral responsibility requires some knowledge of
moral law, Finney argues that the wise Creator has provided
extensive "notices in nature both within and without us of
moral government."[3] In a sermon on "the inner and the outer
revelation" Finney elaborates the claim that

> we possess an intellectual or moral nature which
> as truly reveals great truths concerning God and
> our relations to Him and to law, as the material
> world reveals his eternal power and Godhead.[4]

Finney's description of "the original revelation that God
has made in each human soul"[5] is drawn from the opening
chapters of St. Paul's epistle to the Romans in which the
apostle argues that, apart from the incarnation, God has
revealed himself universally through the evidences of his
creative power and the witness of conscience. Thus, even
those who are ignorant of both the written commandments to
Israel and the incarnate Christ are responsible as moral
agents before God, their consciences "accusing or else
excusing them" (Romans 2:15). In his claim for the
perspicacity of natural revelation, Finney is following
again the "old legal authors," such as Samuel Pufendorf:

> . . . there's no man of proper Years, and Master
> of his own Reason, so desperately dull and stupid,
> as not to comprehend, at least, the most general
> Rules of Natural Law . . . . For these universal
> Edicts are so clearly publish'd and explain'd, and
> so closely interwoven with our Being, that no one
> can be overcome with so Brutal a Sottishness, as
> not to be capable of apprehending and discerning
> them . . . . [6]

In answer to the objection that "to render a Law obligatory, there is a necessity of making it known to the Subject," but not all people have heard the Scriptures, Pufendorf declares, "yet the knowledge of that Law may nevertheless be stil'd Natural, in as much as the necessary Truth and Certainty of it may be drawn from the use of Natural Reason."[7]

Finney, however, draws the same melancholy conclusion about natural law as St. Paul: that the awareness of obligation to moral law is accompanied by the awareness of one's failure to keep its demands. "There is none righteous, no not one . . . for all have sinned and come short of the glory of God" (Romans 3:10, 23). For Finney failure to obey the inner revelation of moral law is a deliberate act of violating the order of one's created nature—an affront to the rightful rule of God over his creation. Following his custom of addressing sinners directly, Finney drives home the point:

> . . . and you are in the position of an outlaw,
> condemned by law and without hope from the
> administration of justice . . . . You have cast
> off His authority, have disowned subjection to His
> law and government; indeed, you have cast all his
> precepts beneath your feet.[8]

The knowledge of God which is disclosed in creation is the idea of the supreme moral governor who rules both the material world and human beings by laws appropriate to the nature of each. Thus, it is as unnatural for a person to disobey moral law as for a stream to flow uphill.

To acknowledge the inner revelation is to awaken to one's true position in the universe as a being who both rules and is ruled. Finney cannot in fact conceive of a world that is not ruled: ". . . if the universe was not worth governing, it was not worth creating."[9] There is no action, from the slightest vibration of a leaf in the wind to the management of a stage-coach line to the raising of a revival, for which there is no directing law. In the case of physical actions and reactions, the laws are established and maintained by the Creator and perceived by clear-headed scientists. In the case of actions affecting the moral relations among people, the laws are established by the Creator but must be perceived and maintained by all moral beings.

The task is made simple by the benevolent wisdom of the Creator in so constituting moral beings that virtue "is both accompanied with and followed by a feeling of complacency and happiness."[10] Indeed, divine providence is evident "everywhere" in "the manifold contrivances for the promotion of happiness . . . happiness is the ultimate end of government."[11] There is then a natural motive to benevolence which is resisted only by a perverse denial of one's own good. The tragedy of human life is not that people are cursed by a dark compulsion to evil, but that they deliberately choose to do what is manifestly not in their own best interests. They act, in the words of St. Paul, contrary to "the work of the law written in their hearts." Thus Finney closes with a plea for inward examination: "Will you allow yourself to go on, bewildered, without considering that you are yourself a living, walking revelation of truth?"[12]

The perception of human life as governed by a rational system of laws designed to promote "the highest practicable well being of the universe" is present also in the "old legal authors." Blackstone agrees with Montesquieu and Pufendorf that the purpose of law is to articulate and

enforce that natural order of human society designed by the
Creator to achieve the highest measure of happiness in the
world. God has "so inseparably interwoven the laws of
eternal justice with the happiness of each individual,"
Blackstone declared, "that the latter cannot be obtained but
by observing the former."[13] By the "mutual connection of
justice and human felicity" God benevolently provides a
natural motive for virtue. God "has been pleased so to
contrive the constitution and frame of humanity, that we
should want no other prompter to inquire and pursue the rule
of right, but only our own self-love, that universal principle of action."[14] It is, then, all the more astonishing
that moral beings reject all the promptings of the created
order--the entire "inner and outer revelation"-- to pursue
their own selfish interests.

Sin

The presence of sin in the world, as Finney tirelessly
preached, is due not to lack of resolution, but to deliberate "stubbornness of will." He was conscious of such
intractableness in his own encounter with the gospel:

> When I came to pray, I found I could not give my
> heart to God. My inward soul hung back, and there
> was no going out of my heart to God. I began to
> feel deeply that it was too late; that it must be
> that I was given up of God and was past hope [MF,
> p. 15].

This passage illustrates what Finney later called the blas-
phemous excuse of inability. In fact, the very attempt to
excuse oneself for unbelief on the ground of lacking the
capacity to repent simply proves that one is unwilling to
meet God's demands. Finney is uncompromising on the point:
"This is the very essence--the true idea of sin: it is
deliberate, intelligent, and intentional rebellion against
God."[16] To persist in unbelief is to refuse to make a commitment of will which requires no other condition than

natural agency. "Those men therefore who plead that they
are willing to be Christians while yet they remain in their
sins, talk mere nonsense."[17] Finney recognized that, left
to himself, the sinner has "a moral weakness that effectually shuts him off from salvation, save as God interposes
with efficient help." However, that help is never beyond
the limits of moral persuasion; it consists in presenting
the truth clearly and vividly to the mind. Any other aid
would violate the "laws of mind" by which God establishes
"moral relations" with human beings.[18]

In Finney's own experience, it was his reluctance to be
"shamed" which appeared to him as sin, "awful, infinite. It
broke me down before the Lord" (MF, p. 16). The ground of
his sin was the failure to search for God, "with all your
heart," as Jeremiah counselled. In his sermons, Finney
interprets the heart, not as "sentiment," as did other
evangelicals, but as the power of moral choice.[19] At one
point Finney defines "heart" as "the will, because it is the
only faculty of the mind which can be said to be set--
fixed--bent, determined upon a given course of voluntary
action."[20] His own experience was that the biblical demand
was "put within the voluntary powers of my mind" (MF, p.
17); and the most insistent theme of his preaching was that
sinners are bound to change their own hearts. One typical
exposition of this demand is in the sermon entitled, "The
Sinner's Excuses Answered." Here Finney argued that, just
as Adam changed his heart to embrace sin, so it is possible
to make the reverse move, to change "the ruling preference,
the governing purpose of the mind," to holiness. Therefore,
God requires people to change their wills.

> He asks you to put your hand on the fountain-head
> of all your own power, to act just where your
> central power lies--where you ALWAYS HAVE POWER so
> long as you have a rational mind and a moral
> nature.[21]

The failure to change one's will is due to selfish resistance to the demands of the gospel, not to any natural

inability. "What is this <u>can</u> <u>not</u>? Nothing less or more
than a mighty <u>will</u> <u>not</u>!"[22]

> Sin is not a mere negation, or a not willing, but
> consists in willing self-gratification. It is a
> willing contrary to the commandments of God. Sin,
> as well as holiness, consists in choosing, will-
> ing, intending. Sin must be voluntary; that is,
> it must be intelligent and voluntary. It consists
> in willing, and it is nonsense to deny that sin is
> voluntary. The fact is, there is either no sin,
> or there is voluntary sin [LST, 122].

Finney would have appreciated Coleridge's declaration that
"Original Sin is a Pleonasm," for every sin must originate
in the will of the sinner, and no where else.[23] The unregenerate person is "one who cannot, because he will not,
conquer himself and his lust" (LST, p. 317).[24] Sin has no
other cause than self-indulgence.

It follows that, given the "simplicity" of moral action, selfishness is present in even the conspicuous acts of
public virtue by the unbeliever. Since one can hold only
one moral intention at a time, the unregenerate act always
from a motive of self-interest. If such a person seems to
perform an act of compassion, Finney insists that he or she
is actually gratifying his or her own desires. The person
is, then, not "the reformer in a virtuous sense, but the
selfish reformer" (LST, p. 187).[25] Finney admits that such
actions may conform to the demands of moral law "so far as
the outward life is concerned . . . but as they do not
proceed from disinterestedly benevolent intention, they are
only specious forms of selfishness" (LST, p. 187).

Selfishness, however, must be distinguished from self-
love, for "self-love is simply the constitutional desire of
happiness. It is altogether an involuntary state" (LST, p.
180). By giving the desire for happiness a natural, and
thus morally neutral, status Finney preserves a point of
contact in the unregenerate to which the preaching of the

gospel can make a legitimate appeal.[26] For the natural
desire for happiness ought to lead the reasonable person to
seek his or her good in submission to the moral law as the
best-adapted means of attaining universal well-being. Thus
in choosing selfishness one is failing to love oneself, that
is, to choose one's own highest good. As Finney explained
the matter in one sermon,

> You have desires correlated to God, yet you deny
> them their appropriate gratification. . . . [A
> person] can no more be happy without God than he
> can be without the sympathy and society of man.
> We all understand this law of human nature . . .
> [There is] a moral side to man's nature, and he
> can never be supremely happy till he becomes
> morally perfect.[27]

By rejecting the counsel of reason and committing one's will
"to gratification of the desires" (LST, p. 183), the sinner
enters into a state of personal disorder which Finney regarded as nothing less than "moral insanity," or "will-
madness."[28]

Throughout his analysis of sin Finney assumes the position of "psychological egoism," i.e., that all people whose
minds are not consciously directed to the moral law are
"selfish." The point may be expressed by use of a Kantian
distinction: while one may act "according to duty," one is
virtuous only if acting "from duty."[29] Even if one practices "commercial justice" in dealings with others, "all his
apparent fairness and justice, are only a specious form of
selfishness. He has, and, if a sinner, it is impossible
that he should not have, some selfish reason for all he
does, is, says, or omits" (LST, p. 195). Whether one
chooses to preach the gospel or follow a murderous career of
piracy, if a person is unconverted, "whichever course he
takes, he takes it for precisely the same ultimate reason;
and with the same degree of light it must involve the same
degree of guilt" (LST, p. 207).

Inasmuch as selfishness is a function of the will it is characterized by "efficiency," i.e., it produces moral actions. "The whole causality of the mind resides in the will. In it resides the power of accomplishment" (LST, p. 189). Here Finney applies the psychological principle established earlier that outward actions, or means, are always consonant with intentions (unless there is some "physical" hindrance). If the will is governed by self-interest, it cannot choose means to a benevolent end; and "God regards nothing as virtue except devotion to the right ends."[30] Thus there is no possibility of good in the sinner. "The end being wrong, all is, and must be, wrong" (LST, p. 191). Finney concludes that selfishness implies "total moral depravity," that "every selfish being is at every moment as wicked and as blameworthy as with his knowledge he can be" (LST, p. 202). Since moral obligation and blame are based upon ultimate intention only, and since the intrinsic value of benevolence is intuited in some degree by everyone, persistence in selfishness constitutes complete rejection of the light of reason. All people accrue to themselves the fullest possible measure of moral guilt; their damnation follows from their selfish intention.

The Excuse of Constitutional Depravity

Given the utter freedom of individual moral choice, how does one explain the universality of moral depravity, the inevitable triumph of self-love? Old School Calvinism argued that all people sin because all are sinners, that is, corrupted by an evil disposition inherited from Adam for which reason they are properly called, in the biblical phrase, "by nature children of wrath" (Ephesians 2:3). In Finney's view, however, the traditional doctrine of original sin presented God as an "infinite tyrant"; and, he protested, "this is a lie."[31]

> Orthodoxy! There never was a more infamous libel on Jehovah! It would be hard to name another dogma which more violently outrages common sense. It is nonsense--absurd and utter NONSENSE![32]

The absurdity of the traditional view is due to its contradiction of the primary intuition of moral agency. Therefore, in the slightly calmer words of the Lectures,

> The thing needed is a philosophy and a theology
> that will admit and explain all the phenomena of
> experience, and not deny human consciousness. A
> theology that denies human consciousness is only a
> curse and a stumbling-block. But such is the
> doctrine of constitutional depravity [LST, p.
> 308].

The first datum of consciousness for Finney is individual freedom; he has very little awareness of the other side of the dialectic of sin, that sense of general human condemnation which was so prominent in the experience of converts in the Great Awakening of the mid-eighteenth century. Jonathan Edwards reported that an intuition of solidarity with Adam's guilt was not at all uncommon among the subjects of "surprising conversions" at Northampton. For example, one Abigail Hutchinson testified that before her conversion it had been her "opinion" that

> she was not guilty of Adam's sin, nor any way
> concerned in it because she was not active in it;
> but that now she saw she was guilty of that sin
> and all over defiled by it; and the sin which she
> brought into the world with her, was alone suffi-
> cient to condemn her.[33]

Edwards himself had argued at great length that depravity is natural to fallen human kind, but that the divine condemnation of Adam's children is nevertheless just because each of them consents to the original transgression. That is, membership in the race entails personal acceptance of the values, perception, and intentions which comprise the governing disposition of the whole. Thus God properly views all humanity as constituting "one complex person, or one moral whole."[34] The act of coming to consciousness as a

moral agent is the act of affirming one's identity with the
unified moral history of Adam's race and the disposition to
sin which is the ground of that history in the mind of God.
To be human, then, for Edwards is to consent to a particular
history of conduct. There is no morally neutral feature of
human existence; no one is exempt from the tragic consequences of solidarity with all other persons, including the
first man.

Finney, however, rejects any communal responsibility as
inconsistent with the principles of moral government according to which each individual is judged solely on the basis
of response to an acknowledged law. Before the bar of
justice there is no provision for moral responsibility
beyond acts of individual disobedience, a point made repeatedly by the best known legal theorists. Hugo Grotius emphasized that "all Obligation to Punishment is grounded upon
Guilt. Now Guilt must of Necessity be personal, because it
results from our Will, than which nothing can be said to be
more directly ours. . . ."[35] Similarly, Samuel Pufendorf
had declared that while the understanding is at times
"Fallacious and Uncertain," and issues in mistaken conduct,
the consequence could not "be charged on us as Guilt, that
we have done a bad Action, if we were not furnished with a
clear Discernment of Good and Evil; and it would be the
highest Injustice to impute that Error as Sinful, which was
beyond our Power to avoid or shake off."[36] If human and
divine ideas of justice are to correspond exactly, which
Finney asserted as a first principle of reason, then praise
and blame can be assigned, on heaven as well as on earth,
only for free and informed choices. Grotius stated the
principle with absolute clarity:

> All punishment, if it be just, must be the Punish-
> ment of some Crime; which is true even of those
> Punishments that are inflicted by GOD . . . he
> that punishes, if he punish justly, must have a
> Right to punish, which Right arises from the Crime
> of the Delinquent.[37]

For Edwards the dialectic of human consciousness between the joy and power of personal belief, and the despair arising from a sense of the history of human sinfulness in which one feels entrapped was a fact of moral consciousness--as real to him as Finney's intuition of the natural ability of the individual to achieve moral perfection, in spite of the common destiny of mankind.[38] Yet on the basis of his reading in the law, Finney firmly rejects appeals to a sense of responsibility beyond the limits of self-determination.

> It is . . . absurd . . . to infer real
> responsibility from a feeling or persuasion of
> responsibility. To hold that men are responsible,
> because they loosely think themselves to be so, is
> absurd. . . . The idea of responsibility, when
> there is in fact real inability, is a prejudice of
> education, a mistake [LST, 356f.].

The first step toward correcting that mistake is to recognize that the true ground of sin is selfishness.

> That men are morally depraved is one of the most
> notorious facts of human experience, observation
> and history. Indeed, I am not aware that it has
> even been doubted, when moral depravity has been
> understood to consist in selfishness [LST, p.
> 232].

The argument is clinched with a high degree of presumption, even for Finney: "I may also appeal to the universal consciousness of the unregenerate. They know themselves to be selfish, to be aiming to please themselves, and they cannot honestly deny it" (LST, p. 234). As in all forms of "psychological egoism," Finney must assume omniscience regarding human motivation. But on the ground of observation he can establish only whether people in fact commit deeds with evil consequences; he can determine nothing infallibly about their intentions. Indeed, for him to do so would contradict a position he took earlier, viz., that deeds

which appear "right" do <u>not</u> necessarily entail benevolent
intentions (and, in the unregenerate, never do). Conversely, deeds which appear evil may not necessarily entail
selfish intention (and, in the sanctified, never do). That
is, there is no discernible correlation between the character of one's actions and intentions. Ultimately, then,
Finney rests his argument on the biblical passages which
teach that "subsequent to the commencement of moral agency,
and previous to regeneration, the moral depravity of mankind
is universal" (LST, p. 233).

These are, of course, the same passages to which
Edwards had appealed in support of an innate human tendency
to sin. Finney's interpretation is governed by the principle that to ascribe sin to human nature "is to overlook the
essential nature of sin, and to make sin a physical virus,
instead of a voluntary and responsible choice" (LST, p.
236). As examples of this error Finney cites Leonard Woods'
essay on "native depravity" (published in Boston, 1835) and
sections of the Westminster Confession and Shorter Catechism. In his critique Finney argues from the admission of
his protagonists that sin is transgression of known law. He
then poses the central question: "Can a voluntary transgression of law be denominated an attribute of human
nature?" (LST, p. 239). If not, then to interpret Scripture as teaching constitutional sinfulness is to "contradict
God's own definition of sin, and the only definition that
human reason or common sense can receive, to wit, that 'sin
is a transgression of the law'" (LST, p. 243).

In addition to the denial of imputed guilt on the
principles of legal responsibility, and the insistence that
the biblical definition of sin is "<u>anomia</u>, a transgression
of, or a want of conformity to, the moral law" (LST, p.
249), Finney offers a familiar objection to the doctrine of
a sinful nature: "To represent the constitution as sinful,
is to represent God, who is the author of the constitution,
as the author of sin" (LST, p. 249). The case is clear-cut.
Adam did not create his own substance, nor any of its acci-
dents. Therefore, if sin inheres in his nature, God is

responsible either for creating Adam's nature sinful or for establishing "the physical laws that of necessity bring about this result" (LST, p. 249). Now, of course, no one held that God directly created evil; but Finney presses the legal principle which would assign responsibility to God if God established the conditions under which sin was necessary. There is no evidence in his theological lectures that Finney had read Jonathan Edwards' treatise on original sin, but he was no doubt familiar with some form of Edwards' argument that God "permitted" Adam to fall into sin by withdrawing those supernatural principles that sustained him in original righteousness. Edwards maintained that God's action was not a positive cause of which Adam's sin was the effect, but a negative condition making the fall possible and, indeed, inevitable.[39] The distinction is too subtle for Finney, since in either case the principles of legal responsibility would assign the blame for sin to God whose willing was the sufficient condition for the result.

There is also a problem in the interpretation of sin as "privation," or lack of "gracious affections." For Finney moral agents cannot justly be held responsible for what has been withdrawn from them, or for what they lack. Sin is a phenomenon of the will, a deliberate and, therefore, culpable choice of self-interest as one's ultimate intention. To present sin in Edwards' terms is in effect to transfer it from the field of human responsibility to the divine. Even if one were willing to do so on the ground that sin is the means to a greater good, Finney would reply that evil means reflect the character of the willing agent. One of the attributes of will is "efficiency," i.e., employment of appropriate means to realize its end. Evil means are appropriate to an evil (selfish) end only. Thus, on the view that God causes sin God stands condemned as evil—an unthinkable conclusion for either side in the dispute.

But for Finney perhaps an equally damning indictment of the doctrine of constitutional depravity is that it undercuts the basis of revival preaching.

It is difficult, and, indeed, impossible for those
who really believe this doctrine to urge immediate
repentance and submission on the sinner. ... It
is a contradiction to affirm, that a man can
heartily believe in the doctrine in question, and
yet truly and heartily blame sinners for not doing
what is naturally impossible to them [LST, p.
251].

The traditional teaching of original sin makes the preaching
of the gospel "an insult to the unfortunate" by demanding
that sinners perform an act of "self-condemnation" on
grounds which are unreasonable.

[This doctrine] must render repentance, either
with or without the grace of God, impossible,
unless grace sets aside our reason. If repentance
implies self-condemnation, we can never repent in
the exercise of our reason. Constituted as we
are, it is impossible that we should condemn our-
selves for a sinful nature, or for actions that
are unavoidable [LST, p. 251].

There is more than a hint of autobiographical reference in
that last sentence. Finney discovered his own resistance to
the theology of the Old School, as well as that of his more
intelligent auditors, grew out of its contradiction of
coherent moral reasoning. If one approaches the bar of
divine justice as a responsible moral agent, then the ground
of condemnation, as well as the means of justification, must
be within the grasp of both reason and will. For only under
those conditions can one make a moral decision--the defining
action of selfhood.

Finney's uncompromising rejection of the Old School
doctrine of original sin is entirely consistent with his
view that each individual is personally responsible to obey
the demands of the gospel immediately upon hearing them. If
impenitence is the result of "inability," then the preacher
cannot warn sinners about their just condemnation; the

terrors of conscience cannot be aroused. It is characteristic that in his closing shot at the idea of constitutional depravity Finney should refer to the aid and comfort it had provided his other chief enemy in the field.

> This doctrine is a stumbling block both to the church and to the world, infinitely dishonorable to God, and an abomination alike to God and the human intellect and should be banished from every pulpit, and from every formula of doctrine, and from the world. It is a relic of heathen philosophy, and was foisted in among the doctrines of Christianity by Augustine. . . . This view of moral depravity that I am opposing, has long been the stronghold of Universalism. From it, the Universalists inveigh with restless force against the idea that sinners should be sent to an eternal hell [LST, p. 252].

The Fall of Adam

But, if the universality of sin is not to be explained by a corrupt disposition, what is its ground and how is it related to the sin of the first man? How is the solidarity of the human race "in Adam" to be understood? First, whatever that solidarity may be, it cannot carry moral significance in itself for the individual. One's membership in the human race is a given condition for moral responsibility, but implies neither guilt nor virtue in itself. Second, Finney emphasizes that

> the Bible once, and only once, incidentally intimates that Adam's first sin has in some way been the occasion, not the necessary physical cause, of all the sins of men. Rom. v. 12-19. It neither says nor intimates anything in relation to the manner in which Adam's sin has occasioned this result [LST, p. 253].

The biblical writers assume that "the quo modo was too obvious to need explanation" (LST, p. 253). For Finney, Adam's sin "consisted in yielding the will to the impulses of the sensibility, instead of abiding by the law of God, as revealed in the intelligence. Thus the Bible ascribes the first sin of our race to the influence of temptation" (LST, p. 253). It is on these grounds that the presence of sin in all persons is to be explained: all have fallen in the same manner Adam fell. "Free, responsible will is an adequate cause in the presence of temptation, without the supposition of a sinful constitution, as has been demonstrated in the case of Adam and of the angels" (LST, p. 245). Sin thus presupposes the attributes of moral agency, as described in the introductory lectures. That is, sin is an "adult" possibility. Infants, in whom the conditions of moral consciousness have not matured, are not, strictly speaking, subjects of moral government. However, as soon as children develop moral consciousness, they invariably lapse into sin, as did Adam; ". . . temptation may be universal, and of such a nature as uniformly, not necessarily, to result in sin . . ." (LST, p. 238).

Adam is the archetypal sinner. It is not that his guilt is imputed willy-nilly to his descendants, but that he introduces sin into the world and so demonstrates the pattern of its origin in every moral being.

> . . . Adam fell into a state of total alienation
> from the law of God, and lapsed into a state of
> supreme selfishness. His posterity have unani-
> mously followed his example. He and they have
> become dead in trespasses and sins [LST, p. 343].

That pattern is summarized by Finney in a passage that traces the emergence of moral consciousness.[40]

> . . . the sensibility acts as a powerful impulse
> to the will, from the moment of birth, and secures
> the consent and activity of the will to procure
> its gratification, before the reason is at all

> developed. The will is thus committed to the
> gratification of feeling and appetite, when first
> the idea of moral obligation is developed. . . .
> as the will is already in a state of committal,
> and has to some extent already formed the habit of
> seeking to gratify feeling, and as the idea of
> moral obligation is at first but feebly developed,
> unless the Holy Spirit interferes to shed light on
> the soul, the will, as might be expected, retains
> its hold on self-gratification [LST, pp. 253f].

The influence of Adam's sin in this process is restricted to
the exposure of his posterity to "aggravated temptation"
(LST, p. 255). That is, the relationship between Adam and
his race (as well as among the members of that race) is one
of "moral suasion." His sin provides a greater persuasive
force to the sensibility, but in no way causes the triumph
of feeling over reason. To be "in Adam," then, is to be a
member of a race whose lower faculties are subject to self-
gratification as "the rule of action previous to the development of reason" (LST, p. 255). This condition is not
subject to legislation (since it is a function of the sensibility) and thus is a form of "physical," not "moral"
depravity. The bias of sensibility toward self-interest is
strong, but not determinative, i.e., it does not sustain a
relation of cause to the will. There is a significant
parallel to Finney's position here in Pufendorf's claim that
the will exercises "Freedom of Determination," despite its
dependence on the understanding for presenting to it the
objects of choice.

> . . . tho' the Reason, which makes a thing desired
> or avoided, does not depend upon the Will, but
> upon the Condition of the Object, according as it
> bears the Face of Good or Evil; yet that Appetite
> and that Aversion, which thus follow the
> Appearance of the Object, are not of so much Force
> and Sway, but that there still remains in the Will
> a Liberty, whether or no it shall determine itself
> to any external Act about such an Object. . . .[41]

Nevertheless, Finney recognizes that, apart from the assistance of the Holy Spirit, strengthening the reason, "the lower propensities will of course influence the will" (LST, p. 256).

Thus Finney recognizes that there is a predisposition to selfishness, located in the infantile drive for self-gratification prior to the development of rational capacities; the disposition is not an act of will, and thus carries no moral responsibility. Yet this appetite for self-indulgence is so strong that it uniformly overcomes the weak objection of the embryonic reason and leads the will into the choice of sinful intention. The process of initial moral choice is conceived by Finney as if it were a courtroom debate carried on in the inner chambers of the mind. The will, or "heart," as the jury, must decide between the opposing attorneys representing the interests of the self (sensibility) and of God and the universe (reason). The contest is tragically uneven since "sensibility gets the start of reason" (LST, p. 257) and invariably brings decisive "arguments" (in fact, impulses) against the inexperienced attempts of reason to persuade the heart to benevolence.

To overcome moral depravity, then, what is required is that the persuasive influence of reason be strengthened by the presentation of truth by the Divine Advocate, the Holy Spirit. Regeneration consists in the successful appeal of the truth to the will so that one decides for benevolence. What is essential to Finney's interpretation is an image of psychological processes following courtroom procedure, in which human nature is divided into distinct "faculties," each representing to the will particular, and conflicting, interests. The essence of the moral agent is identified with the will whose judgments define the whole moral character of the individual. The will stands between the "natural propensities and appetites" and the "idea of reason" (i.e., consciousness of the moral law), and in each moment of life one is called upon to choose between the persuasive influences of each. Whether one decides for selfishness or benevolence, the outcome is a result of moral influences and is in no way determined by constitutional dispositions.

But, if the internal courtroom is governed by moral suasion only, why does everyone decide for selfishness? Surely reason would triumph, even over the persuasive example of Adam's sin, in at least a few cases. Finney's answer is that the will is influenced by the prior development of selfish appetites which are stronger than reason. Thus moral agents surely fall into sin; but they do so voluntarily, on the basis of a proper trial. Yet given the underdeveloped resources of reason as the advocate for God and the universe, moral defeat seems inevitable. The outcome seems dictated by the "laws of mind" which Finney recognizes as requiring that the strongest motive presented to the will is always decisive.

The dilemma which Finney faces is a result of conflicting interests in maintaining individual responsibility for sin, on the one hand, and acknowledging the inevitability of sin on the other. His solution consists of assigning the origin of sin to each individual; sin arises in an unconditioned choice between the persuasion of reason and the impulses of sensibility, a choice which invariably, but not necessarily, favors the lower instincts. Finney describes the process of moral apostasy, but does not provide any more satisfactory explanation for its source than traditional theologians have offered for the fall of Adam. G. C. Berkouwer's comment on Pelagius applies as well to Finney: "the problem of the origin of sin is made acute, and even intensified, for every single member of the race."[42] Each person, in coming to mature moral consciousness, re-enacts the drama of Eden, yielding to the lure of "being like gods." Moral depravity, then, does not "consist in anything back of choice, and that sustains to choice the relation of a cause. Whatever is back of choice is without the pale of legislation . . . moral character belongs only to choice, or intention" (LST, p. 231).

Moral Necessity?

In order to preserve the principle that legal responsibility requires conscious choice Finney works out a detailed criticism of Jonathan Edwards' famous treatise on <u>Freedom</u> <u>of</u> <u>Will</u> in which Edwards argues that the will is under "moral necessity" to act according to the strongest motive which affects it.[43] The problem, as Edwards sees it, is that, since Adam, the human will has necessarily fallen under the influence of sinful affections, and thus exhibits a "propensity . . . which really amounts to a fixed, constant, unfailing necessity" to sin.[44] Finney's response assumes that what Edwards means by "affections" is either a) irresistible "objective motives" which determine the will, or b) that passive faculty of the self which Finney calls "sensibility." In both forms Finney interprets Edwards' schema of moral action to be necessitarian, and thus false to the meaning of moral responsibility. If one labors to obey the divine will under a "moral necessity" to disobey, then human freedom is an illusion and the call to repentance a cruel joke. For Finney the ultimate outcome of Edwards' position is a denial of human nature, a denial of that very capacity which gives one the dignity of personal existence, viz., the liberty to originate one's own response to the moral law. We shall examine each of Finney's interpretations of Edwards.

a) "Objective Motives"

Finney interprets Edwards' motto, "the will is as the greatest apparent good," to mean that there is a causal relation between the motives presented to the mind and the movement of the will. "Edwards held that motive, and not the agent, is the cause of all actions of the will. Will, with him, is always determined in its choices by motives as really as physical effects are produced by their causes" (LST, p. 329). Finney rightly notes the parallel in Edwards' view between physical and moral causation. What he

fails to understand is Edwards' nontraditional view of causation as the reciprocal relation among entities within a
complex system of being. Working from the Newtonian model
of the physical universe, Edwards explained that moral decisions are affected not only by the motive which is presented
to the agent but also by the prior moral character of the
agent which shapes how the motive is apprehended. The
affections, which are formed in a complex process of human
response to being acted upon, determine what appears to the
mind as the greatest good and so either incline or disin-
cline the will from the motive. The agent, Edwards argued,
is still free to will as he pleases, but he is not free to
be pleased in any way he will. Nevertheless, the agent is
responsible for his preferences. It will not excuse me if,
upon striking you, I were to explain that my action was
caused by my hating you. For the most part we are held as
responsible for hatred as for battery.

Edwards attempts through a brilliant synthesis of Newton's physics and Locke's psychology to defend the position
that one can justly be held responsible for one's disposition, even though it is prior to conscious intention, or in
Finney's terms, "without the pale of legislation." What
Edwards proposes is a notion of complex causation by which
moral evil can be understood to proceed from the field of
powers both acting upon and exercised by the individual
agent.[45]

Finney, however, has little patience with such metaphysical subtleties. He understands the term "cause" in the
ordinary sense of the sufficient condition of an "effect,"
such that an effect has one, and only one, cause. For
example, if I strike you as the result of a muscle spasm, or
the effect of a third person's forcibly directing my arm,
then I am not the "cause" of the act. In that case I am not
acting as a moral agent for what happened was beyond the
control of my will. As Finney reads Edwards' discussion of
"motive," human actions are always caused by something other
than the will of the agent; thus, there is no ground of
responsibility.

It is denied, at least by me, that either reason
or divine revelation affirms moral obligation or
moral character of any state of mind, that lies
wholly beyond both the direct and indirect control
of the will (LST, p. 337).

It seems clear to Finney that Edwards has adopted the "capital error of denying the proper causality of moral agents."

This error is fundamental. Every definition of a
moral agent that denies or overlooks, his proper
causality is radically defective. It drops out of
the definition the very element that we
necessarily affirm to be essential to liberty and
accountability [LST, p. 334].

Finney's criticism presupposes the utter independence
of the will from perception and disposition. His psychology
has no provision for the interpenetration of mental powers.
Consequently, he fails to appreciate Edwards' argument that
the way an object appears to the mind is a function of the
affections, which in turn elicit the consent of the perceiv-
ing subject. Thus, the motive for moral action is itself
shaped by the vision and the disposition of the agent. For
Edwards, then, the relation among the constituents of the
self cannot be adequately described as a linear sequence of
causation. For Finney, however, the suggestion that any
element of experience, other than the self-determining power
of the will, should affect moral decisions is to obscure and
reduce the moral responsibility of the agent.

b) "Sensibility"

In the second case, Finney translates Edwards' term
"affections" to mean emotions or feelings. This misreading
was common among Edwards' opponents in the Great Awakening,
and the error is sustained by Finney.[46] If Edwards taught
that whatever operations of the mind do not belong to the
understanding must be attributed to the will, and if the

will is necessarily moved by the strongest desire, then it
is moved irresistibly by whatever most strongly impresses
itself upon the affections, or in Finney's terms, the sensibility or feelings. However, because the sensibility is
entirely passive in Finney's psychology, the moral agent has
no control over what impresses the feelings and thus has no
responsibility for the actions which result.

Finney's own psychology deals with those functions of
consciousness under the direct control of the will. Sin,
then, is the individual's failure to keep the faculties in
order. "Moral depravity, as I use the term, consists in
selfishness; in a state of voluntary committal of the will
to self-gratification" (LST, p. 231). Thus Finney rejects
the notion of "moral inability" as a contradiction in terms:
any action which lies beyond the control of the will is
without character (LST, p. 337).[47] The inability to will
aright could not be the ground of condemnation, but a state
in which the condition of moral agency is missing. Finney's
position depends upon two presuppositions: the strict separation of the person into distinct mental faculties which
are related in causal sequence; and the absolute separation
of moral action as originating in freedom from all physical
actions which occur necessarily, including those of perception and feeling. The decisions of a moral agent are ultimately unconditioned, or absolutely free. It is only on
these grounds that Finney thinks the defense of moral government is possible.

Finney represents an extreme development of the "volun-
tarist" position in which the self is identified with conscious acts of willing: each successive volition springing
from unconditioned freedom of choice. Thus Finney rejects
Edwards' distinction between natural ability to do as one
pleases and the moral inability to will other than what
appears most agreeable. The only morally relevant ability
is the ability to form right intentions, i.e., to will
according to one's duty. "If there is no ability to will,
there is, and can be no ability to do . . . " (LST, p.
322).[48] Finney concludes that "moral inability" is either a

physical defect, and thus without moral obligation, or it is
the natural ability to disobey, and thus culpable under
moral law (LST, pp. 332-334). If moral inability is simply
disobedience, then it is within the sinner's natural power
to overcome.

Benevolent Punishment

But if obedience to God is the happy fulfillment of human
nature, and if the law of God is the expression of his
benevolent will, then is it not reasonable to expect that
the Creator will finally forgive the apostasy of his creatures and receive them into the loving arms of the father
welcoming the prodigal? No sooner has Finney dispatched the
forces of traditional Calvinism than his other ideological
opponents rush on to the field. This last sentimental wish
of the Universalists, however, Finney also attacks on the
basis of "governmental principles." In moral government
sins must be surely and severely punished.

Already in the Skeletons, Finney had argued that the
sanctions attached to moral laws are the natural consequences of either obedience or disobedience to those laws.
As such, sanctions are "an expression of the benevolent
regard of the law-giver to his subjects: the motives which
he exhibits to induce in the subjects the course of conduct
that will secure their highest well-being."[49] Sanctions
also undergird confidence in the justice of divine rule, and
"confidence in the government is the sine qua non of all
virtue." The positive implication of the principle is that
the recognition of the unconditional benevolence of the
ruler inspires sacrificial obedience to the law, for the
subjects know that such obedience is, in the long run, most
productive of their own happiness. God would not require
anything but what will eventually result in his subjects'
highest well-being. The negative implication of the principle is that the ruler is obligated to punish any who threat-
en his government. At the end of one horrific portrayal of
the agonies of the damned, Finney exclaims that "the only

thing that can secure public confidence in a ruler is fidelity in the execution of his law. Hence it is to them [angels observing hell] no wonder that, there being sin to punish God should punish it with most exemplary severity."[50]

Any violation of moral law is an expression of distrust in the divine government, a denial of God's benevolence. It follows that "under moral government there can be no small sin, as every sin is a breach of the whole and only law of benevolence, i.e., it is a violation of the principle which constitutes the law of God."[51] The enormity of sin, requiring the severity of unending punishment, is that it strikes at the very foundation of the divine rule, and thus at the heart of God himself. In an analogous fashion Blackstone had argued that "public wrongs" are more serious than private ones because they strike "at the very being of society." In cases of murder or treason, for example, "the private wrong is swallowed up in the public."[52] Finney extends the principle to include every violation of moral law. Inasmuch as God's rule over human life is universal and comprehensive, every sin is a "public wrong," a damnable betrayal of divine government.

In the Skeletons he emphasizes that sin "tends to overthrow all government, all happiness. And as all rebellion is aimed at the throne and the life of the sovereign, the natural tendency of sin is not only to annihilate the authority, but the very being of God."[53] Thus, to the objection that "man is so diminuitive a creature, so much less than the Creator, that he cannot deserve his endless frown," Finney answers that "the higher the ruler is exalted above the subject in his nature, character, and rightful authority, the greater is the guilt of transgression in the subject."[54] Thus, Finney warns in one sermon, that "any one form of sin persisted in is fatal to the soul."[55]

Since sin is a direct frontal assault on God himself, the divine anger is not with "sin" in the abstract sense of a universal human condition, but is directed toward the sinner.[56] Despite the deicidal intention of the sinner, however, God's wrath is not merely a matter of personal pique. Rather, God is required to punish the sinner by the principles of his own government, which are in turn grounded in the infinite value of their end, viz., universal happiness. Now the true crime of the sinner can come to light: "Sin is the violation of an infinitely important law--a law designed and adapted to secure the highest good of the universe."[57] Indeed, the sinner seeks to replace the general good by his or her own selfish interest; and "each sinner maintains that his own will shall be law."[58] In defense God must uphold the moral law, not only for his own sake, but for the sake of his entire creation whose supreme happiness depends upon its maintenance. For God to allow sin to go unpunished, far from being an act of commendable mercy, would constitute culpable neglect of his responsibility as the just and benevolent Governor of the universe.

Granted the punishment of sin is both benevolent and necessary, however, why must it entail endless suffering? Is it not enough, the persistent Universalist might argue, that humans must undergo the pain and indignity of death? Is not the penalty of the final dissolution of the body sufficient "wages" for the dissolute acts of the will? To Finney such questions reveal a mind insensitive to the demands of justice. In the first place, death comes indiscriminately upon all creatures, but not all have committed sinful acts: "infants and animals suffer this penalty as well as the most abandoned transgressors."[59] Nor will it do to say that sin is punished by "annihilation," for then sinners escape their just deserts by being dismissed from existence. The only view which Finney believes honors both the demands of the law and the integrity of moral agents is that sinners are punished with "eternal death," or "that misery which renders existence an evil."[60] In a sermon of considerable rhetorical power Finney explains that "this death is endless misery, corresponding to the death-penalty in human governments."

Everybody knows what this is. It separates the criminal from society forever; debars him at once

and utterly from all the privileges of the government, and consigns him over to hopeless ruin. . .
There can be no doubt that death as spoken of in
our text is intended to correspond to the death-
penalty in human governments.[65]

The punishment which makes one's existence so abhorrent is
consistent with the crime of denying the proper end of that
existence: "the natural vindicatory sanction of the law of
God is misery resulting from the violation of man's own
moral nature."[62]

Finney emphasized that the sinner's misery is demanded
by the penal sanctions of law and is not designed to improve
the sinner but to serve the public good. A staunch defender
of capital punishment, both in this world and the next,
Finney argues that the suffering of the wrongdoer both
encourages public respect for government and discourages
further law-breaking. The principle was clearly enunciated
by Blackstone in his comments on "the end, or final cause of
human punishments":

This is not by way of atonement or expiation for
the crime committed; for that must be left to the
just determination of the supreme being, but as a
precaution against future offences of the same
kind.[63]

Hugo Grotius had earlier distinguished three ends of punishment: for the benefit of the offender, for the benefit of
the offended, and for "the Good of the Publick." Capital
punishment fulfills the last end, "that others may not be
encouraged, by the Hopes of Impunity, and be alike injurious."[64] The defense of capital punishment as a deterrent
of crime was commonplace in the late nineteenth century.
Levi Beardsley, who read law in Ostego County a decade
before Finney, called capital punishment "an example that
shall serve as a 'terror to evildoers.'"[65] One St. Louis
attorney flatly declared that "persons convicted of murder
in the first degree shall suffer death. It is not the

object of the law to punish or retaliate for the crime committed, but to set an example, and to deter others from committing such crimes."[66] In contrast to the American penchant for the noose, however, Blackstone insisted that the extreme preventive of capital punishment "ought never to be inflicted, but when the offender appears incorrigible."[67] For Finney God is no less merciful in the administration of justice and offers the sinner every opportunity to correct himself, until the moment of death. "After that," as the Bible warns, comes "the judgment" (Hebrews 9:27). Yet even after the gates of mercy are forever closed, the sinner may yet render some public good.

In a sermon dishearteningly entitled, "Salvation of Sinners Impossible," Finney argues that, while those in a state of rebellion against God cannot possibly be saved, in hell "sinners can be made useful."

> This principle is partially developed in society here, under civil government. The gallows is not the greatest evil in the world, nor the most unmixed evil. Murder is much worse. State prisons are not the greatest earthly evils. Government can make great use of those men who will not obey law. It can make them examples and lift them up as beacons of warning, to show the evil of disobeying wholesome laws. . . . If so under all the imperfections of human government, how much more under the perfect administration of the divine![68]

If one refuses to repent, then "there is no other way for God to meet the demands of the public weal" than to use "every groan and every throb and pang of your agonised soul" as a demonstration of "the bitter misery of sinning." Thus in the irony of cosmic justice "sinners in hell must preach for God and for his truth." They "will tell over and over the dreadful story of mercy abused and sin persisted in, and waxing worse and worse, till the bolts of vengeance broke at last upon your guilty head!"

Both the ideas and the language are designed as measures to evoke the dread awareness of deserved punishment, and all reports testify to their disturbing effect on Finney's hearers. According to an eye-witness,

> He preached the "Law" in a way that thrilled with awe and terror, as all who have heard his first sermon on "The wages of sin is death," will bear witness. He pictured the world of darkness, lit up only by lurid flames, by the light of which the damned read on the high walls, from which they could not escape, Wages! Wages! WAGES![69]

The sinner who, by his or her own choice, has refused the only way of life which could secure personal happiness and that of all other creatures, can expect no further benefit from the divine government, save the sure payment of those awful wages. To make matters worse, as Finney urged his trembling auditors, "the established law of our mental and sentient being" requires that, as the doomed sinner becomes increasingly aware of the happiness that has been forfeited, his or her sufferings will be intensified.[70] Thus Finney appeals to "these known and changeless laws of mind in their progression onward through the endless cycles of eternity" to justify his claim that "when a soul is lost" only endlessly deepening anguish is to be expected from the moral governor of the universe.[71] Finney does not speculate on the exact nature of the suffering, whether the sinner is tormented by literal fire or not is unimportant, he declares. It should be sufficient to realize that "once in hell, you will know that, while you continue to sin, you must continue to suffer."[72] It appears that, as life in heaven is the unending progress in virtue and happiness, the "eternal death" in hell is precisely the opposite.

The Universalists' hope in some future good for the sinner is, therefore, the result of a sentimental confusion between disciplinary action which aims to rehabilitate the miscreant and vindicatory punishment. The latter is for the sake of maintaining the proper authority of government; as

for the former, Finney notes that it would be futile in
reclaiming sinners for "punishment has no tendency to beget
disinterested love in a selfish mind towards him who
inflicts the punishment."[73]

But it is exactly such love which the moral law
demands.

> God's rule requires universal benevolence. . . .
> God requires men to devote themselves not to their
> own interests, but to His interests and those of
> His great family. He has set up but one great
> end--the highest glory of His name and kingdom.
> He asks them to become divinely patriotic, devot-
> ing themselves to their Creator and to the good of
> His creatures.[74]

Disloyalty to God's interests lays sinners under infinite
obligation and gains them the "strongest opposition" of the
divine will to their very lives.[75] Well might sinners cry
out, in a paraphrase of St. Paul, "If God be against us, who
can be for us?"

The answer is simple: as sinners have voluntarily
placed themselves under the judgment of divine law, so they
must remove themselves from condemnation by taking a new
"ruling preference" in their conduct.[76] Since the required
"change of heart is a voluntary thing," conversion is a
matter of transferring one's loyalty from one realm of
government to another. Finney preached that sinners have
"of choice belonged to Satan's government on earth: at
least, in the sense of doing precisely what he would have
them do. . . ."[77] Now, the good news is that people may "of
choice" belong to God's government, "in the sense of doing
precisely what he would have them do," viz., obey the moral
law. For God "rules the universe by righteous law and our
race also on a Gospel system which magnifies the law and
makes it honorable."[78]

NOTES

1. _Systematic Theology_ (New York: Harper & Row, 1957),
Vol. II, p. 56.

2. _Of the Law of Nature and Nations_, p. 27.

3. _Skeletons_, p. 43.

4. _Gospel Themes_, p. 232.

5. _Gospel Themes_, p. 231.

6. _Of the Law of Nature and Nations_, p. 21.

7. _Of the Law of Nature and Nations_, p. 118.

8. "The Inner and the Outer Revelation," _Gospel Themes_,
pp. 234f.

9. _Skeletons_, p. 64.

10. _Skeletons_, p. 79.

11. _Skeletons_, pp. 150, 166.

12. "The Inner and the Outer Revelation," _Gospel Themes_,
p. 244.

13. Jones, ed., _Commentaries_, p. 29.

14. _Ibid._

15. "The Excuses of Sinners Condemn God," _Gospel
Themes_, p. 85.

16. "The Wrath of God," _So Great Salvation_, p. 49.

17. "The Excuses of Sinners Condemn God," _Gospel
Themes_, p. 81.

18. "So Great Salvation," _So Great Salvation_, pp. 63f.

19. Perry Miller notes that Finney does not indulge in
"a rhetoric of romantic communication" characteristic of
other evangelicals (_Life of the Mind in America_, p. 61).
The reason is that, under the influence of the classic legal
interpretation of human nature, Finney interprets the biblical term "heart" to mean the will, not the seat of emotions.
Thus his appeal is made directly to the conscience of his
hearers through a "legalistic" account of their moral obligations.

20. "The Wicked Heart Set to Do Evil," _Gospel Themes_, p.
129.

21. "The Sinner's Excuses Answered," _Gospel Themes_, p.
114.

22. "The Wicked Heart Set to Do Evil," Gospel Themes, p. 134.

23. Aids to Reflection (New York: William Gowans, 1863), p. 203.

24. G. F. Wright interprets this definition of sin as control by the chaos of desire and thus as a denial that there is "a unity of object in the sinful choice" (Finney, p. 234). Wright approves this interpretation of sin to what he admits is Finney's more generally expressed view that sinful choices are unified by a consistent end, viz., self-interest. By rejecting the latter definition Wright misunderstands Finney entirely. For Finney the sinner, if he or she is to be accountable, must be be an intelligent agent making coherent decisions and not the subject of uncontrollable impulses. The impulses are a passive faculty and have no moral status until organized around a consciously chosen end. In the sinner this organizing interest is selfishness.

25. As an example of "the selfish reformer" Finney points to Daniel Webster, "a man ruled by ambition," for whom he seems to have a special antipathy (Gospel Themes, pp. 157, 354).

26. William McLoughlin attributes this influential notion in the development of evangelical theology to the "Scottish School of Realism," led by Thomas Reid. "Underlying all Scottish thinking was the conviction that God had implanted in man a sense of self-love or the capacity for pleasure and pain by which man learned to pursue happiness and avoid misery. Moral Philosophy thus defined itself in American textbooks as the science by which men learned to pursue happiness or moral well-being by learning those fundamental laws of duty to which they must conform in their personal life, their family, their occupations, and their governments" (introduction to American Evangelicals, pp. 2-4).

F. H. Foster notes that Nathaniel Taylor had also made a distinction between "self-love" and "selfishness" in order to establish the former as a "neutral point in the mind to which the motives of the gospel could be addressed and the pulpit make its appeal" (New England Theology, p. 283). Inasmuch as people value happiness, they may be persuaded to

submit to moral law as the best means of gratifying this
constitutional desire. Taylor presents the argument in the
same terms Finney employs: "So certain as man is a moral
agent and is properly addressed by motives to holiness, so
certain is it that he has constitutional susceptibilities to
that good which these motives proffer; and that, if he is
led at all to prefer this good to every other, he is primarily prompted to the choice by the desire of happiness or
self-love" (from Quarterly Christian Spectator, March 1830,
quoted by Foster, pp. 385f). Cf. Sidney Mead, Taylor, pp.
121f, 227f.

27. "The Wants of Man," So Great Salvation, pp. 123f.

28. "Moral Insanity," Gospel Themes, p. 148. Finney is
quick to add that moral insanity is "altogether voluntary.
It results not from the loss of reason, but from the abuse
of reason" (p. 155).

29. Critique of Practical Reason, tr. L. W. Beck,
original edition, 1788 (Indianapolis: Bobbs-Merrill, 1956),
p. 84.

30. "Men Often Highly Esteem What God Abhors," Gospel
Themes, p. 349.

31. "The Excuses of Sinners Condemn God," Gospel
Themes, p. 75.

32. "The Excuses of Sinners Condemn God," Gospel
Themes, p. 80.

33. Jonathan Edwards, A Faithful Narrative of Surpris-
ing Conversions, in The Great Awakening, ed. C. C. Goen, The
Works of Jonathan Edwards, vol. 4 (New Haven, Conn.: Yale
University Press, 1972), p. 193.

34. Jonathan Edwards, The Great Christian Doctrine of
Original Sin, ed. C. A. Holbrook, The Works of Jonathan
Edwards, vol. 3 (New Haven, Conn.: Yale University Press,
1970), p. 391. For an exposition of Edwards' imaginative
interpretation of the "guilt of the species," see D. L.
Weddle, "Jonathan Edwards on Men and Trees, and the Problem
of Solidarity," Harvard Theological Review 67:2 (April
1974), 155-175.

35. The Rights of War and Peace, pp. 468f.

36. Of the Law of Nature and of Nations, p. 20.

37. The Rights of War and Peace, pp. 402f. Pufendorf
follows Grotius closely on this point: " . . . no Man can
be justly punish'd by any civil court for another Man's
Offense, when he is free from Guilt of it. And the Reason
is, because that Aptitude which disposes a Man for Punishment proceeds from Demerit, and Demerit in the last Resort
is founded in the Will, which is certainly, or nothing is,
at a Man's own Command, and which cannot contract any Guilt,
but by some internal Motion of its own" (Of the Law of
Nature and of Nations, p. 50).

38. Cf. John Wesley, "On the Fall of Man," Sermons on
Several Occasions (New York: Carlton and Porter, 1825),
vol. II, pp. 31-37. Finney was influenced by Wesley's
argument that sin issues from a person's "liberty; a power
of directing his own affections and actions; a capacity of
determining himself, or of choosing good and evil."

39. Edwards, Original Sin, pp. 381-383.

40. F. H. Foster notes the close parallel with Nathaniel Taylor's explanation of the rise of moral depravity (New
England Theology, pp. 376, 467f).

41. Of the Law of Nature and of Nations, p. 28.

42. Sin, tr. Philip C. Holtrop (Grand Rapids, Mich.:
Wm. B. Eerdmans, 1971), p. 431.

43. Jonathan Edwards, Freedom of Will, ed. Paul Ram-
sey, The Works of Jonathan Edwards, vol. 1 (New Haven,
Conn.: Yale University Press, 1957), pp. 156-162.

44. Edwards, Original Sin, p. 123. Finney focuses his
attack on Edwards' view of moral inability at the point of
the support it provides the doctrine of natural depravity.
Thus he anticipates the advice of C. Conrad Wright that the
Arminians "should have dismissed the Freedom of the Will,
and concentrated on the treatise on original sin which
complemented it. Moral necessity without total depravity
loses all its sting" [The Beginnings of Unitarianism in
America (Boston: Beacon Press, 1966), p. 104].

45. The sources for my interpretation of Edwards here
are primarily A Treatise Concerning Religious Affections
[ed. John Smith, The Works of Jonathan Edwards, vol. 2 (New
Haven, Conn.: Yale University Press, 1959)]; and his late
essays, The Nature of True Virtue [ed. Wm. Frankena (Ann

Arbor: University of Michigan Press, 1960)], and "A Dissertation Concerning the End for Which God Created the World"
[ed. E. Williams and E. Parsons (London, 1817), vol. 1, pp.
443-533]. As are all students of Edwards, I am deeply
indebted to Perry Miller, Jonathan Edwards (New York: Dell
Publishing Co., 1949). The most illuminating study of the
synthetic achievement of Edwards is Herbert W. Richardson,
"The Glory of God in the Theology of Jonathan Edwards: A
Study in the Doctrine of the Trinity" [unpublished Ph.D.
dissertation (Harvard University, 1962)].

46. For example, Charles Chauncy, the most able critic
of the Great Awakening, argued against Edwards that if the
Holy Spirit were to give men's "Passions the chief Sway over
them," the result would be to "invert their Frame." Rather,
Chauncy proposed a view of conversion much like Finney's
inasmuch as it is based on the same understanding of psychological processes: "One of the most essential Things neces-
sary in the new-forming Men, is the Reduction of their
Passions to a proper Regimen, i.e., the Government of a
sanctified Understanding." [Seasonable Thoughts on the
State of Religion in New England (Boston, 1743), reprinted
in The Great Awakening, ed. Alan Heimert and Perry Miller
(Indianapolis: Bobbs-Merrill Co., Inc., 1967), p. 297].
For an account of the controversy between Edwards and
Chauncy see Edwin S. Gaustad, The Great Awakening in New
England (New York: Harper & Row, Publishers, 1957), pp. 80-
101. George Wright notes that Finney had read Edwards'
Treatise on Religious Affections early in his career
(Finney, p. 178). When he quotes from it in his sermon on
"Christian Affinity" (1826), however, Finney does so to
support his claim that it is necessary in revivals to excite
the "emotions" (McLoughlin, Modern Revivalism, pp. 34f.).

47. Here Finney departs significantly from Nathaniel
Taylor who had argued that "men themselves had the power to
act rightly but it is a certainty that until they underwent
a miraculous change of heart they would never use that power
to act virtuously. We are physically able, but morally
unable to obey God" (McLoughlin, introduction to American
Evangelicals, p. 9). Finney abandons this untenable compromise with Old School Calvinism to assert that religion is

not in any way miraculous, but consists entirely in the right exercise of human powers. It is Finney's willingness to attribute to the sinner a natural capacity for faith that convinced the Old School theologians that his revival measures were the practical consequences of the "Pelagian New Haven Theology." See M. L. Vulgamore, "Charles G. Finney: Catalyst in the Dissolution of Calvinism," Reformed Review 17 (June 1964), 33-42.

48. Finney's emphasis on intention as the ground of moral responsibility corresponds to a generally accepted legal principle. "Proof of criminal intent--often, of a specific criminal intent--was the general requirement in the standard catalog of crimes in the first half of the [nineteenth] century. . . . The requirement of a guilty mind as an essential to make out a crime had very old roots. Partly it responded to a belief in the freedom of the human will and the consequent moral responsibility attending its exercise. But, also the requirement was, as Mr. Justice Jackson observed, 'as congenial to an intense individualism, and took deep and early root in American soil'" (Hurst, Law and the Conditions of Freedom, p. 18).

49. Skeletons, p. 203.

50. "Salvation of Sinners Impossible," So Great Salvation, p. 41. Cf. Blackstone: "Of all the parts of a law the most effectual is the vindicatory. . . . The main strength and force of a law consists in the penalty annexed to it. Herein is to be found the principal obligation of human laws" (Jones, ed., Commentaries, p. 43.).

51. Skeletons, p. 204.

52. Jones, ed., Commentaries, p. 190.

53. Skeletons, p. 209.

54. Skeletons, p. 207.

55. "When Sin Is Fatal," Guilt of Sin, p. 105.

56. "God's Anger," Guilt of Sin, p. 84.

57. "God's Love for a Sinning World," Gospel Themes, p. 1.

58. "On the Wages of Sin," Gospel Themes, p. 38.

59. Skeletons, p. 206.

60. Skeletons, p. 205.

61. "On the Wages of Sin," Gospel Themes, p. 43.

62. Skeletons, p. 205.

63. Jones, ed., Commentaries, p. 195.

64. The Rights of War and Peace, p. 412.

65. Reminiscences, p. 51.

66. George Ritter, An Essay on the Law, p. 12.

67. Jones, ed., Commentaries, p. 195.

68. So Great Salvation, p. 39.

69. Shumway, Oberliniana, p. 70.

70. "When a Soul Is Lost," Guilt of Sin, pp. 62-65.

71. Ibid., p. 67.

72. "So Great Salvation," So Great Salvation, p. 66.

73. Skeletons, p. 210.

74. "Men Often Highly Esteem What God Abhors," Gospel Themes, p. 348.

75. "God's Anger," Guilt of Sin, p. 83.

76. "The Sinner's Excuses Answered," Gospel Themes, p. 114.

77. "Salvation of Sinners Impossible," So Great Salvation, p. 35.

78. "On Trusting in the Mercy of God," Gospel Themes, p. 26.

Chapter VI

THE PLAN OF SALVATION

Finney's interpretation of the human condition is designed
to awaken both shame and guilt: shame because one has
failed to live according to the moral dictates of one's own
nature, and guilt because those dictates are expressions of
the exalted will of God and carry inescapable punishments.
Or so it seems. For while the letter of the law condemns
all violators, "the spirit of the moral law allows and
requires that upon condition of satisfaction being made to
public justice, and the return of the sinner to obedience,
he shall live and not die" (LST, p. 259). The "good news"
Finney proclaimed was that God can forgive his lawless
creatures, through the atonement of Christ, in such a way
that the moral law is confirmed rather than set aside, that
the integrity of the divine government is preserved, and
that the "highest possible moral influence" is brought to
bear on sinners. By gracious persuasion God calls, through
the voice of the preacher, all persons to place their faith
in his government and follow his example of self-denying
benevolence.

As the principles of moral government require that God
rule only through means of persuasion, Finney must deny the
Old School view of irresistible grace as unconditionally as
he rejected the notion of constitutional depravity. No
moral agent should be either forgiven or punished for any
other reason than one's own free choices. Grace, then, is
manifest in all those ways by which God seeks to persuade
sinners to submit to the law. Since obedience to the law
brings the greatest happiness, it is the proof of God's love

that he brings gracious influences to bear upon his subjects, usually through the "new measures" of revival preaching. Grace does not consist of an act of divine "illumination" which provides a "supernatural" capacity to understand
and obey the truth, as Jonathan Edwards had so eloquently
argued. Rather, grace is the dramatic presentation of the
truth designed to move the sinner to use "natural ability"
to obey the moral law.

Correspondingly, Finney revises the notion of faith as
a divine gift one must prayerfully and anxiously await to be
bestowed. Faith just is the determination to "seize" the
truth and align all one's intentions and actions with its
demands. To arouse the human will to the heroic sacrifice
of self-interest and the consistent dedication to the discipline and goals of moral government requires the "highest
possible moral influence." It is just such influence, presenting "overpowering motives to repentance," that the
atonement, rightly understood and proclaimed, brings to bear
on the mind and will of all moral agents.[1]

Atonement

The purpose of the doctrine of atonement in Christian theology is to explain the possibility of a restored relationship between sinful humanity and a holy God through the
person and work of Jesus Christ. The word "atonement" is
derived from the Greek term which is translated "reconciliation" in the New Testament, and is closely related to the
Hebrew verb, "to cover," as the blood of a sacrifice covers
the sins of the people in ancient Jewish ritual.[2] The
English word is taken directly from the Middle English,
atonen, a compound of "at" and "one" which means literally
"to bring into accord." The task of the theologian is to
explain and define the process by which the career of Jesus
overcomes the alienation of humankind from God and reestab-
lishes the harmony of the created order. In so doing the
theologian seeks to understand the biblical faith that "God

was in Christ, reconciling the world unto himself, not
imputing their trespasses unto them" (2 Corinthians 5:19).

The three types of theories about the atonement that
have proved most influential in the history of Christian
doctrine can be distinguished according to the element in
the career of Jesus each claims as the basis of his atoning
work.[3] The exemplarist theory, associated with St. Abelard,
emphasizes the inspiring example of Jesus' compassionate
love and patient suffering as a moving disclosure of divine
love, encouraging the weak human will to imitate his virtue.
Jesus' life reveals that God desires to forgive his creatures and so overcomes their ignorant fear of his wrath and
restores their lost communion. This theory emphasizes the
"subjective" effect of Christ's life and death on the human
mind and will, and belongs to the tradition beginning with
the Christian humanism of the Renaissance, through the
experiential theology of Schleiermacher to modern Protestant
liberalism.

The transactional theory, found in its classic form in
St. Anselm, focuses on the death of Christ as the perfect
sacrifice "which none but God can make and none but man
ought to make."[4] By dying in the place of guilty sinners,
Jesus gives himself as the offering of infinite value which
alone can compensate God for the loss of his honor caused by
sin and satisfy the demand of justice that offenses against
his law must be punished. As the substitute, Christ takes
upon himself the infinite guilt of humanity and pays the
full penalty of sin, "having become a curse for us," in the
words of St. Paul (Galatians 3:13). This theory has been
the consistent favorite of Western Christianity, although
the two major branches divide on the question of how one
appropriates the benefits of Christ's death. For the Protestant it is through identification with Christ by faith and
for the Roman Catholic it is through participation in Christ
by sacrament--but in both cases the believer receives the
righteousness of Christ as his or her own. The followers of
Calvin inherited the Anselmic theory of the atonement, but
in light of their growing emphasis on the divine "decrees"

of predestination, they drew the extreme logical conclusion that Christ was the substitutionary sacrifice for only those whom God had, from eternity, chosen to be saved. The Old School view, against which Finney so adamantly set himself, thus accepted the notion that the scope of the atonement was "limited" to the elect.

The triumphalist theory, which Gustav Aulen argues is the "classic" view of atonement in the New Testament and the Greek fathers (especially Athanasius and Irenaeus), places the resurrection of Christ at the center of the work of reconciliation. Through sin, according to Athanasius, humanity falls under the law of corruption which governs the lower orders of creation. The physical result of the fall, therefore, is death; the spiritual symptom is decline into lawlessness and moral chaos.[5] Further, the fear of death leads humans to desperate acts of self-interest in the vain attempt to preserve themselves from the inevitable sentence of the curse, and so they entangle themselves ever more helplessly in the snares of Satan. The only hope is for the power of death itself to be broken and the grip of Satan thus loosened, so that God's creation can be restored to his rightful rule and not waste away into nothing. Through the resurrection Christ triumphs over death, having paid the "ransom" for Satan's victims, and establishes his right to impart immortality to those "who through fear of death were all their lifetime subject to bondage" (Hebrews 2:15). Christ reconciles humankind to God by defeating the enemies whose power of corruption separates sinful creatures from the holy and incorruptible Creator. The means of sharing in Christ's victory, according to the fathers, is through incorporating Christ's divinized flesh in the Eucharist, "the medicine of immortality," in Irenaeus' phrase. In Luther's version of the theory God's Law and his Wrath were added to the list of enemies of humankind from which only God's triumphant grace, like a thunderbolt from heaven, could rescue.[6] The "classic" theory has provided the foundation of Orthodox theology and liturgy for centuries and is undergoing something of a revival in contemporary "theologies of liberation."

Finney's own view is an original combination of the emphasis on the "objective" standard of moral law in the second theory and the "subjective" effect of Christ's death in the first. Finney neglects almost entirely the "triumphalist motif" of the third theory since his principles of moral government do not allow, as we have seen, for admitting that sin is an alien power which is greater than the sinner's natural ability to overcome; nor could he ever appreciate Luther's terrifying frustration in the face of the demands of the Law. Why search desperately for "a gracious God," Finney would ask, when the only obstacle to your forgiveness is your own willful rebellion? Reconciliation takes place only and always when the rebel repents. For Finney the death of Christ provides both a powerful incentive for the sinner to repent and also the necessary condition for God to accept that repentance as the basis for forgiveness. Christ thus overcomes the separation between God and the sinner in complete accord with the principles of moral government.

Finney recalled that before his conversion the teaching that divine forgiveness is conditioned upon a transaction between an "implacable" God and an innocent substitute "had stumbled" him. "But afterwards I saw the answer so plainly that it left nothing to be desired."[7] The answer is that the Calvinist formulation is mistaken! At the time he had not worked out his own interpretation fully, but its main outlines were clarified during his long conversations with the Reverend George Gale. Finney says that he had read nothing on atonement "except my Bible; and what I had there found upon the subject, I had interpreted as I would have understood the same or like passage in a law book" (MF, p. 42). Consequently, he found that the Old School views of George Gale "were much less definite and intelligible than those to which I had been accustomed in my law studies" (MF, p. 43). Relying on the legal views of guilt and punishment Finney concluded that the claim that Jesus' death was a vicarious sacrifice required by retributive justice was indefensible. "On the contrary it seemed to me that Jesus

only satisfied public justice, and that was all the government of God could require" (MF, p. 42). The Memoirs provide
a summary of Finney's version of the "governmental theory"
of the atonement:

> . . . Christ died simply to remove an
> insurmountable obstacle out of the way of God's
> forgiving sinners, so as to render it possible for
> him to proclaim a universal amnesty, inviting all
> men to repent, to believe in Christ, and to accept
> salvation; that instead of having satisfied
> retributive justice, and borne just what sinners
> deserve, Christ had only satisfied public justice,
> by honoring the law, both in his obedience and
> death, thus rendering it safe for God to pardon
> sin, to pardon the sins of any man and of all men
> who would repent and believe in him [MF, p. 50].

Finney's view of atonement, like other formal elements
of his theology, is not without precedent. Some form of the
"governmental theory" of atonement had been current in New
England theology since the days of Joseph Bellamy, and the
notion of the death of Jesus' satisfying "public justice"
was elaborated by the younger Jonathan Edwards.[8] Joseph
Haroutunian argues that the governmental theory "never really became a part of popular religion," however, because it
transmuted the gospel of divine love, suffering in place of
sinners, into "a glorification of divine vindictive justice
and obedience to the moral law." The New School Calvinists,
according to Haroutunian, reduced the richly imagistic piety
of substitutionary atonement to a bleak moralism.

> Christian living became identified with obedience
> to the moral law of God as revealed to Moses, and
> the fear of God's vindictive justice was made its
> foundation. All things revolved around the "moral
> law". God became the Great Enforcer of the moral
> law, the blood of Christ became the evidence that
> God will punish transgression. Holy love faded

into conformity to the moral law, and such
conformity was now the measure and substance of
"true virtue."[9]

While it is true that Finney abandoned the notion that Jesus
paid the debt of suffering which retributive justice demanded, the charge that his alternative formulation was the
expression of a moribund piety is hardly justified. On the
contrary, the governmental theology gave Christian preaching
a new purchase on the hearts of men and women by providing a
form of its central doctrine that was intelligible to a new
and more self-reliant generation, and by encouraging the
development of persuasive techniques of evangelism. The
categories of moral law thus announced piety in a new key:
the trembling wonder before a holy Mystery was being replaced by the confidence in, and respect for, a wise Governor.
One may certainly not presume upon Finney's God any more
than upon Edwards', but at least one can know what in the
world he wants and can proceed to follow his commands with a
sense of their rational justification and a reasonable hope
of success in achieving their ends.

In developing his governmental theory Finney begins
with those aspects of the doctrine of the atonement which
can be worked out in part through deductions from moral
consciousness, or as he called them in the Lectures on
Systematic Theology, "a priori affirmations of reason."
That is, given the intuition of the existence of God and his
benevolence, as well as his "moral relations" to the universe, "it might have been inferred . . . that an atonement
of some kind would be made to render it consistent with his
relations to the universe, to extend mercy to the guilty
inhabitants of this world" (LST, p. 262). In the Skeletons
Finney referred his students to Buck's Theological Dictionary for evidence that "all nations have felt the necessity
for expiatory sacrifices," thus establishing the requirement
of atoning death as a provision of "common law" recognized
by all systems of government.[10] The need for the provision
is self-evident; without it, people would be greatly tempted
to sin with impunity.

Now what is true of human governments, Finney argues, is also true of the divine. If forgiveness were conditioned upon repentance alone, without requiring some further compensation, the sinner would be encouraged in the delusion that "his forgiveness was secure, however much he might trample on the divine authority, upon a single condition which he could at will perform" (LST, p. 264). That is a consequence which the moral government of the universe could not tolerate. Rather, "if pardon is to be extended, it should be known to be upon a condition not within the power of the offender" (LST, p. 261). It is not adequate to interpret the atonement as calling for a mere subjective change in the sinner; the atonement must also fulfill an objective condition.

If the intuitions of moral consciousness are to be trusted, then, divine forgiveness must be offered on such conditions that respect for moral order is sustained. Finney states in his list of "governmental principles" in the Skeletons that "disobedience cannot be pardoned unless some equally efficient preventive be substituted for the execution of the law." Such a preventive must "as fully illustrate and manifest the righteousness of the government, as the execution of law would do."[11] In the Lectures on Systematic Theology Finney expands the point:

> Public justice, by which every executive magistrate in the universe is bound, sternly and peremptorily forbids that mercy shall be extended to any culprit, without some equivalent being rendered to the government; that is, without something being done that will fully answer as a substitute for the execution of penalties. This principle God fully admits to be binding upon him . . . [LST, p. 264].

The atonement is necessary, then, not to "satisfy any implacable spirit in the divine mind," but to maintain the integrity of moral government and to guarantee the appropriate means of achieving its chief end, viz., the happiness of all moral agents, by encouraging their obedience.

It is further clear that, if there were no atonement, the mere execution of the penalty of sin upon the guilty could not in itself achieve the proper end of moral government. Since "penal inflictions, do not as a matter of fact, subdue the heart, under any government, whether human or divine," the result of "the law, without Atonement, was only exasperating rebels, without confirming holy beings."[12] The mere suppression of rebellious spirits, however, does not produce the greatest happiness and, therefore, cannot constitute an adequate administration of the divine government. "Hence, a fuller revelation of the love and compassion of God was necessary, to guard against the influence of slavish fear."[13]

That fuller revelation occurs in the death of Christ, which acts as a "preventive" of sin "by demonstrating the righteousness of the lawgiver, and thus begetting confidence and heart obedience."[14] The _fact_ of atonement, as opposed to its possibility, is "purely a doctrine of revelation, and in the establishment of this truth appeal must be made to the scriptures alone" (LST, p. 266). Although the subsequent citations fill three and one-half pages, the chief text for Finney is Romans 3:24-26 in which the death of Christ as a propitiatory sacrifice is said to have taken place so that God "might be just."

Before explaining how the death of Christ provides the possibility of "just" forgiveness under moral government, Finney must first refute the claim that Jesus died as the literal payment for sin in some kind of "commercial transaction." In his conversations with George Gale Finney argued that "this was absurd; as in that case he suffered the equivalent of endless misery multiplied by the whole number of the elect" (MF, p. 42; LST, p. 271). There are two reasons why Christ's death is not the payment of the sinner's debt. First, Christ himself owed perfect allegiance to the moral law; therefore, it was "impossible for him to perform any works of supererogation" (LST, p. 270).

Second, even if Christ could accumulate surplus merit to pay the debt of sinners, it would be unjust for God to accept the payment. Here is Finney's main criticism of the Old School view: that it disrupts the principles of moral government by transferring the guilt of an evil party to an innocent party and vice versa, in defiance of the clear demands of justice. "Neither wisdom nor enlightened benevolence could consent that an innocent being should suffer, as a substitute for a guilty one, the same amount that was due to the guilty."[15] The notion of literal substitution assumed that, since moral obligation is grounded in the divine will, God can choose arbitrarily to impose its penalties upon Christ, although he is innocent, and cancel its demands on the elect, even though they are guilty. Finney argues, on the contrary, that "the moral law did not originate in the divine will. . . . He cannot therefore repeal or alter it" (LST, p. 271). Nor would he wish to do so, since the maintenance of legal order is the only appropriate means by which infinite love can be exercised. Thus, despite the death of Christ, "the punishment of sinners is just as much deserved by them as if Christ had not suffered at all"; and their forgiveness is "just as much an act of mercy as if there had been no atonement."[16]

But in that case how can God extend mercy to sinners without violating the claims of justice upon them? Finney would seem to find himself at the familiar impasse between love and law: how can God forgive the sinner's infinite guilt of transgressing the moral law without requiring that he or she suffer eternal punishment as just compensation? A good many theologians had racked their brains over that problem. The most promising solution thus devised seemed to be some variant of Anselm's position that Christ was the exact substitute for the sinner so that either Christ's sufferings were accepted by God in place of the sinner's punishment or Christ's perfection as a sacrifice was imputed to the sinner as his or her own. All such schemes of moral transference, however, were manifestly unlawful; and it was unthinkable to Finney that God would, or indeed could, violate the principles of law in the plan of salvation. How then can the law breaker be lawfully delivered from deserved punishment?

The theological problem is parallel to the question that can be raised about pardons which are sometimes given to criminals under human government. Hugo Grotius defended governmental pardons on the grounds that the immediate ends of punishment, viz., the satisfaction of retributive justice on the offender, "be not in a Moral Sense necessary, or if quite contrary ends do occur no less Profitable or Necessary, or the Ends proposed by Punishment can be obtained Another Way, then it plainly appears, that there is nothing, which can strictly oblige us to exact Punishment."[17] That is, the sanctions of the law are not ends in themselves, but means which, under certain circumstances, may be replaced by more efficient means, in this case, pardon.

But what end is it which both punishment and pardon serve as means? The answer is, in a phrase, "public justice."

By public justice is intended, that due administration of law, that shall secure in the highest manner which the nature of the case admits, private and public interests, and establish the order and well-being of the universe. In establishing the government of the universe, God had given the pledge, both impliedly and expressly, that he would regard the public interests, and by a due administration of the law, secure and promote, as far as possible, public and individual happiness.[18]

As Finney consistently argues, God aims at the universal happiness of moral beings and is bound to pursue that aim by moral means only, that is, by persuasive and not coercive means. If it is possible then to convince people that it is

in their best interests to submit to moral law by offering
pardon on the condition of Christ's suffering, then it is
not, as Grotius said, "in a Moral Sense necessary" to punish
them. Thus Finney concludes that Christ did not suffer the
"literal penalty of the law," but he endured such suffering
as was sufficient to satisfy public justice and so "to
render the universal offer of forgiveness to all the penitent consistent with the due administration of justice."[19]
The purpose of Christ's death is to guarantee that God may
accept the sinner's repentance as a condition of forgiveness
without compromising the authority of divine government.

What distinguishes Finney's version of the governmental
theory of the atonement from others current in his day is
precisely the consistency with which he adheres to principles of law, especially in his denial that Christ's death
satisfies retributive justice on behalf of sinners. The
younger Jonathan Edwards had made a distinction between
"general or public justice" and "distributive justice,"
affirming that Christ's death satisfied the requirements of
the public good in such a way as to make the punishment of
sinners unnecessary. Joseph Haroutunian argues, however,
that it is impossible to show that the sufferings of Jesus
established public order by exhibiting God's vindictive
justice, without also claiming that in some sense Christ was
punished in the place of sinners.[20] Finney would agree for
he flatly denies that vindictive, or retributive, justice
must be literally satisfied at all. Retributive justice
"visits on the head of an individual sinner a punishment
corresponding to the nature of his offense."[21] It could be
realized only if each guilty party were punished according
to his or her crime. "Retributive justice makes no exceptions, but punishes without mercy in every instance of
crime" (LST, p. 259). On this definition Christ could not
have borne the sinner's penalty on the cross. "Punishment
implies crime--of which Christ had none. Christ, then, was
not punished."[22] In fact, the sufferings of Christ have
only an indirect relation to sin; their primary end is to
display God's "high regard for His law and for obedience to
it."[23]

Since the highest well-being of the universe depends upon the maintenance of moral government, the whole scheme of redemption requires universal respect for the authority of moral law. While divine forgiveness is grounded in benevolence, it cannot be exercised in a way that would undermine the moral law by ignoring its sanctions. The public good, then, requires that the penalty of the law be executed or a suitable alternative means of assuring continued respect for law be provided. Finney is well aware that no government can survive which does not enforce its laws for people are disposed to presume upon any laxity in the restraints placed upon their "natural" selfishness.

> The influence of law, as might be expected, is found very much to depend upon the certainty felt by the subjects that it will be duly executed. It is found in experience, to be true, that the exercise of mercy in every government where no atonement is made, weakens government, by begetting and fostering a hope of impunity in the minds of those who are tempted to violate the law [LST, p. 260].

Thus in one sermon he commends the "remarkably able state paper" in which Napoleon rebuked Jerome Bonaparte, who was then monarch of Spain, for pardoning certain criminals. Finney urges his audience to reflect upon "those principles, as they were grasped and presented so vigorously by the mighty mind of Napoleon."[24] The difference between Napoleon and God, fortunately, is that God is able to provide an alternative to execution as a means of honoring the law. That alternative is "the governmental substitution of the sufferings of Christ for the punishment of sinners" (LST, p. 261).

It must be emphasized that Christ did not suffer _for_ the sinner: neither his obedience nor his sufferings can be "transferred" to the "account" of sinners. Rather, Christ died for the sake of moral government, to preserve the integrity of moral law in the face of the divine forgiveness

of sinners. But how did Christ's sufferings constitute an
equivalent to the deserved punishment of the guilty? (This
is the problem Haroutunian raised in connection with the
younger Edwards.) Finney's answer must be quoted at some
length:

> The relation of Christ to the universe renders his
> sufferings so infinitely valuable and influential,
> as an expression of God's abhorrence of sin on the
> one hand, and his great love to his subjects on
> the other, than an infinitely less amount of suf-
> fering in him than must have been inflicted on
> sinners, would be equally, and no doubt vastly
> more, influential in supporting the government of
> God, than the execution of law upon them would
> have been. Be it borne in mind, that Christ was
> the lawgiver, and his suffering in behalf of sin-
> ners is to be regarded as the lawgiver and execu-
> tive magistrate suffering in the behalf and stead
> of a rebellious province of his empire. As a
> governmental expedient it is easy to see the great
> value of such a substitute; that on the one hand
> it fully evinced the determination of the ruler
> not to yield the authority of his law, and on the
> other, to evince his great and disinterested love
> for his rebellious subjects [LST, p. 272].

Finney's argument is that a display of the willingness of
the Moral Governor himself to fulfill the sanctions of the
law, even though he does not deserve to suffer, is an infinitely "influential" expression of the ultimacy of the law
in the mind of God. As such, the death of Christ fulfills
the same function as the execution of sinners, viz., to
enforce respect for the divine government, thereby fulfilling the requirements of public justice: "Whatever can
effectually reveal God, make known his hatred of sin, his
love of order, his determination to support government, and
to promote the holiness and happiness of his creatures, as
the execution of his law would do, is a full satisfaction of
public justice."[25] The purpose of the crucifixion is to

persuade all moral agents to take the demands and warnings of the moral law with ultimate seriousness, as does God himself. "An atonement was needed," Finney argued in the Skeletons, "to manifest the sincerity of God, in his legal enactments."[26] Furthermore, because "the atonement demonstrates the superior efficacy of love, as a moral influence, over penal inflictions," it is a "higher expression of [God's] regard for the public interests than the execution of law. It is therefore a fuller satisfaction to public justice."[27] Blackstone had argued in a similar vein that when a magistrate occasionally mitigates punishment for the deserving, he exhibits the fundamental humaneness of the law and so counteracts "the general disrespect for law."[28]

Unlike some modern versions of the exemplarist theory, then, Finney's interpretation requires a "high" Christology:

> Christ is God. In the Atonement God has given us the influence of his own example. . . his own self denial . . . the Atonement is the most impressive revelation of God, of which we have any knowledge.
> . . . .[30]

The death of Christ is not a tragic martyrdom, setting before us the example of a man perfectly submitted to the will of God. It is rather the poignant event in which God reveals both his "abhorrence of sin" and his "disinterested benevolence" toward all moral beings by himself undergoing great suffering. The crucifixion of Christ has "unbosomed God before the universe," exposing the depth of his love and the intensity of his commitment to moral law.[31] Christ dies, not as the innocent victim of divine wrath, suffering the penalty due to sinners--such a transaction would make a mockery of just government--but as the greatest conceivable means of upholding moral government while, at the same time, persuading the recalcitrant to submit to its demands.

By his obedience and death, then, Christ upheld the honor of the law, while demonstrating that God "is personally ready to forgive, and needs only to have such an

arrangement made that he can do it safely as to His government."[32] Thus, the work of Christ is "not to prevent the
conviction of the sinner, but to prevent his execution."[33]
The sinner is already "civilly dead" under the law; the
advocate appeals to the merciful disposition of the Judge to
stay the deserved penalty. In building his case the advocate cannot argue against the justice of the sentence for
that would be to impugn the law which represents the eternal
nature of God. Rather, he must "volunteer a gratuitous
service" which will compensate the honor of God while providing "a condition upon which our release is honorable to
God." In response the sinner must now "retain" Christ as
his own advocate. The only "fee" required, Finney preached,
is "your heart."[34] The death of Christ presents to the
sinner a strong motive to obey the divine law and provides
the "tax" on sin (if not the entire principal) in order to
maintain "Jehovah's government."[35] The precise relation
between the sinner's pardon and Christ's death in this
"governmental transaction" is analogous to that between the
favors conferred on the children of public servants and the
accomplishments of their distinguished fathers. Thus all
who are "united to [Christ] by faith" receive the "rewards
of the righteous" he has earned by "the public service he
has rendered the universe by laying down his life for the
support of the divine government" (LST, p. 274).

How the atonement supports divine government, and so
satisfies "public justice," becomes clearer as we reflect
upon the essential conditions of any lawful society. H. J.
Berman argues that chief among those conditions is a wide
spread recognition that the law is administered impartially
and consistently and that it is grounded in "an ultimate,
transcendent reality."[36] Where the law is viewed in merely
secular terms, as an instrument of social manipulation, the
ground of ultimate respect for it is cut away, and society
loses control over crime. Only in a society where the
ideals of legal justice are supported by "shared emotions,"
including fidelity to law as the foundation of that society's integrity, can there be reliable order. As Berman
observes, in elaborate courtroom rituals and reliance on

authoritative traditions, "law draws on the sense of the holy partly in order to commit people emotionally to the sense of the just."[37] Blackstone had similarly noted that, although the British monarch is himself subject to the law, he is also invested by tradition with sufficient dignity to inspire "awful respect" in his subjects. Such respect for the office of the King assures the continuity of order in the empire as power passes from the current ruler to his heir.[38] The same principle applies, _mutatis mutandis_, to the "legal emotions" shared by the citizens of a democratic republic. Where such emotions run deep and strong in the life of the society, justice is approved and respected, while injustice is both condemned and contemned.

> the sense of rights and duties, the claim to an impartial hearing, the aversion to inconsistency in the application of rules, the desire for equality of treatment, the very abhorrence of illegality. Such emotions . . . are an indispensable foundation of every legal order . . . . They require the sustenance of a belief in their inherent and ultimate rightness.[39]

Applying Berman's description to Finney's governmental theory of atonement, we might say that the death of Christ supports "Jehovah's government" precisely by reinforcing the legal emotions of its citizens. Without such legal emotions in his subjects, calling forth their active faithfulness to the moral law, God himself could do no more than sadly but relentlessly punish them for every wrong-doing. His wisdom and goodness are evident, Finney claims, in that the natural sense of moral consciousness, which he implanted in the human mind as the Creator, is strengthened and fulfilled in the revelation of his love and justice in the crucifixion which he endured as the Redeemer. Thus Finney lists among the thirty-two points of the influence of the atonement the fact that "it has more fully developed those laws of our being upon which the strength of moral government depends."[40] The atonement reveals the continuity between human moral consciousness and the divine nature, "the true

character and designs of the lawgiver." The point of contact between God and his subjects, the image of God reflected in the creatures, is precisely the set of values and
intentions which Berman calls "legal emotions."

Through his exemplary devotion to moral law, manifest
in his unconditional benevolence, Jesus exerts "an amazing
influence over moral beings" (LST, p. 273); but that influence never exceeds the limits of persuasion allowable under
moral government. The atonement, in fact, is "an auxillary
to law, adding to the precept and sanction of law an overpowering exhibition of love and compassion."[41] Yet the
influence is not so "overpowering" that there is no possibility of resisting both the command itself and the divine
"exhibition" of obedience to it. Thus, while Finney says
that the influence of the atonement can be properly called
"moral omnipotence," it "cannot compel a moral agent, and
set aside his freedom, for this is not an object of moral
power." Nevertheless, while "it is the most moving, impressive, and influential consideration in the universe,"[42] the
atonement can secure no one's redemption without one's own
determination to follow the example of faith and virtue in
Christ. Indeed, "if the benevolence manifested in the atonement does not subdue the selfishness of sinners, their case
is hopeless" (LST, p. 273).

The atonement does not guarantee forgiveness to any
individual, or elect group of people, but the benefits of
Christ's death are available to all. The "amazing influence" of his moral example is accessible to anyone who will
read or hear. The satisfaction of public justice by
strengthening legal emotions makes it possible for God to
forgive any one who will repent without weakening respect
for his government. The Old School notion of a limited
atonement, on the contrary, contradicts "the desire for
equality of treatment," one of the emotions which "are an
indispensable foundation of every legal order." The Old
School view of limited atonement brings into question the
fundamental fairness of divine government, thus working at
cross purposes with the governmental theory. For "if the

atonement is not intended for all mankind, it is impossible
for us not to regard God as insincere, in making them the
offer of salvation . . ." (LST, p. 275).

For Finney the final test of doctrine is its power to
strengthen confidence in the divine moral order and so
encourage faithful action. As the teachings of Universalism, which lead to unjustified optimism about one's destiny,
had failed the test, so too does the Old School doctrine,
which leads to despair over one's salvation and to laxity
among preachers. The sinner falls into despair over the
impossibility of discovering whether the atonement applies
to him as one of the elect and is tempted to abandon his
moral duty. Preachers lose their enthusiasm for urgent and
direct appeals to each of their hearers. "If ministers do
not believe that it was made for all men, they cannot heartily and honestly press its acceptance upon any individual,
or congregation in the world . . ." (LST, p. 275).

The development of Finney's innovative restatement of
the doctrine of the atonement is influenced at every point
by his insistence on the principles of moral government,
enforced by analogies to the operation and defense of human
systems of legal order, and grounded in the conviction that
the most appropriate mode of relationship between personal
beings is one established through moral law. What Finney
sees revealed in the cross of Christ is exactly the divine
intention to form such a relationship with all moral agents.

Grace

Finney's view of the atonement seeks to account for both the
grace of God in suspending the execution of the deserved
penalty upon the sinner and assigns full responsibility for
appropriating the divine forgiveness to the sinner's act of
faith. His views are the consequence of submitting the
religious imagination, stirred by the drama of Christ's
death, to the discipline of legal principles. His criticisms of alternative views of the atonement are uniformly

based on the charge that they fail to meet the standards of
reason and conscience. Throughout his theology Finney remains alert to the dangers of mysticism and antinomianism.
The source of his "governmental principles" was not the
Bible, since his interpretation of the Scriptures was itself
guided by those principles. Rather, they came from Finney's
study of the law; and they were rooted in the regulating
idea that each person, including the Deity himself, is
directly responsible to moral law. Thus, when Finney turns
from the question of how it is possible for God to forgive
sinners, to the question of how sinners receive that
forgiveness, his answer in no way compromises human responsibility.

As in the doctrine of sin, so in the doctrines of grace
and faith, Christian theologians have recognized a puzzling
dialectic. Early on, St. Paul stated the matter straight
forwardly: " . . . work out your own salvation with fear
and trembling. For it is God which worketh in you both to
will and to do of his good pleasure" (Philippians 2:12f).
The divisions in the history of Christian doctrine between
Augustine and Pelagius, Luther and Erasmus, Calvin and
Arminius stem from a fundamental disagreement about the
extent to which sinners are to work out their own salvation
and the extent to which it is God who works in them. The
same issue arises in the theological disputes between New
School Calvinists, like Taylor and Finney, and the Old
School, represented by the faculties of Andover (typified by
Leonard Woods) and Princeton (led by Charles Hodge). In
practical terms how one stood on the "new measures" of
revivalism indicated whether one lay greater stress on human
faith and so favored a direct appeal to the sinner's will,
or on divine grace and so preferred to wait for the gift of
salvation without encouraging sinners to presume that they
can exercise faith on their own.

There can be no question about which side of the debate
Finney takes. In one sermon he recounts the conversion of
"a lawyer who had been greatly offended with the gospel."
Under the influence of Finney's preaching, the man was

converted, and later testified, "I snatched at [the Gospel]--I put out my hand . . . and seized it--and it became mine."[43] In another sermon Finney draws the following analogy: "Ordinary food must be taken into the system by our own voluntary act. We take and eat; then the system appropriates. So faith receives and appropriates the bread of life."[44] With such a strong statement of natural ability, however, how can Finney adequately account for the myriad Scriptural references to the necessity of divine grace in the plan of salvation? How is it possible for God to abide by governmental principles and still bestow unmerited favor?

What Finney understands as the only acceptable meaning of grace is that undeserved assistance which God gives moral agents by presenting the truth of the gospel to their minds. Finney hopes to eliminate, by this interpretation, any compromise of God's moral relations with the universe. As he put the issue in a sermon on the moral suasion of the Holy Spirit: "If God should in any way set aside our voluntary agency, he would of necessity terminate at once our moral and responsible action."[45] Thus, no matter how vividly the truth is presented, "the will has still the same changeless power to yield or not yield. . . ."[46] As Finney argued earlier, not even the "moral omnipotence" of the example of God's love in the atonement can "compel a moral agent, and set aside his freedom."

Finney retains the traditional view that "grace is unmerited favor"; however, he explains that "its exercise consists in bestowing that which, without a violation of justice, might be withheld!" (LST, p. 341). Thus grace cannot be the creation of the ability to obey God since that ability could not be taken from a moral agent without undercutting one's obligation to obey: ". . . the bestowment of power adequate to the performance of that which is commanded, is an unalterable condition of the justice of the command" (LST, p. 347). On the principles of moral government, the Old School claim that grace provides the possibility of faith through a "constitutional change" (by granting "gracious ability") is shown to be "an absurdity and an impossibility" (LST, p. 347). For if people were without the power of moral agency, then God could not justly demand that they submit to moral government.

Given the natural ability to obey however, God's act of placing people "in circumstances to render holiness and consequent salvation possible to them" is "properly a matter of grace" (LST, p. 347). That is, grace represents the action of God in providing the means for a virtuous exercise of will, primarily by a persuasive presentation of the truth to human reason. Grace seeks to change one's "mind" in a way that does not lessen one's responsibility to change one's own "heart." Finney concludes his critique of the idea of "gracious ability" in this way:

> I admit the ability of man, and hold that he is
> able, but utterly unwilling to obey God. There-
> fore I consistently hold that the influences
> exerted by God to make him willing, are of free
> grace abounding through Christ Jesus [LST, p.
> 352].

Finney's definition of grace is compatible with moral government in which the nature of moral agents is respected, while at the same time they are provided every opportunity and encouragement to turn from sin to virtue. Grace provides, not the possibility of repentance, but the means. People are saved by the perfection of their natural capacities, not by the infusion of supernatural powers: "the sinner has all the faculties and natural attributes requisite to render perfect obedience to God. All he needs is to be induced to use these powers and attributes as he ought" (LST, p. 285).

In conversion, then, there is a "simultaneous exercise of both human and Divine agency . . . God draws him, and he follows . . . the sinner puts forth his activity, and God draws him into life . . ." (LST, p. 284). However, the word simultaneous is misleading since Finney understands the

process of conversion as a linear sequence from presented
truth to obedient compliance; regeneration is a voluntary
change of moral character in response to the truth presented
by the Holy Spirit, usually through the instrumentality of a
preacher (LST, p. 285). "God has so constituted man as to
limit himself to one mode of government over him. This must
be moral, and not physical. . . . Such being the case, the
great difficulty is to persuade sinners to choose right."[47]
The conditions of moral government create a close alliance
between divine grace and the office of preaching.[48] Finney
thus made explicit what had all along been implied in the
"new measures" of revival preaching: the sermon is God's
chosen sacrament, the most appropriate means of grace under
moral government. The believer is one who responds to the
moral suasion of the truth presented in the sacramental task
of preaching.

> The work accomplished is a change of choice, in
> respect to an end or the end of life. The sinner
> whose choice is changed, must of course act. The
> end to be chosen must be clearly and forcibly
> presented; this is the work of the third person,
> and of the Holy Spirit. The Spirit takes of the
> things of Christ and shows them to the soul. The
> truth is employed, or it is truth which must
> necessarily be employed, as an instrument to in-
> duce a change of choice [LST, p. 288].

Finney recognizes that in this schema the subject is
"passive in the perception of the truth presented by the
Holy Spirit" (LST, p. 290). What he denies is that the
"perception" itself provides the power of spiritual rebirth;
it merely "induces" regeneration. Perception of truth is
the "condition and occasion of regeneration"; but as a
function of the intellect, it is wholly passive and without
moral status. What determines the moral identity of the
self is the willed response to what is given by the intellect. "The Spirit acts upon him through or by the truth:
thus far he is passive. He closes with the truth: thus far

he is active" (LST, p. 290). Thus, to be "in Christ" involves a continuing consent of the will to presented truth:

> When the scriptures require us to grow in grace
> . . . the spirit of the requirement must be, that
> we should acquire as much knowledge as we can of
> our moral relations, and continue to conform to
> all truth as fast as we know it. This, and noth-
> ing else, is implied in abiding in our first love,
> or abiding in Christ, living and walking in the
> Spirit [LST, p. 291].

To alternative "philosophical theories" of regeneration
which entail some prior action of the Holy Spirit within or
upon the individual Finney replies that they deny the moral
integrity of the self.

> Free agency, according to them, consists in doing
> as we will, while their theory denies the power to
> will, except as our willings are necessitated by
> God. . . . All freedom of will must . . . consist
> in the sovereign power to originate our own
> choices . . . it is absurd to affirm, that a being
> is a moral or a free agent, who has not power to
> originate his own choices [LST, p. 295].

Finney calls his own theory of grace, "Divine Moral
Suasion" (LST, pp. 298-299). In its defense he makes the
familiar appeal to the moral intuition of his converts.
"They are conscious of no other influence than light poured
upon the intelligence, or truth presented to the mind" (LST,
p. 299). This is in accordance with biblical teaching in
which truth is said to be the instrument of conversion.
Finney concludes that to say that God "exerts any other than
a moral influence, or the influence of divine teaching and
illumination, is sheer assumption" (LST, p. 299). His is a
theory of conversion to correspond to the facts of the
revival and particularly with the "new measures," including
"clear exhibition of the truth," pressing for conversion
"upon the spot," and denial of original sin and physical

regeneration as "relics of a most unreasonable and confused philosophy" (LST, pp. 229f).

Indeed, Finney claims that the "new measures" grew out of his belief that the influence of the Spirit in conversion was "moral, that is persuasive," and that "the Holy Spirit operates in the preacher" through the proper use of means "calculated to convert" the people (MF, pp. 154f). Since human depravity is "a voluntary attitude of mind," it can be corrected by appeals through the reason to the will. The preacher is the human medium through whom the Holy Spirit presents truth to the mind of the sinner in a way designed to elicit consent. The object of the Spirit's work "is always the same--namely, to produce voluntary action in conformity to His law."[49] Finney pictures the "striving of the Spirit" in terms that express the strength and integrity of the human will in the process as strongly as possible:

> [The striving of the Spirit] is an energy of God, applied to the mind of man, setting truth before his mind, debating, reasoning, convincing, and persuading. The sinner resists God's claims, cavils and argues against them; and then God, by his Spirit, meets the sinner and debates with him, somewhat as two men might debate and argue with each other.[50]

The influence of the Spirit is not to create a special capacity for perception, nor is it even a distinct object of consciousness. One becomes aware of the Spirit's work when he "finds his attention arrested to the great concerns of his soul. The solemn questions of duty and responsibility to God are continually intruding themselves upon his mind."[51]

Although Finney insists all the while that salvation is wholly a matter of grace, he views the work of the Spirit in conversion as primarily an appeal to natural principles. Grace lies in the divine provision of the conditions of forgiveness in Christ; the sinner can expect no more direct

action from God. The work of the Spirit is to produce
conviction of sin and to make "a personal application of the
truth." Since the means by which this work is accomplished
is preaching, Finney can interpret resistance to revival
measures as hardening of the heart against the Spirit.
Further, because the Spirit respects the "laws of mind" in
his persuasion there is a point beyond which he cannot
affect the sinner, viz., when the sinner's determination to
reject the truth makes further attempts at persuasion
futile. Further patience would be injurious to moral government. "No government could possibly be maintained which
should push the indulgence of a spirit of forbearance toward
the guilty beyond all limits."[52] If the truth of the moral
law, which has already been inscribed by the hand of the
Creator in the conscience of every moral agent, does not
elicit obedience even when it is pressed upon the mind in
the clearest and most forceful manner by the gracious supply
of preaching, there is nothing more God can rightfully do to
secure the allegiance of a moral agent.

In his own experience Finney discovered that conversion
was a matter of submitting his will to the truth of the
Gospel. What the intellect received, the will enacted.
Both are essential, since Finney takes it as the first
principle of government that "the precept of the law must be
intelligible."[53] Whatever is not accessible to human reason
cannot be obligatory for the human will. As Blackstone
said, a law cannot be binding unless the "resolution be
notified to the people who are to obey it."[54] Finney's
understanding of the relation between reason and will is the
psychological correlate of his claim that the truth is
presented to the human mind in the form of moral law.[55]
Truth addresses one's will only through reason; thus divine
revelation must necessarily be the communication of certain
propositions about the divine purposes in the form of laws
or commands. The Bible then stands as a legal document
whose provisions are open to any person capable of coherent
reasoning. Finney affirms not only the priesthood of
believers, but also a democracy of exegetes.

By addressing every auditor as capable of understanding and responding to a reasonable account of the moral government of the universe, Finney rejected any idea of the mediation of truth through a scale of religious authorities. His own career as a revivalist was guided by the conviction that the individual stands directly responsible to the truth.

> Christ . . . is presented in the gospel . . . to the individual acceptance of men. He is embraced by the world no further than he is embraced by individuals. He saves the world no further than he saves individuals [LST, p. 376].

The truth of divine government is accessible to any being possessed of "common sense," that is, moral consciousness or practical reason. If one's acceptance of that truth is to be genuine, it must be a conscious decision to submit to moral law. The truth is presented in the form of law because it is appropriated through an exercise of will informed by moral consciousness. To believe the truth of the gospel is not passive assent to a set of doctrines, legitimated by religious tradition, but active obedience to the principles of moral government prompted by direct intuition of their authority. Thus, while grace provides the object of trust, it is the sinner who must turn his or her heart to the Lord.

Faith

Finney's understanding of faith as "voluntary--a will-trust" provided the basis for the "new measures" of his revival activity.[56] The meetings in general, and the sermons in particular, were organized around the conviction that belief is a response of the will to a clear moral demand. What is required, then, is a "reasoned" presentation of truth to the unregenerated mind. Finney's position raises two major questions: a) The question of faith and reason: How is the believing response of the will related to the reasoning

capacities of the natural mind?   b) The question of justification by faith: How is the human act of believing
related to the divine pronouncement of forgiveness before
the law?

a) The Question of Faith and Reason

     Finney's preaching is distinguished from that of many
of his colleagues in the revival by a lack of sentimentality
and an emphasis on logical rigor. For Finney the movement
of the will in repentance and faith must by informed by the
reason.

> Such is the correlation of the will to the intel-
> lect, that repentance must imply reconsideration
> or after thought. . . . Repentance implies the
> giving up of the attention to the consideration
> and self-application of these first truths, and
> consequently implies conviction of sin, and guilt,
> and ill-desert, and a sense of shame and self-
> condemnation. It implies an intellectual and a
> hearty justification of God, of his law, of his
> moral and providential government, and of all his
> works and ways [LST, p. 365].

Repentance involves both a judgment and a decision: the
perception of the truth and the "act of turning; the changing of the heart, or of the ruling preference of the soul"
(LST, p. 365). However, Finney resists any suggestion that
the truth itself, or the mode of its presentation, is the
cause of the movement of the will. The truth provides the
occasion for repentance, but not until the will has so
directed the attention of the intellect is there any conscious reflection upon the truth. The intitial appeal of
the truth then must be not to the intellect, but directly to
the will. The psychological analysis when carried out in
this way becomes hopelessly abstract; we are left with the
will as a totally unconditioned power of the self with no
end or direction.

But in accord with Blackstone's analysis of the psychological basis of legal order, Finney assigned a definite
conatus to the will, viz., the natural desire for happiness,
or self-love. Thus in its primary sense "will" means the
power of self-affirmation, the drive to establish one's
individual well-being. The decision required in repentance
is a reasoned judgment about which means are best adapted to
achieve self-fulfillment: selfishness or benevolence. Finney's reference to reason in this context must be interpreted in the light of his preaching in which rational
appeals are appeals to moral intuition. What is reasonable
is relative to what satisfies the condition of one's sense
of moral obligation to seek universal happiness. While
faith does not acknowledge self-love as the supreme value,
the will is initially attracted to obedience to the truth as
the means of restoring moral order within one's own being.
Faith then consists in "the embracing of the truth by the
heart or will. It is the will's closing in with the truths
of the gospel. It is the soul's act of yielding itself up,
or committing itself to the truths of the evangelical system" (LST, p. 374). Since that commitment alone achieves
the conformity to moral law and concomitant happiness which
is the proper end of every moral agent, faith is the only
means of fulfilling the demands of practical reason.

In one of his sermons given at Oberlin Finney argued
that "faith implies three things. 1) Perception of truth 2)
An interest in it 3) The committal or giving up of the mind
to be interested and controlled by these objects of
faith."[57] The truth of the gospel calls for moral consent,
and not merely intellectual assent. Here is a distinction
essential to revival theology, which appears in some form in
all evangelical writers, between intellectual judgement and
decisions of the "heart." "Heart-faith" is that appropriation of the truth which "involves an earnest committal of
one's self and interests to the demands of the truth believed."[58] Only such interested perception can "deal fairly
with the evidence of [God's] works and ways," disclosed in
the "inner revelation" of moral consciousness.[59] "Heart-
faith" trusts God despite contradictory evidence in the form

of philosophical "reasonings" which question the "practical truths" the believer has "experienced." When faith loses its moorings in practical reason, the intellect may wander into false speculations, such as Jonathan Edwards' claim that "God absolutely and supremely controls all the moral actions of all his creatures." It is to the credit of Edwards' piety that "the absurdities of this philosophy did not shake his faith in God."[60] The discrepancy between a deterministic philosophy and an active religious confidence in Old School theologians demonstrates to Finney's mind the "very wide and essential distinction" between "reason" and reasonings."

> The intuitive affirmations of their reason were one thing; the points which they reached by their philosophical reasonings were quite another thing. The former could not lie about God, the latter could. . . . While these reasonings pushed them on into the greatest absurdities, their reason held their faith and piety straight.[61]

It is clear, then, that what Finney means by "reason" is neither formal logical coherence nor metaphysical explanation, but the power of moral consciousness to recognize the first principles of its own operation, including the obligation to practice unconditioned benevolence in the pursuit of universal happiness. The reason which holds faith and piety straight is the intuition of Christian doctrines as "practical truths." Reason, in this sense, is a natural ability of all moral agents, as is faith or obedience to the moral law. Both faith and reason are rooted in the conscience and exercised through the will. Since, as we have seen, the will constitutes the essential center of the self, it is the ground of unity between reason and faith. One whose will is submitted to the moral law is both reasonable and faithful. Such a person alone can be regarded as "morally sane." For such a person there can be no conflict between faith and reason--only between the two of them, representing the claims of moral law, and the intellect which, in Finney's psychology, is a merely passive faculty of the mind.

Because it does not actively judge the veracity of claims by their practical value, the intellect can be seduced by "philosophical reasonings," like those of the Old School. Indeed, Finney blamed the "speculations" of Edwardeans for providing sinners with intellectual puzzles which could be offered as "reasons" for unbelief.[62] For Finney the "demand for reasons" is "one of the tricks of the devil" to "embarrass our faith."[63] But "the virtue of faith" is "that it trusts God on the ground of his general character, while the mind can be no means comprehend his reasons for particular acts," like the call to Abraham to sacrifice his son.[64] The astounding premise underlying this routine-sounding position is that human reason is capable of grasping not only "the general character" of God as absolute benevolence, but also the very "ground" of that character! Moral agents who are alert to the "inner revelation" of conscience know why God can be trusted; they recognize that God is bound to be benevolent as the best means of achieving the goal of his government of the universe. Based on this profound intuitive knowledge, the believer's trust in and obedience of God--in short, one's faith--can hardly be touched by the superficial objections of mere intellect. Thus, while Finney insists that faith is perfectly reasonable, he pleads with his audience not to hesitate over intellectual problems:

> If the thing required were intellectual faith, I could explain to you how it is reached. It must be through searching the evidence in the case. But heart-faith must be reached by simple effort-- by a voluntary purpose to trust. Ye who say, I cannot do this, bow your knees before God and commit yourself to his will; say, "O my Saviour! I take thee at thy word." This is a simple act of will.[65]

But if the intellect is not the final arbiter of the decisions of the will, is there not a danger that in fact the other "faculty" of the mind will become determinative, viz., the sensibility? Certainly most critics of revival preaching--both religious and secular--have focused on its excessive emotionalism. There is no question that many revivalists consistently and intentionally did, and still do, manipulate the emotions of their audience to elicit "decisions for Christ." The skillful use of music by evangelistic teams (such as Moody and Sankey, Sunday and Rodeheaver, Graham and Shea) is but one example of a highly developed technique for such manipulation.

While Finney himself employed means of arousing passion in his audiences, he was wary of the danger involved. For, according to his own understanding of psychology, a person moved to a profession of faith through excited emotions is not acting in a morally responsible way. If one's will is moved by the influences of sensibility, then one's action is determined by a passive faculty of the mind and is not a free decision. It is, therefore, not merely more sophisticated taste or more genteel audiences that cause Finney to grow increasingly critical of undue emotionalism, but a firmer understanding of the psychology of conversion. In the midst of one sermon on the persuasive influence of the Holy Spirit, he explains the delicate balance of reason and emotion required:

> There must be excitement enough to arouse the mind to serious thought--enough to give the truth edge and power; but it is always well to avoid that measure of excitement which throws the mind from its balance and renders its perceptions of truth obscure or fitful.[66]

In his own practice Finney eschewed written sermons, holding that "the impassioned utterance of a common exhorter" was more effective (MF, p. 91). Yet he addressed his audiences according to remarkably detailed chains of reasoning,[67] delivered with an animation shocking to traditional ministers and with a dignity beyond the reach of most itinerants. It was a combination, however, perfectly familiar to those acquainted with the forms of spirited advocacy within the limits of traditional decorum in the courtroom. It is in his adaptation of the rhetorical style of the lawyer to evangelical preaching that Finney achieves a practical synthesis of intellect and emotion by focusing on the task of bringing persuasive means to bear on the will, in the form of evidence.

The evidence Finney presents is the intuitive awareness of the moral truths of Christianity--an awareness awakened, but not distorted, by emotional interest. To Finney's mind such evidence is reasonable for it is self-authenticating. One need only consult one's own moral consciousness. For Finney truth is revealed through moral intuition and reason is the power to reflect upon that intuition and move the person to appropriate action. Thus it is reasonable to believe in hell if one's conscience, under the influence of revival preaching, is quickened by a sense of infinite obligation. It is likewise reasonable to believe that one is eternally forgiven of sins if one is filled with peace and love.

The success of revival preaching depends on its ability to evoke such "heart experience" in the hearers. Jerome Frank's general observation about the power of revival preaching is directly applicable to Finney's: "Only the emotionally detached are immune."[68] Consequently, Finney will argue for hours with unbelieving critics, but when a person loses interest, when his or her heart "turns cold," Finney concludes that the Spirit has abandoned the person. In a state of indifference one is invulnerable to evangelical persuasion; there is no opportunity "to give the truth edge and power."[69] As always for Finney the ultimate illustration of the way of salvation was his own conversion. While confined to the theological arguments in the books George Gale loaned him, Finney remained unconvinced of the truth. It was not until God "so revealed himself to me personally that I could not doubt the truth of the Christian religion" that he was rescued from infidelity (MF, p. 53).

To return to Finney's three-fold description of faith
it can now be seen that by "perception of truth" he means
the intuition of the contents of moral consciousness as he
has set them out; by "interest in the truth" he means that
concern for happiness which "shall wake up the mind to fixed
and active attention"; and by "voluntary committal of the
mind to the control of truth" he means that "within our very
souls we receive Christ to live and energize there," that
is, Christ is the object of all one's willing.[70] Thus faith
necessarily entails holiness, or moral purity.

b) The Question of Justification by Faith

Insofar as faith is the purification of one's intention, it is an indispensable condition of justification.
God could not justly regard one who was not perfected in
holiness as righteous. Thus Finney criticizes the notion of
justification as a "forensic" proceeding on the ground that
"to be justified judicially or forensically, is to be pronounced just in the judgment of law. This is certainly an
impossibility in respect to sinners" (LST, p. 383). This
criticism entails the rejection of the imputed righteousness
of Christ (the usual basis for forensic justification) because it is as destructive of principles of legal responsibility as is the imputation of Adam's guilt. Finney calls
the notion that Christ's "obedience was altogether a work of
supererogation, and might be made a substitute for our own
obedience" a "false and nonsensical assumption" (LST, p.
385). For Christ also was "under infinite obligation to be
perfectly benevolent." Therefore, it was "naturally impossible" for him to do more than what was required to justify
himself (LST, p. 385).

Rather, justification consists in "a governmental
decree of pardon or amnesty--in arresting and setting aside
the execution of the incurred penalty of the law--in pardoning and restoring to favor those who have sinned, and those
whom the law had pronounced guilty . . ." (LST, p. 384).
This decree has its ground, or "procuring cause," in the

"benevolence and merciful disposition of the whole Godhead,
Father, Son and Holy Spirit" (LST, p. 386). However, the
love of God does not provide the sufficient condition of
justification.

> The Godhead desired to save sinners, but could not
> safely do so without danger to the universe,
> unless something was done to satisfy public, not
> retributive justice. The atonement was resorted to
> as a means of reconciling forgiveness with the
> wholesome administration of justice [LST, p. 386].

As we have seen, Christ's sufferings provided a vindication
of the divine moral government by honoring its sanctions; in
thus assuring respect for divine authority the atonement
makes it possible for God to justify sinners without seeming
lax toward moral law. Yet while the atonement is a necessary condition for justification, the principles of moral
government demand additional conditions, all of which require exercises of the will of the believer, viz., repentance, faith, present sanctification and perseverance (LST,
pp. 389-393).

In an important sense it can be said that these conditions are comprehended in the full meaning of "faith."
"Faith is often spoken of in scripture as if it were the
sole condition of salvation, because, as we have seen, from
its very nature it implies repentance and every virtue"
(LST, p. 390). That is, faith fulfills the condition of
justification as an active, sanctifying, persevering virtue.
As Finney put it in one sermon: "That faith is justifying
which is sanctifying. True faith works by love; it purifies
the heart . . . ."[71] Is faith then the cause of the sinner's justification before God? Finney is certainly not
prepared to defend such a straight forward moralism. Faith
is an indispensable condition of justification, but it presupposes others (the gracious persuasion of the Spirit and
the satisfaction of public justice in the sufferings of
Christ). The point that Finney is so concerned to establish

that he seems willing to overstate it, is that faith is a
form of moral action, specifically obedience to law.

Consequently, Finney is sensitive to the antinomian
implications of any view of faith in which the believer is
brought into "a covenant and mystical relation to Christ,[72]
in consequence of which his righteousness or personal obedience is imputed to us" (LST, p. 390). Finney regards any
scheme of imputation as antinomian insofar as the forgiven
individual is not required to submit personally to moral
government as a condition of forgiveness. For him the
definition of faith as commitment of will to the law of
benevolence means that

> the faith that is the condition of justification,
> is the faith that works by love. It is the faith
> through and by which Christ sanctifies the soul.
> A sanctifying faith unites the believer to Christ
> as his justification; but be it always remembered,
> that no faith receives Christ as a justification,
> that does not receive him as a sanctification, to
> reign within the heart [LST, p. 390].

Finney intends to emphasize as strongly as the Puritans that
the only genuine saint is a "visible" saint: evangelical
faith is a commitment to a holy intention as the ruling
preference of one's life; faith "must imply the existence in
the soul of every virtue . . . a state of present sinlessness."

> When contemplated in the wider sense of universal
> conformity of will to the will of God, it is then
> synonymous with entire present sanctification. . .
> Faith is an attitude of the will, and is wholly
> incompatible with present rebellion of will
> against Christ [LST, p. 377].

This identification of justifying faith and sanctifying
virtue in the Lectures is the final result of Finney's
developing notion of Christian perfectionism. His own

"second baptism" of the Spirit had occurred a few years earlier during one of his revival tours, but he had become convinced that if converts were to be sustained in piety the necessity of entire sanctification must be made clear from the first moment of faith.

> While I inculcated the common views, I was often instrumental in bringing Christians under great conviction, and into a state of temporary repentance and faith. But falling short of urging them up to a point where they would become so acquainted with Christ as to abide in him, they would of course soon relapse again into their former state. I seldom saw, and can now understand that I had no reason to expect to see, under the instructions which I then gave, such a state of religious principle, such steady and confirmed walking with God among Christians, as I have seen since the change in my views and instructions [LST, p. 423].

Indeed, the faith which sanctifies is simply the continuation of that same movement of the will in obedience to the moral law which is the condition of justification. In each moral decision one is re-making one's religious identity, determining anew one's posture toward the demands of benevolence at that moment. As "different occasions arise, faith will secure conformity to all truth on all subjects, and then every modification of virtue will exist in the heart, and appear in the life . . . " (LST, p. 381).

This expansion of the meaning of faith to include the whole range of Christian virtues was anticipated already in the Skeletons where Finney taught that "the Atonement tends in the highest manner to beget in the believer the spirit of entire and universal consecration to God."[73] Finney's view of Christian perfectionism, then, follows with irresistible logic from the first principles of moral government.

NOTES

1. Skeletons, p. 214.

2. Finney cites these derivations in one of his rare etymological notes in Skeletons (p. 212).

3. The standard statement of this typology is Gustav Aulen, Christus Victor, original ed., 1931 (New York: Macmillan, 1969).

4. Cur Deus Homo in St. Anselm: Basic Writings, tr. S.N. Deane (La Salle: Open Court Publ. Co., 1962), p. 245.

5. On the Incarnation, tr. a religious of C.S.M.V. (London: A. R. Mowbray, 1953), pp. 29-32.

6. Aulen, Christus Victor, pp. 111-116.

7. "The Sinner's Excuses Answered," Gospel Themes, p. 107.

8. Wright acknowledges the source of the term "public justice" and suggests that Finney interjected it inadvertently into the record of his early thought (Finney, p. 22).

9. Piety Versus Moralism, p. 176.

10. Skeletons, p. 212. The first American edition of A Theological Dictionary by the Rev. Charles Buck was published, from the second London edition, at Philadelphia in 1807. Revised editions were issued regularly until 1836, attesting to the widespread use of the work as a standard reference.

11. Skeletons, p. 211.

12. Skeletons, p. 213. Cf. LST, p. 273.

13. Skeletons, p. 213. Cf. LST, p. 274.

14. Skeletons, p. 211.

15. Skeletons, p. 221.

16. Skeletons, p. 231.

17. The Rights of War and Peace, p. 424.

18. Skeletons, p. 213. Cf. LST, p. 265.

19. Skeletons, p. 221.

20. Piety Versus Moralism, p. 171.

21. "On the Atonement," Gospel Themes, p. 206.

22. Ibid., p. 207.

23. Ibid., p. 208.

24. "The Inner and the Outer Revelation," Gospel
Themes, p. 236.
    25. Skeletons, p. 222
    26. Skeletons, p. 214.
    27. Skeletons, p. 217.
    28. Commentaries, quoted in Boorstin, The Mysterious
Science, p. 151.
    29. Skeletons, p. 216.
    30. Skeletons, pp. 224-225. Cf. LST, p. 266: "I shall
here take it as established, that Christ was properly 'God
manifest in the flesh.'"
    31. Skeletons, p. 277. Don S. Browning's comment on
the "moral influence" theory of Horace Bushnell applies also
to that of Finney: "Both God and man are undergirded by a
common moral law that constitutes the crystalline essence of
both" [Atonement and Psychotherapy (Philadelphia:
Westminster Press, 1966), p. 70].
    32. "On the Atonement," Gospel Themes, p. 211.
    33. "Christ Our Advocate," Gospel Themes, p. 293.
    34. Ibid., p. 305.
    35. "God's Love for a Sinning World," Gospel Themes,
p. 13.
    36. Berman, Interaction of Law and Religion, p. 25.
    37. Ibid., p. 45.
    38. Jones, ed., Commentaries, pp. 91-100.
    39. Berman, Interaction of Law and Religion, p. 25.
    40. Skeletons, p. 230.
    41. Skeletons, p. 223.
    42. Skeletons, p. 225.
    43. "Conditions of Being Saved," Gospel Themes, p. 190.
    44. "The Essential Elements of Christian Experience,"
Gospel Themes, p. 410.
    45. "Quenching the Spirit," Gospel Themes, p. 247.
    46. Ibid.
    47. "Salvation Difficulties," So Great Salvation, pp.
13-14.
    48. Lyman Beecher had emphasized this connection in
his insistence that the appeal of moral law is "the influence of motives upon accountable creatures . . . it is the
influence of persuasion only, and results only in choice,

which in the presence of understanding and conscience, is free agency" (Works, cited by Mead in Taylor, p. 126). Mead comments that "the reduction in effect of God's power over his creatures to 'persuasion only'" made the revivalists "co-workers with the Spirit to effect that persuasion—and how they worked at it."

49. "Quenching the Spirit," Gospel Themes, p. 246.

50. "The Spirit Not Striving Always," Gospel Themes, p. 266.

51. Ibid.

52. Ibid., p. 282.

53. Skeletons, p. 211.

54. Jones, ed., Commentaries, p. 33.

55. This observation clarifies Finney's claim that God elicits the sinner's consent through persuasion of truth "in perfect harmony with the laws of mind" ("Converting Sinners a Christian Duty," Gospel Themes, p. 338). The moral law moves the will inasmuch as one recognizes its perfect correspondence to one's own intuitions. Thus, "conversion consists precisely in this: the heart's consent to these decisions of the conscience. It is for the heart to come over to the ground occupied by the conscience, and thoroughly acquiesce in it as right and true" ("Where Sin Occurs God Cannot Wisely Prevent It," Gospel Themes, p. 225). That is, the harmony of mental faculties depends upon the appeal to the will through "practical reason," or moral intuition.

56. "Believing with the Heart," So Great Salvation, p. 93.

57. "Victory over the World through Faith," Gospel Themes, p. 371.

58. "Believing with the Heart," So Great Salvation, p. 77.

59. Ibid., p. 78.

60. Ibid., p. 84.

61. Ibid., p. 85.

62. "The Excuses of Sinners Condemn God," Gospel Themes, pp. 72-102.

63. "Believing with the Heart," So Great Salvation, p. 89.

64. Ibid., p. 90.

65.   Ibid., pp. 93-94.

66.   "Quenching the Spirit," Gospel Themes, p. 251.

67.   A typical "skeleton" of one of Finney's sermons contains fifty-two numbered points! (MF, between pages 96 and 97).

68.   Persuasion and Healing: A Comparative Study of Psychotherapy (New York: Schocken Books, 1963), p. 80.

69.   Similarly, Finney wasted no words in satisfying idle curiosity in religious matters. Shumway recalls the time when "a conceited young infidel" came to the inquiry room to engage in argument. "The great preacher saw at a glance that the tyro merely wished to display himself. He had no time to witness such a silly pageant, as a hundred anxious inquirers were waiting for him; he therefore gave the fledgling just one long look of mingled scorn and pity, and passed on." The result was to bring the fellow under "genuine conviction" (Oberliniana, p. 72).

70.   "Victory over the World through Faith," Gospel Themes, pp. 371-372.

71.   "When Sin is Fatal," The Guilt of Sin, p. 109. George F. Wright notes that on this point Finney agreed with Nathaneal Emmons, "who regarded the sanctification of believers as 'precisely the same as continued regeneration'" (Finney, p. 240).

72.   This eccentric phrase illustrates Finney's lack of concern for theological precision which often characterizes his presentation of opposing arguments. Yet his main point seems clear: any view of faith which minimizes the necessity of individual conversion by associating salvation with "owning the covenant" of church membership, or which understands faith as a form of passive receptivity of moral power beyond one's natural ability is to be utterly excluded.

73.   Skeletons, p. 235.

Chapter VII

THE DUTY OF PERFECTION

There can be little doubt about the prevailing passion of
Charles Finney's life. A graduate of Oberlin College recalled that "when the first mill on Main Street was burned
one night about forty years ago, the President was present
with the rest. On his way home, after the fire was extin-
guished, he met a young man to whom he said: 'Good evening,
we've had quite a fire, haven't we? Are you a Christian?'"[1]
It was the same question he put to thousands of people in a
career that exceeded half a century. Friends, colleagues,
students, total strangers--none were exempt from that direct
inquiry into the state of their souls. For to pose that
question and to press for an affirmative answer was to
Finney's mind the inescapable duty and the unmistakable sign
of the true convert, who is faithfully following the plan of
salvation to the end of Christian perfection.

In a sermon entirely devoted to proving the proposition
set forth in its title, "Converting Sinners a Christian
Duty," Finney declares,

> Every truly converted man turns from selfishness
> to benevolence, and benevolence surely leads him
> to do all he can to save the souls of his fellow-
> man. This is the changeless law of benevolent
> action.[2]

It follows, conversely, that the lack of evangelistic zeal
is evidence that one is still in an unregenerate state.
Finney closes his sermon with the question: "For unless you

live to save others, how can you hope to be saved yourself?"
The minor premise of the "practical syllogism," in which the
Puritans used to identify those works which characterize the
elect, assumes a highly specific form for Finney.

> Often I ask persons how they are getting along in
> religion. They answer, pretty well; and yet they
> are doing nothing that is really religious. They
> are making no effort to save souls--are doing
> nothing to serve God.[3]

In the sermon entitled, "Bound to Know Your Own Character," he claims that "activity in religion is indispensable
to self-examination."[4] The test of true conversion then is
not introspection but one's willingness to "go out and warn
sinners." In fact "the more an individual goes out from
himself, and makes things not belonging to himself the
subject of thought, the more piety he will have, and the
more evidence of his piety" (LPC, p. 206). Consequently,
Finney dismisses the talk about revival or missions from
those who make no effort to convert their neighbors as
"fictitious imaginings" (LPC, p. 205).

In Finney's revival sermons the entire question of the
authenticity of conversion rests on one's interest in "saving souls." He pressed upon his New York congregation also
the claim that perfect love

> uniformly shows itself in great efforts for the
> sanctification of the church and the salvation of
> souls. When a person is negligent or deficient in
> either of these, he is by no means perfect in
> love, whatever may be his pretensions [LPC, p.
> 432].

Thus Finney can say that the desire to convert sinners is
"the leading and fundamental characteristic of true piety"
(LPC, p. 81), the standard by which the value of all other
activities is judged. At times Finney can speak of reform
movements as merely measures for more effective evangelism.

The saint is a tireless reformer, "continually devising new means and new measures for doing good"; that is, he "cannot rest till he has found something that will succeed in the salvation of souls" (LPC, p. 85).[5] Even personal devotion is shaped by evangelistic concern. The true saint "is never so copious and powerful in prayer as when he gets upon his favorite topic--the conversion of sinners" (LPC, p. 83). In the most private exercises of the mind, the saint presents to God labors in the field.

In the sermon, "Prayer and Labor for the Gathering of the Great Harvest," Finney insists that the true Christian must have "the same compassion that Jesus Himself had for souls. His heart was gushing with real compassion for dying souls, and He was conscious that His own was a right state of mind." The "same mind" in the believer takes the form of "a sense of personal responsibility in respect to the salvation of the world."[6] Finney put the challenge of the Christian life to one audience this way: "What is really worth living for but to save souls?"[7] What is remarkable is that Finney thought the answer as obvious to every genuine believer as it was to him, viz., that conversion involves not only submitting oneself to the moral law of God, but also accepting the vocation of persuading others to submit as well.

Because the moral law comprehends all of one's actions, conversion is a total dedication to the aims and principles of divine government. Further, since God's government extends to all "moral relations" among his creatures, the true Christian should accept responsibility for conforming all areas of life to the requirements of moral law. "To uphold and assist good government is not being diverted from the work of saving souls," he lectured his students at Oberlin. On the contrary, "the promotion of public and private order and happiness is one of the indispensable means of doing good and saving souls" (LST, p. 218). The result, as Finney came to see with increasing clarity, should be the entire sanctification of individuals and, through their strenuous efforts, the moral perfection of social institutions. The revival would thus produce the final reform. The exalted task called for a special anointing of the Holy Spirit, the divine power of moral suasion.

Baptism of the Holy Spirit

As Finney's Lectures on Systematic Theology demonstrate, his understanding of "Christian perfection" was the logical extension of his interpretation of faith as the determination to obey the law of love. Timothy Smith notes that "the ethical earnestness native to revivalism attained fullest expression in the doctrine of entire consecration to God's will, an idea which was the pith and marrow of the holiness crusade. At the high tide of revivalism, perfectionism was the crest of the wave."[8] The same relation did not develop in the Great Awakening, due to the very different view of faith in the theology of Jonathan Edwards. Finney's emphasis on natural ability, however, invited the literal interpretation of the biblical admonition, "Be ye therefore perfect, even as your Father which is in heaven is perfect" (Matthew 5:48). Finney's unyielding commitment to the legal principle that obligation entails ability led him to a position which was viewed as shockingly extreme even by most of the New School who also accepted a certain degree of human responsibility in salvation. Finney, however, persisted in his perfectionist teachings, convinced by his own spiritual experiences that the "common sense" reading of Scripture allowed for nothing less.[9]

Finney announced the possibility of consistent holiness in a series of sermons, delivered to the congregation of the Broadway Tabernacle in New York City during the winters of 1836-38, while he was on leave from Oberlin. Transcribed by Joshua Leavitt, who gave them wide circulation in the New York Evangelist, they were later published under the title, Lectures to Professing Christians. In his Memoirs Finney recalls that "those sermons to Christians were very much the result of a searching that was going on in my own mind"--a searching which culminated in an experience of "that divine

sweetness in my soul, of which President Edwards speaks as
attained in his own experience. That winter [1837] I had a
thorough breaking up . . . " (MF, pp. 339, 341). The motive
for his seeking this "more stable form of Christian life"
was the recognition that Christians, "as a general thing,
were making very little progress in grace"; as well as what
he confessed was "a state of great dissatisfaction with my
own want of stability in faith and love" (MF, p. 340). By
1837 Finney could no longer ignore the fact that his converts were too often like the young plants in Jesus' parable: " . . . forthwith they sprung up, because they had no
deepness of earth; and when the sun was up, they were
scorched; and because they had no root, they withered away"
(Matthew 13: 5-6).

The criticism has been a standard one against revivalist enthusiasm: that it is impossible to maintain the glow
of passion after the first flush of conversion has faded.
Those who have produced a "profession" of faith under the
operation of revival machinery, the critics claim, often
fail to maintain it once the tent is folded and the last
echoes of the evangelist's shouts die away. Only steady
spiritual growth, under the gentle nurture of an established
ministry, will produce the deep roots required to sustain
faith through the trials of a life-time. The difficulty
with the theory of nurture, as Finney and other thoughtful
revivalists have argued, is that it may be effective for
those who are "brought up" in a Christian congregation; but
it cannot touch those, particularly of adolescent age and
beyond, who are not disposed to darken the door of a church,
let alone sit patiently for years of weekly instruction.
Thus the dilemma as the revivalists perceive it: established churches have the means of nurture, but no aggressive
techniques for adult conversion; the revivalists have effective measures for recruiting converts, but no means of
sustaining their spiritual growth.

Finney recognized that to leave young converts without
instruction is "as unphilosophical as it is unscriptural."[10]
Therefore, he emphasized that converts should join a church

immediately, even if its official teachings were not entirely "the doctrines of God." For Finney accepted the rule of
thumb that "ordinarily, if a person does not desire to be
associated with the people of God, he is rotten at the
bottom."[11] Nevertheless, while Finney attempted to work
closely with local churches in his revivals, the relationship was not always smooth—particularly when he insisted
that "the church cannot maintain her ground, cannot command
attention, without very exciting preaching, and sufficient
novelty in measures, to get the public ear."[12] Predictably,
converts brought into the churches by revival novelties were
very often impatient with the less spectacular offerings of
local clergy; and their vocal criticisms of spiritual "dead-
ness" were rarely as welcomed, or as effective in promoting
revivals, as Finney thought they should be.

The sad fact is that, while Finney taught that revivals
should unite churches in a renewed spirit of commitment,
congregations were often left divided and exhausted by the
intense passions aroused by "the work" and the bitter controversies over its appropriateness. Further, while Finney
emphasized that "the very idea of being a Christian is to
renounce self and become entirely consecrated to God," and
that converts "should not rest satisfied till they are as
perfect as God," the new believers all too quickly fell into
the old sin of "backsliding."[13] Thus, when the recognized
master of revival preaching stepped into the New York pulpit, in the winter of his forty-fifth year, he faced his
audience with an unaccustomed heaviness of spirit.

In the thirteen years he had devoted to pleading the
case of Jesus Christ, Finney had enjoyed virtually unqualified success in raising revivals. He had spent his early
adult life, abandoning his chosen profession and risking his
health, in ceaseless travel to meet the insatiable demand
for his services. Notwithstanding a bout with cholera, he
had arrived at middle age in far better shape than many
other preachers and crusaders of his time: his voice was
still strong, his eyes as clear and penetrating as ever, his

frame tall and straight, and his mind agile. Having overcome the determined opposition of the leading New School
Presbyterian clergy to his revival techniques, he had led
major campaigns in cities from Rochester and Philadelphia to
Boston and New York. Charles Finney had, apparently, every
reason to entertain at least some faint sense of satisfaction. Indeed, a person of less consuming dedication might
have been positively beaming. Finney, however, was troub-
led. He had aimed at nothing less than the complete moral
reformation of his generation--the unconditional surrender
of the American will to the law of God. For then, in fulfillment of biblical prophecy, "a nation shall be born in a
day. Only let [the churches] feel as the heart of one man,
and be agreed as to what ought to be done for the salvation
of the world, and the millennium will come at once."[14]

But everywhere he saw lapses into self-indulgence among
church members. The use of wine, tobacco, coffee, tea--on
however small a scale--was an intemperance which betrayed
their claims to self-denial. "But I tell you it is a great
mistake of yours, if you think these are little things, when
they make the church odious in the sight of God, by exposing
her hypocrisy and lust."[15] In New York Finney had sadly
concluded that his audience had "never known the radical
principle of serving the Lord" (LPC, p. 35). Therefore, he
could not address them as genuine believers, but only as
"professing Christians."

As disappointing as was the inconstancy of most church-
goers, Finney was even more discouraged by a growing doubt
about the authenticity of his own profession. That uncertainty had no doubt been deepened by criticism from colleagues who feared his preaching was becoming less the
fervent pouring out of his spirit and more the calculated
application of right means. Theodore Weld, who continued to
hold Finney in high esteem even after Weld had left the
revival campaign to devote himself to the abolition crusade,
felt compelled to warn his "father in Christ" with a penetrating series of questions that in one less sincerely pious
would have been presumptuous. The letter is addressed to

Finney in Philadelphia, during the beginning of the revival
there in 1828.

> Now brother beloved how is it with your own soul?
> . . . Dear brother do tell me what mark you are
> pressing towards? The same that Paul did? Per-
> fect sinlessness? . . . My dear father in Jesus,
> you are in such a maddening whirl of care, respon-
> sibility and toil, I do dreadfully fear that you
> neglect the culture of personal holiness. . . . I
> fear [revivals] are fast becoming with you a sort
> of trade, to be worked at so many hours every day
> and then laid aside. . . . The machinery all moves
> on, every wheel and spring and chord in its place;
> but isn't the main spring waxing weaker? Who has
> witnessed such exhibitions of almightiness in
> God's moral kingdom as you? . . . O dear Finney
> had I not rather go to the stake than to see you
> shorn of your locks. "And he wist not that the
> Lord had departed from him."[16]

Following these strong words, Weld urges Finney to set aside
an hour a day to "enter into the secret chambers [of] your
soul and solemnly debate this matter with your conscience in
the fear of God." The advice had particular force coming
from one who was also unceasingly active, but so assiduously
modest that his own monumental efforts went largely unrecog-
nized.[17]

    For Finney such warnings only increased the gnawing
anxiety about the value of his work, which is the dark side
of success at any age, but which throws its longest shadow
when youth has undeniably passed and the inevitability of
death must be fully acknowledged. That critical moment
arrived in 1843, again in the dead of winter, when he was
conducting a revival in Boston and his beloved wife lay
seriously ill in Oberlin. He found that he was unable to
offer what had become a routine prayer of dedication, offering "my family all upon the altar of God." It appeared that
the Lord was about to accept the sacrifice of his wife; and

Finney suddenly saw "clearly what was implied in laying her, and all I possessed, upon the altar of God; and for hours I struggled upon my knees, to give her up unqualifiedly to the will of God. But I found myself unable to do it." Here was a serious test of his theology, as well as his piety: "the bitterness, almost of death seemed, for a few moments, to possess me, at the thought that my religion might be of the sensibility only, and that God's teaching might have taken effect only in my feeling" (MF, p. 375).[18]

As Finney now sought for himself that power of "pre-vailing prayer" he had long admonished others to exercise, the cumulative effects of concern about the fidelity of his converts and thus the value of his own career precipitated a crisis in his spiritual life. He was close to despair--a condition all the more disturbing for being unfamiliar. The occasion for his agony was the recognition that his feelings of affectionate attachment to his wife were inconsistent with his duty willingly to detach himself from everything and everyone in order to fulfill his divine calling without distraction. Finney's understanding of psychology was that a person is capable of controlling the feelings through a careful application of the will; his theology demanded that one do so; but his own experience was threatening to betray his theories, or at least complicate beyond recognition his fairly simple notions about "mental philosophy." If there are any dark recesses in the human heart or mind which remain unillumined by the "inner revelation," and thus resistant to the claims of reason and law, they would con-stitute the functional equivalent of original sin. And what supreme irony if these strongholds of a depraved selfishness should be disguised with the facade of conjugal love! In a lecture on the Pauline command to "be filled with the Spirit," Finney acknowledges that "you will sometimes find your own corruptions making strange headway against the spirit."[19]

While Finney is not unaware of the forbidden subterran-ean impulses that sometimes surface and threaten to over-whelm the mind, neither does he regard them as invincible.

Rather he offers a regimen--a course of mental hygiene--for subduing and cleansing the "imaginations of the heart." The key to spiritual health, as one might expect, is the proper alignment of the "faculties" with the law of God.

The moral law requires that one be truly benevolent. The term for the chief Christian virtue, which had been prominent in American moral philosophy since the days of Edwards, was "disinterested benevolence." To love others disinterestedly is to love them "in God," that is, to act toward them as God does by seeking their true good which consists, of course, in their being submitted to the divine government. Thus, every action toward others, or feeling about them, should have as its object nothing less than the total happiness of the universe of moral beings. As Edwards himself said, "no affection limited to any private system, not dependent on, nor subordinate to being in general, can be of the nature of true virtue."[20] To be truly universal in one's benevolence, however, requires a heroic abstraction of virtue beyond the emotional discipline of all but a few saints. One can do good only for some particular others; and the choice of certain individuals as objects of benevolence--insofar as it is a conscious choosing among alternatives--always proceeds from some interest in them.

Timothy Dwight, in the generation following Edwards, recognized the problem, and cheerfully accepted the common sense maxim that charity begins at home. Specifically, Dwight argued that God has wisely placed humankind in families so that each individual has opportunities to practice benevolence immediately at hand. In one sermon he expounded the "consistency of benevolence with providing peculiarly for our own."

> Were there no families, there would be no country: were there no little spheres of beneficence; there would be no great one: and were good-will not exercised first toward those, who are near; it would never be extended to those who are distant.[21]

Such a frankly utilitarian argument, however, even from
a respected leader of the New Divinity in New England, could
not have quieted the turmoil in Finney's soul. For while he
was a firm believer in the guidance of common sense in moral
questions, he was also an idealist. If the moral law required that benevolence be entirely disinterested, and that
love of every particular being be subordinated to the love
of the universal Lord, then such virtue must be literally
possible. If so, Finney must bring himself to give up his
wife--gladly--to the sickness with which Providence seemed
determined to slay her. No temporizing argument about the
utility of partial benevolence could deliver him from the
crisis he faced. How could he find, or create, the proper
feelings of joyful surrender to accompany and support the
decision to lay his wife on the altar of duty? Finney knew
something of the pain Kierkegaard was discovering at about
the same time in the "movement of infinite resignation"
which the "knight of faith" is required to make.

What went through Finney's mind as he prayed through
that long night in Boston we do not know in detail; neither
does he mention any visions which passed before his eyes.
But he did experience what he called a "baptism of the Holy
Spirit," and before morning he had determined to "give up
everything to the will of God." This was the second time
Finney had been baptized by the Holy Spirit, and his report
of the experience is much less dramatic than that of his
first baptism. Following his conversion, he had been inun-
dated by "waves and waves of liquid love" and had shed tears
of ecstatic joy. Upon reflection he recognized the experience as the confirmation of his decision to "get my own
consent to give up my sins." Consistently enough, the
second baptism, while less traumatic, also served to confirm
Finney's decision to submit himself wholly to the divine
will. As he had earlier admitted to his New York congregation: "How great a thing it is, for the proud heart of man
to give up its wisdom, and knowledge, and will, and everything, to God. I have found this the greatest of all difficulties. Doubtless all find it so" (LPC, p. 375). The
resolution of "the greatest of all difficulties" came about

when Finney was impressed with feelings of inner peace and
joy which were appropriate to, and therefore confirmatory
of, his act of willing. The "baptism of the Holy Spirit" is
for Finney the symbol of the blessed reconciliation of
sensibility and will: the gift of joy in duty.

At the moment of entire consecration Finney writes that
he fell back, "in a deeper sense than I had ever done before
upon the infinitely blessed and perfect will of God" (MF, p.
375). He abandons not only his wife to the disposition of
Providence, but also his own soul: "I . . . recollect
telling the Lord, that I did not know whether he intended to
save me or not. Nor did I feel concerned to know. I was
willing to abide the event" (MF, p. 376). Finney appears to
assume the very posture of unquestioning humility before a
despotic monarch which he mockingly attributed to those who
accepted the doctrine of unconditional election. His confession in fact seems but another version of the Hopkinsians' reported willingness to be damned for the glory of
God. Appearances in this case however, if not in all, are
deceiving. Finney repeatedly states that his submission to
God is conditioned upon his own rational judgment that God
is trustworthy.

> . . . I had such perfect confidence in his good-
> ness and love, as to believe that he could consent
> to do nothing, to which I could object . . . he
> would not do anything that was not perfectly wise
> and good; and therefore, I had the best of
> grounds for accepting whatever he could consent
> to, in respect to me and mine . . . I went no
> farther in pledges and professions than was
> reasonable [MF, pp. 376f].

As we have seen, Finney holds that all of God's actions are
conformed to the moral law, and therefore are reasonable and
efficient means of achieving the ultimate good, viz., the
true happiness of the moral universe. He can confidently
offer himself, even for eternal condemnation, since his
reason assures him that it is "impossible" for God to send

anyone to hell who so entirely submits to his will. Finney
has now reached the point of personal wholeness; his will,
feelings, and intellect are in complete agreement. He has
arrived at the end toward which the plan of salvation aims;
he has been perfected. "My confidence in God was perfect,
my acceptance of his will was perfect, and my mind was as
calm as heaven" (MF, p. 377).

His account of the process concludes with a touching
image of trusting innocence.

> I have felt since then a religious freedom, a
> religious bouyancy and delight in God. . . . My
> bondage seemed to be, at that time, entirely bro-
> ken; and since then, I have had the freedom of a
> child with a loving parent. It seems to me that I
> can find God within me, in such a sense, that I
> can rest upon him and be quiet, lay my heart in
> his hand, and nestle down in his perfect will, and
> have no carefulness or anxiety [MF, p. 381].

The cycle is complete. The child struggles to achieve
legitimate autonomy, to be released from the parental embrace, becoming a guilty rebel in the process, but then
returns in a voluntary act of submission to rest in "the
everlasting arms." The return does not mean, however, that
the sanctified person lapses into inactive contemplation, a
state Finney could regard only as a kind of spiritual coma.
On the contrary, Finney finds in sanctification a release
from anxiety about tangible "results," including "the interests of the church, the progress of religion, the conversion
of the world, and the salvation or damnation of my own soul"
(MF, p. 376). He is now free to be more active in the work
than ever, for now nothing could shake his loyalty to the
divine government or cause him to doubt the worth of his own
place in its operations. He is also released from the
almost overwhelming personal responsibility for the conversion of the nation. The season of millennial blessing will
come in God's own time; in the meanwhile Finney will

continue to labor as if it were autumn and the fields were
white unto harvest.

As in his conversion, so in reaching sanctification,
Finney passes through a crisis of will: a struggle of the
self-determining individual to conform himself to the demands of moral law. Indeed, entire sanctification is the
extension of the movement of faith into the continuous
exercise of adherence to the will of God, as the expression
and enactment of the moral law. The spiritual insight in
which the doctrine of entire sanctification is grounded is
that divine providence disposes all things according to the
ultimate end of the moral law, and that therefore the divine
will may be accepted with the confidence that it is good.
The emotional ecstasy accompanying this act of commitment is
a "natural" effect of the proper alignment of the will;
understood in terms of Finney's psychology, it is the joy of
self-fulfillment. Finney testified that, as a result of the
baptism of the Spirit, "it seemed as if my desires were all
met." Accordingly, in his theological lectures he identi-
fies one of the points "wherein saints and sinners must
differ" as the former's proper sense of self-satisfaction:

> Conscious as he is of conformity to the moral law,
> he cannot but affirm to himself, that the Lawgiver
> is pleased with his present attitude. . . . The
> harmony of his own being is a witness to himself,
> that this is the state in which he was made to
> exist. He is a peace with God, because he and God
> are pursuing precisely the same end, and by the
> same means [LST, pp. 310f].

Insofar as humans conform to the same law as God, viz., "to
love as impartially, with as perfect love," they reflect the
image of God. "This, and nothing less than this," Finney
declared, "is Christian Perfection" (LPC, p. 342).

When Finney sought to "bear witness" to his new
insights before his Boston congregation, "as a general
thing, the testimony that I bore was unintelligible to them"

(MF, p. 379). This had been the case in New York as well
and had led Finney to address his sermons on holiness to
"professing Christians." Only in the atmosphere of spiritual excitement at Oberlin did Finney find "a larger number
of persons, by far, that understand me, and devour that
class of truths, than I have found elsewhere; but even here,
the majority of professors of religion do not understand-
ingly embrace those truths" (MF, p. 384). Finney's complaint is ironic, for during the school year of 1836 he had
himself, from the pulpit at Oberlin, ridiculed the idea of
achieving perfection. A few students who had made a covenant among themselves to grieve God no longer by sinning
were rewarded by Finney's public declaration that "he would
creep a hundred miles upon his hands and knees, to see a man
who was living without a sin."[22]

His colleagues at Oberlin, however, were attracted by
the possibility of Christian perfection. Later that year,
the highly respected Asa Mahan answered a student's question
with the statement that a Christian could attain "freedom
from voluntary failures, positive and present sin." The
subsequent discussion among students and faculty deeply
impressed Finney, and he took the new ideas with him to New
York where they provided the basis for his lectures on
Christian perfection. James Fairchild reports that the
essence of what became widely known as the "Oberlin doctrine" was that perfection is found "in the continuity or
permanency of obedience, and not in the heartiness or genu-
ineness of obedience while it exists."[23] That is, perfection refers to constancy of will, always choosing to
follow the moral law, and not to any emotional state. Even
when Finney refers to perfect love as "affection" for God he
adds sternly, "I use the term . . . in the sense of President Edwards . . . an affection in his treatise is an act of
the will or a volition" (LPC, p. 421). The saints may not
continually bubble with enthusiasm, but they can be counted
on always to do the right thing for the right reason.

Thus, when a group from Oberlin, including Finney as a
prominent member, held a convention in Rochester in July

1841 to clarify their views, they issued a statement which
emphasized fidelity of the will.

> The advocates of this doctrine affirm that
> obedience to the moral law, or a state of entire
> consecration to God in this life, is in such a
> sense attainable as to be an object of rational
> pursuit with the expectation of attaining it.[24]

Such complete devotion of the moral agent is demanded by the
very nature of the moral law, according to their statement;
but the conferees are careful to add that the state of
entire consecration is attained only through continual
effort in "constant dependence upon the grace of our Lord
Jesus Christ, and the agency and indwelling of the Holy
Spirit." Their caution on this point was in response to
critics, including other New School Presbyterians, who
accused those at Oberlin of teaching Pelagianism. Finney
found it "amazing" that Beecher, for example, should charge
him with minimizing the believer's need for grace. Yet
Finney's defense hardly met the objection: "Entire sanctification, instead of implying no further dependence on the
grace of Christ, implies the constant appropriation of
Christ by faith as the sanctification of the soul . . .
entire sanctification, as I understand the term, is identi-
cal with entire and continued obedience to the law of God"
(LST, p. 406).

Given Finney's interpretation of grace as "divine moral
suasion," the emphasis on moral law in the Oberlin statement
was very much to his taste. His Lectures to Professing
Christians, accordingly, are designed to instruct believers
in the necessity of perseverance in obedience. As such,
they struck many hearers "as rather an exhibition of the
Law, than of the Gospel."

> But I did not, and do not, so regard them. For me
> the Law and Gospel have but one rule of life . . .
> I have long been satisfied that the higher forms
> of Christian experience are attained only as a

result of a terribly searching application of
God's Law to the human conscience and heart [MF,
p. 339].

Finney repeatedly emphasizes in his sermons that the difference between a mere "professor," whose expectations and
attainments in holiness are satisfied with the bare possession of justification, and the dedicated Christian is exactly the complete devotion of the latter to the law of benevolence. For thereby one exercises true virtue in a state of
entire sanctification.

But the highest happiness belongs to the believer whose
determination is graced with the feeling of being embraced
and supported by the divine presence. The baptism of the
Holy Spirit represents for Finney the integration of will
and feelings and intellect (inasmuch as the experience is a
reasonable warrant for belief) which constitutes the perfection of the moral agent. It is not surprising, therefore,
that at Oberlin "the doctrine of sanctification by special
experience, gradually gave place to a presentation of the
baptism of the Spirit as a condition of a more efficient and
permanent Christian life."[25] Specifically, for Finney the
baptism of the Spirit was a necessary condition for evangelical ministry and the basis of true and lasting moral reform. Timothy Smith comments that "the experience was [for
Finney] normative for all Christians; it was the source of
divine grace which sanctified their hearts and minds. . . .
By this means alone could such righteousness prevail in
individual and social life, in church and nation, as the
Lord has ordained for his people."[26]

The baptism of the Spirit initiates the believer into a
"higher form of Christian experience": joyful and consistent
obedience. As Finney explained, "The liberty of the gospel
does not consist in being freed from doing what the law
requires, but in a man's being in such a state of mind that
doing it is itself a pleasure instead of a burden" (LPC, p.
279). That is, saints love to do their duty and they recognize love as the highest duty.

The Law of Love

Sanctification, like faith, is primarily for Finney a moral action, not to be confused with any merely passive "state of sensibility." Thus, while he commends A Plain Account of Christian Perfection by John Wesley, Finney adds that "I find some expressions in it to which I should object but I believe it is rather the expression than the sentiments" (LPC, p. 358). It is not hard to imagine Finney's disapproval of the enthusiasm with which John Wesley pressed his views and of the "impressions" made upon the sensibilities by the affecting hymnody of his brother Charles. Yet there is more than a difference in style at stake in Finney's critique of Wesleyan perfectionism. In the Memoirs Finney rejects "the view of sanctification entertained by our Methodist brethren" on the ground that, "as their idea of sanctification seemed to me to relate almost altogether to states of the sensibility, I could not receive their teaching" (MF, p. 340).

> Yet [he continues] I was satisfied that the doctrine of sanctification in this life, and entire sanctification, in the sense that it was the privilege of Christians to live without known sin, was a doctrine taught in the Bible, and that abundant means were provided for the securing of that attainment [MF, p. 341].

The chapters on sanctification in Finney's lectures do not refer to Wesley at all, but it is clear that there are passages in the Plain Account which Finney could regard only as a threat to the integrity of moral agency.[27] The most obvious example is Wesley's teaching about the "indwelling of Christ," in terms which suggest that the human spirit is replaced by the Spirit of Christ in conversion. The suggestion is made explicit in one hymn co-authored by John and Charles Wesley:

Heavenly Adam, life Divine,
Change my nature into Thine;
Move and spread throughout my soul,
Actuate and fill the whole.[28]

Further, in his final advice to his readers, Wesley writes, "True humility is a kind of self-annihilation; and this is the centre of all virtues" (PA, p. 100). Elsewhere Wesley speaks of that "deep gratitude, which plunges the soul in Him as in an abyss . . . as rivers seem willing to empty themselves when they pour themselves with all their waters into the sea" (PA, p. 105). If these passages are taken as teaching a literal absorption of the human subject into the divine, or as an identification of the Christian's will with that of the indwelling Christ, they could only lead to what Finney called a passive form of spirituality, a "mystic relation" to God. it is probably such expressions as these, as well as the introspective "quietism" of nineteenth-century Methodism, that made Finney qualify his approval of the Plain Account. Finney's understanding of sanctification is one of active obedience to moral law, not a supernatural infusion of divine virtue: "It is self-evident, that entire obedience to God's law is possible on the ground of natural ability" (LST, p. 407).[29]

The "indwelling of Christ", however, is only one of four descriptions of Christian perfection in Plain Account. The other three—"circumcision of the heart," "obedience to God," and "perfect Love"—refer to the ethical union of the believer with the will of God, expressed in the law and exhibited for human emulation in Jesus Christ, "our grand Exemplar." Wesley recalls that early in his ministry, "I generally considered religion, as a uniform following of Christ, an entire inward and outward conformity to our Master" (PA, p. 6). Wesley was as insistent as Finney that entire sanctification is single-minded obedience of the divine commandments from a perfect love of God (PA, pp. 13f). Where love is "the sole principle of action" (PA, p. 43), sin cannot find entrance, "there being no room for this in a soul which is full of God" (PA, p. 23). Sin is a

function of conscious intention; therefore, it is in principle conquerable through the purification of the inward person by faith (PA, p. 33). Perfection, understood in these
terms, is the very opposite of antinomianism. Wesley reminds his followers that while Christ is the end of the law,
"he has adopted every point of the moral law, and grafted it
into the law of love" (PA, p. 91). Wesley emphasizes the
"third use" of the law; the distinguishing mark of the
sanctified person is not a greater freedom from the law, but
a more stable motive of perfect love in its obedience. This
love is directed to God through the neighbor.

> One of the principal rules of religion is, to lose
> no occasion of serving God. And since He is
> invisible to our eyes, we are to serve Him in our
> neighbor: which He receives as if done to Himself
> in person, standing visibly before us [PA, p.
> 103].

Finney did not draw his understanding of "perfect love"
as directly from a theology of the incarnation as did Wesley, but he agreed that the Christian's character should be
shaped by the image of the historical Jesus in the gospels.

> Suppose a person is naturally penurious . . . he
> will never remedy that defect, until he receives
> Christ as his pattern, and the selfishness is
> driven out of his heart by imbuing his very soul
> with the infinite benevolence of the Saviour [LPC,
> p. 376].

The believer can expect no divine aid except that given in
the persuasive example of Christ; and this, as we have seen,
is the meaning of grace under moral government. Although
Finney insists that Christ is "the immediate cause of our
being sanctified," still "he works our works in us, not by
suspending our own agency, but he so controls our minds, by
the influence of his Spirit in us, in a way perfectly consistent with our freedom, as to sanctify us" (LPC, p. 391).
"The act of the mind, that thus throws the soul into the

hand of Christ for sanctification, is faith" (LPC, p. 392). As Finney emphasizes in the sermon on "Sanctification by Faith," faith is a response to the exhibition of divine benevolence in the death of Christ. The gospel

> exhibits God as making the greatest sacrifice to reconcile sinners to himself. . . . Nothing is so calculated to cut down an enemy, and win him over, and make him a friend. This is what the gospel does to sinners. It shows that not withstanding all they have done to God, God still exercises toward them disinterested love [LPC, pp. 312, 314].

The appeal for sanctification is in accordance with the "laws of mind" upon which the "moral relation" between God and his creatures depends. "God has so constituted the mind, that it must necessarily do homage to virtue. It must do this, as long as it retains the power of moral agency" (LPC, p. 315). The sanctifying influence of the gospel, then, is to stabilize the moral consciousness by eliciting a consistent exercise of faith, or obedience to the law.

Thus, the gospel does not in any way dispense with the moral law of the Old Testament: "The very first sentence of the gospel, the command to repent, is in effect a re-enactment of the law, for it is a command to return to obedience" (LPC, p. 273). As the divine will was expressed in the Mosaic commandments, so "the gospel is but a republication of the same will, in another form" (LPC, p. 347). This is the insistent theme in the theological lectures as well: "Sanctification is nothing more nor less than entire obedience, for the time being, to the moral law" (LST, p. 405). Finney inverts the routine interpretation of the relation between law and love, namely that lawful conduct is the spontaneous expression of a loving heart. Instead, Finney argued that love is the primary form of obedience to moral law. Thus, he resists the temptation (to which John Humphrey Noyes yielded) to redefine what constitutes lawful conduct on the basis of some "higher experience" of love.

Finney begins with the clear and unchangeable provisions of moral law and defines perfect love as consistent obedience to them.

There is a further implication in the priority of law to love which has great significance for Finney's attitudes toward social reform. If it is true, as H. J. Berman argues, that law is "love's reliable servant" in the sense that law guarantees the minimal conditions of social order required for the exercise of love, then the establishment of a lawful society is a necessary condition for the exercise of Christian virtue.[30] Since true love is a social activity, its sustained practice presupposes at least a rudimentary form of human community. Under conditions of social anarchy, the sacrifices of love may produce martyrs, but not the kingdom of God. The leading concern of a true Christian, therefore, should be the establishment of respect for moral law as the foundation of a social order in which love may attain its perfect exercise as the sum of all Christian virtues. Individual believers, then, have a large stake in social reforms as the condition for their own sainthood becoming fully visible.

Thus, in describing the exercise of entire sanctification Finney is fond of the metaphor of loyal citizenship: the true saint shows "the same ardor to promote God's honor and interest, that the true patriot does to promote the honor and interest of his country" (LPC, p. 78). "God requires men to devote themselves not to their own interests, but to His interests and those of his great family . . . . He asks them to become divinely patriotic, devoting themselves to their Creator and to the good of His creatures."[31] Religious revivals have aroused hopes in the glorious destiny of America in each period of national awakening. Edwards had written the "history of redemption" as reaching its fulfillment in the New World; and Finney stands as well "for the old principle; the hope of the coming of the kingdom of Christ."[32] The end result of spiritual patriotism is the dawning of the kingdom of God in America.

Consequently, while all reform activities are welcomed by Finney insofar as they encourage the self-denial that is appropriate for the Christian, he insists that they always be subordinated to the revival which is the divinely appointed instrument of moral transformation. Obedience to the law of benevolence requires first of all a concern for the "souls," or "hearts," or moral character, of others. For it is only as people's "hearts" are "turned to the Lord," that they can attain sanctifying virtue and that the divine government can be extended in the world. It is Finney's hope that, as the truth of the gospel persuades people to submit to the law of love, peace will increase, greed and exploitation will be overcome, and the age of universal well-being will dawn. The eschatological community of righteousness depends on the success of the revival in achieving individual righteousness now; the kingdom of God on earth will be macrocosm of the reign of Christ in the believing heart.

The Final Reform

Finney made many changes in his career, affecting methods, colleagues, and alliances with reform causes, yet he consistently saw revival as the normal state of the Church and evangelism as the vocation of every Christian. He was little aware of the theological significance of history, in which the waters of salvation not only flow, but also ebb. His own career, as he recounted it, was an unbroken series of victories. He had little cause to reflect upon the ambiguities of human experience, including the complexity of moral choice. So he saw no reason to doubt that individuals, and the society they constitute, are capable of complete dedication to moral law.

He was not, of course, the only preacher to make the connection between the traditional Reformed "use" of the law of God to discipline the believer's conduct and the application of that law to the political, economic, and cultural activities of the society at large. John Calvin's own attempt to organize a theocratic government in Geneva was emulated by the Puritans in New England. By the early nineteenth century, however, the divorce between religious vision and political power was final. If America were to be governed by the moral law, as interpreted by its Protestant clergy, the people would have to accept its demands voluntarily. Under the provisions of constitutional democracy, law cannot be imposed from above, but only through the elected representatives of the people. The triumph of moral law thus depended upon persuading people, particularly those whose professional or economic status made their example attractive to others, to follow its legislation.

To step forward in response to the evangelist's invitation, therefore, was to cast one's ballot for the divine government. When Finney speaks of his efforts to raise revivals as a "campaign," he uses the term in the political, rather than the military, sense. Finney, along with almost the entire company of New School Presbyterians, set out to promote divine government with the means available to members of a constitutional democracy, the "moral means" of persuasion.[33] Unlike an ordinary politician, whose ambition is limited to local improvement through the "art of the possible," Finney sought, through the sacramental power of rhetoric, to effect the "impossible dream" of national perfection: the final reform.

Finney's grand project rested upon two premises: first, that all societal evil is the result of the selfishness of individuals; second, that the coming of the kingdom of God will be the result of the gradual increase of moral government in the world by the means of revival preaching.

In relation to the first point Finney has been criticized for holding a "naive individualism," usually defined as the unrealistic hope of solving the whole range of human problems by appealing to the reason and good will of each person. H. Richard Niebuhr, for example, argued that the evangelical program of moral reform was inadequate to solve

the complex social problems of the later nineteenth century
because it proceeded from the premise that "the human unit
is the individual."[34] What about those problems which, it
is claimed, cannot be traced to the evil intentions of any
one moral agent, but seem to be produced by some impersonal
malignant power, such as a political "institution" (Congress, the Department of War) or an economic system (the
Southern mercantile economy), or the "forces of history"?[35]

Just as Finney had rejected the "theological fiction"
of a depraved nature which compels people to act badly, so
he refused to accept what he might have called today the
"sociological fiction" of evil institutions which force
their members to violate moral law. Finney remained convinced that it is the responsibility of each individual to
resist any law or policy of human government that is inconsistent with the divine rule. If an institution or social
system is designed to perpetuate the selfish interest of one
group or class of people at the expense of others, then it
should be dismantled as an act of repentance. Indeed, the
fact that governments are sometimes corrupt should be an
impetus to righteous action. "Instead of destroying human
governments," Finney taught his eager students, "Christians
are bound to reform them."[36] Thus, as John Hammond rightly
notes, the revivalists sought a national consensus, but one
based, not on practical political considerations, but on
commitment to the absolute ends of the revival. Finney was
accordingly willing to support positions which were highly
controversial out of loyalty to the unconditional demands of
the moral law.

> In brief, the revivalists attempted to moralize
> politics . . . they are convinced that they are
> under obligation . . . to God to make the world
> express his will. The revivals created not com-
> placent patriots but people committed to the real-
> ization of their ideals within the nation, however
> much they might violate social order and national
> harmony.[37]

The evangelical prophets have the courage of their calling
to criticize both the political leaders and the people
themselves.

In his theological lectures, Finney did not hesitate to
provide two concrete examples of public policies which are
evil because they are based on selfishness: the war with
Mexico and the practice of slavery.[38] Finney rejected the
claim that the war should be carried on as a matter of
national honor and found contemptible the rationale that
slavery should be sustained, even though a recognized evil,
in the interest of preserving the Union.

> To adopt the maxim, "Our country right or wrong,"
> and to sympathize with the government, in the
> prosecution of a war unrighteously waged, must
> involve the guilt of murder. To adopt the maxim,
> "Our union, even with perpetual slavery," is an
> abomination so execrable, as not to be named by a
> just mind without indignation [LST, p. 227].

Finney's condemnation of slavery was clear and consistent. He argued that the practice is based on the selfishness of those how exploit their neighbors for their own
profit; as such, it is an unqualified evil which no legislative sanction can legitimate. Indeed, "God cannot authorize
it. The Bible canot sanction it, and if both God and the
Bible were to sanction it, it could not be lawful" (LST, p.
227). The moral evil of slavery is located in the selfish
intention of the slaveholders, as the moral evil of the war
lies in the self-interest of a particular region. Because
slaveholding is a sin, Finney declared that the decision of
his congregation in New York to exclude slaveholders from
communion was required by both piety and logic.

> If I do not baptize slavery by some soft and
> Christian name, if I call it SIN, both consistency
> and conscience conduct to the inevitable
> conclusion, that while the sin is perserved in,
> its perpetrators cannot be fit subjects for
> Christian communion and fellowship.[39]

Finney's analysis of the evil of slavery reduces the moral issue to the choice of the slaveholder. He does not deny that there are other issues involved--political, economic, cultural--but they do not engage his attention as an expositor of moral government. For Finney even freeing the slaves, if done for selfish reasons in the master and received with selfish delight by the slaves, cannot be judged a morally good act. The context of ethical judgment is limited to the motives of the agents.[40]

It is not so surprising, therefore, that the devil is not mentioned in the Lectures on Systematic Theology. Since "that old adversary" of God's rule does appear in Finney's sermons, one might expect his sulphurous image on the pages of Finney's theology. But the conspicuous lack of reference to cosmic "principalities and powers" is entirely consistent with Finney's insistence that the moral failure of human beings is attributable to no other energy than their own wills. Satan may cleverly present temptation to move the will toward selfishness--what the Bible calls "the wiles of the devil"--but he cannot force anyone to sin.[41] The claim that "the devil made me do it" is but another excuse of inability, like the deluded attempt to blame one's transgressions on the curse of original sin.

To put the matter another way: the notions of original sin and of an irresistible demonic power are both illusions created, perhaps subconsciously, as strategies for evading responsibility for one's actions. Neither notion is of any practical value for encouraging moral virtue and, taken together, they are the greatest hindrance to the progress of divine government in the world. The doctrine of original sin throws a stumbling block in the way of revival and the idea of Satanic control of human institutions discourages the enthusiastic and hopeful support of reforms that will turn the kingdoms of this world, in the language of the New Testament prophet, into "the kingdom of our Lord and of his Christ" (Revelation 11:15). Conversely, the denial of the curse of original sin and of some supra-human power of evil is absolutely necessary to insure the salvation of souls and the coming of the millennium.

Finney must admit, however, that there are some moral
agents who, although they do not fall under the control of
demonic power, do so continually resist the witness of
conscience that moral truth loses all influence on their
will. There are limits to forbearance under moral government, and those whose consciences are "seared" are abandoned
by the Spirit. Having cauterized the tender flesh of the
heart, such hardened sinners are insensitive to the persuasive touch of the Holy Spirit: "although their intelligence
affirms that sin is wrong, yet they do not feel it or care
for it."[42] Further repentance is impossible, for God will
not violate "the laws of mind" which require that the will
be influenced by no force other than the truth itself. Such
sinners are responsible for the greatest horrors of human
history and will be punished eternally for the crimes
against humanity which they have perpetrated in their life-
times. What is essential to understand, however, is that
for Finney, such evildoers, despite the depth of their
depravity, have, like Pharaoh of old, hardened their own
hearts.[43]

Occasionally, Finney encountered such "hopeless"
individuals; but he always regarded them as tragic
exceptions. Certainly he did not accept the view that an
entire group of people had so "gone to the devil" that there
was no chance for their repentance. His basic optimism
about human nature underlies his insistence that even the
evil of slaveholding could be eliminated through moral
suasion. It is in this context that Finney's well-known
letter to Theodore Weld must be understood. Finney harbored
a prescient fear that Weld's aggressive "mode of abolition-
izing the country" would lead to "civil war." The letter
continues as follows:

> To suggest to some minds what I have here said
> would be evidence either of a pro slavery spirit,
> or of cowardice. But D[ea]r Weld you think, and
> certainly you can not but discern the signs of the
> times. Now what is to be done? How can we save
> our country and affect the speedy abolition of

slavery? This is my answer. What say you to it?
The subject is now before the publick mind. It is
upon the conscience of every man, so that now
every new convert will be an abolitionist of
course. Now if abolition can be made an
append[a]ge of a general revival of religion all
is well. I fear no other form of carrying this
question will save our country or the liberty or
soul of the slave.[44]

As a precedent for this strategy, Finney reminds Weld of the
success in Rochester with making "temperance an appendage of
the revival." As for Finney's own dedication to the cause,
there could be no serious doubt.

We can now, with you and my theological class,
bring enough laborers into the field to, under
God, move the whole land in 2 years. If you will
all turn in I will get dismissed from my charge in
N. York if need be, and lay out what strength I
have in promoting the work. When I am unable to
preach I will counsel and pray and, the Lord
willing, we will make thorough work of it. I
believe we are united in the opinion here that
abolition can be carried with more dispatch and
with infinitely more safety in this indirect than
in any other way.[45]

The perception of the evils of slavery, however, sharpened by ghastly accounts of barbaric cruelty which circu-
lated widely in the North, was far too vivid to allow the
crusade for their eradication to be conducted by indirect
means. Indeed, some of the students in Finney's theological
class were among the dissidents from Lane Seminary. They
were in no more mood than Weld himself for indirection; and
they cast aside considerations of safety when they spread
out over the entire state of Ohio, a "bevy of Anti-Slavery
lecturers," as Fairchild later described them.[46] Even the
big tent Finney had brought to Oberlin from New York, designed to accommodate 3,000 anxious sinners at a time, was

bought by the Anti-Slavery Society. At the time the revivalists were moving indoors, the abolitionists were hitting
the road. While Finney still had his "holy band" of student
evangelists at Oberlin, the cause of abolition inspired the
greater enthusiasm which usually accompanies more immediate
goals. The kingdom of God lies in the unspecified future,
but the emancipation of slaves seemed as close as the determined efforts of "anti-Slavery men" could make it.

Finney persisted, however, in the pursuit of the highest goal: not merely to achieve the particular good of
emancipation, but to "GO ON, and let us have the United
States converted to God."[47] Finney would settle for nothing
less than the entire sanctification of the nation. He
supported the cause of abolition because he considered the
continued tolerance of slavery to be the primary hindrance
to that end: "the revival in the United States will continue and prevail, no farther and faster than the church
take right ground upon this subject. . . . The fact is that
slavery is, pre-eminently, the sin of the church."[48] While
Finney admitted in the 1868 edition of the Lectures on
Revivals that "the church was too late in her testimony to
avoid the war," he also claimed that "revival influences"
aroused slave-holders to take up arms "to defend and perpetuate the abomination and by so doing abolished it."[49] The
call to repent, when it fell upon hardened consciences,
provoked the sinners to even greater evil; and from that
monumental sin of civil war came finally the good of emancipation. Finney did not dwell on this interpretation of the
war; he refers to "the rebellion" only once in his Memoirs
(MF, p. 431). His contemporaries struggled to understand
how the children of promise, heirs of the covenant, could
turn the New World into as bloody a battlefield as Europe
had ever been.[50] Finney, however, saw in the war merely
another illustration of the principles of moral suasion.

The only acceptable response to the war, in Finney's
mind, was to increase efforts to reform the nation through a
general revival of religion. He is happy to report in 1868
that "since these lectures [on revivals] were delivered

great progress has been made in all benevolent enterprises in this country."[51] With slavery abolished, the greatest obstacle to the entire sanctification of the nation was removed. In Finney's mind, all that remained was for dedicated volunteers to pool their energies in the many charitable associations and reform societies which had sprung, like lush foliage, from the strong taproot of the revival. The result of this concentrated effort would be the dawning of the kingdom of God, the universal rule of moral law.

Finney's optimism rested on the promises of the Bible, interpreted, as always, according to "legal principles." For many Christians the prophecies of the coming kingdom of God have been sources of hope in divine deliverance from the tragedy of history. Finney, however, insists that the promises are conditioned upon the faithful obedience of believers in any particular "dispensation." The prophecies of universal moral reformation in Jeremiah 31 and Ezekiel 36, for example, cannot be fulfilled apart from the willing repentance of individuals. Finney, therefore, rejects any chiliastic view of the prophecies which holds that their fulfillment must await the return of Jesus or the universal transformation of human character through supernatural intervention. Legal reasoning drives him to the conclusion that the promises of a "new heart" can be fulfilled only through moral means, i.e., through present agencies of persuasion. Thus the advent of the millennium depends upon the use of revival measures to elicit obedience to the moral law throughout the whole range of individual and social life. The eschatological passages in the Bible--which have inspired visions of a new world order in some and have led others to retreat from the present evil world--impressed Finney as exacting moral admonitions.

It is not surprising that in his "Bible argument" for entire sanctification he cites the prophecies which foresee universal moral reformation as the basis of the kingdom of God on earth (LST, pp. 410-414). He does not draw from the more extravagant predictions of miraculous transformations of nature or of the violent overthrow of human governments, for they depict events which do not occur through moral means. Such apocalyptic visions are told in the language of myth, a language which is not easily translated into moral commands.

Finney's understanding of the kingdom of God is stated clearly in his encounter with William Miller, the leader of an influential adventist movement. When Finney arrived in Boston in the fall of 1843, he found wide spread excitement over Miller's teaching "that Christ would come personally, and destroy his enemies," in that very year (MF, p. 370). In fact, Miller had calculated that Christ would return on March 21, 1843. By the time he met with Finney, therefore, Miller had already seen history refute his arithmetic once; and he and his followers were only six months away from the "Great Disappointment" which led to the collapse of his popular movement. Nevertheless, Finney found him adamant:

> . . . it was vain to reason with him, and his followers at that time. Believing, as they most certainly did, that the advent of Christ was at hand, it was no wonder that they were too wild with excitement, to be reasoned with to any purpose [MF, p. 371].

What Finney failed to do was to convince Miller that the traditional apocalyptic interpretation of the second advent of Christ is mistaken.

Finney wasted no time quibbling over the precision of the date, but attacked directly Miller's view of the advent of Messiah as a coercive intrusion of divine power. While thousands of "Millerites" divested themselves of possessions, businesses, even homes, in frenzied preparation for the end of the world, Finney invited Miller himself for serious discussions, over an open Bible, in the privacy of his room. The focus of disagreement was the book of Daniel, which had provided, next to its New Testament companion, the Revelation of John, the basis of Miller's calculations. One imagines Finney pointing to the text of Daniel 2 in which

the Hebrew seer interprets the Babylonian king's dream of a
stone "cut without hands" destroying "a great image" of a
man composed of gold, silver, brass, and iron. The prophet
identified the metallic figure as a symbol of Nebuchadnezzar
and his successors; later Christian exegetes saw the Messiah
in the stone which "became a great mountain and filled the
earth." The crucial question for Finney was the identity of
the powerful and enduring stone. Leaning forward, his
intimidating eyes narrowed upon his guest, Finney insisted
"that it was not Christ that was going to destroy those
nations, but the kingdom of God."

> I then asked him if he supposed that the kingdom
> of God would destroy those nations, in the sense
> in which he taught that they would be destroyed,
> with the sword, or with making war upon them? He
> said, no, he could not believe that. I then
> inquired, "Is it not the overthrow of the govern-
> ments that is intended, instead of the destruction
> of the people? and is not this to be done, by the
> influence of the church of God, in enlightening
> their minds by the Gospel? And if this is the
> meaning, where is the foundation for your teach-
> ing, that, at a certain time, Christ is coming in
> person to destroy all the peoples of the earth?
> [MF, p. 371].

Ironically, Finney took the more radical position.
Although Miller was widely denounced as a fanatic for setting the date of Christ's coming, even his critics agreed
that Jesus would someday return to earth in splendid glory,
bringing down wrath with his left fist on the heads of the
ungodly, and holding out rewards in his right hand for the
faithful. What the established clergy and their settled
congregations opposed was the notion that the day of judgment might actually arrive before the year's crop was har-
vested or the latest inventory was sold--in short, before
they had completed all those projects by which humans seek
to stake some claim on the future. The problem was not a
new one. Ever since the Christian Church found a home and a

future in the Roman Empire, it has both confessed a hope in
the return of its Lord and castigated every prophet who
dared to bring the present moment under the threat of final
judgment.

Charles Finney resolved the dilemma through the application of "legal reasoning" to the biblical prophecies,
concluding that the kingdom of God is no threat to the
continuity of history after all. For if God directs present
human affairs according to the principles of moral government, he will not violate those principles in the future.
The transformation of the social order will come about
through the gradual spread of the light of moral law by
means of persistent and reasoned persuasion. The kingdom of
God will dawn in the welcome glow of a new day; it will not
crash into our world with the terrifying flash of a lightning bolt at midnight. For Finney there is sufficient
terror in the thought of the sudden crisis each individual
faces at the moment of death. The human enterprise as a
whole will rather progress steadily toward its destiny: to
become the righteous kingdom worthy to receive Christ as
king.

Finney's interpretation of the kingdom of God serves as
a powerful impetus toward action in the world for God
invites believers to join him in the task of persuading
others to accept the rule of moral law. The work of the
Church, then, in transforming culture is a necessary condition for the coming of the kingdom. Finney thus teaches
what is called "postmillennialism."

In the history of Christian thought the thousand-year
reign of Christ over the earth, prophesied in the
apocalyptic writings of the Bible, has been understood as
the symbol of the rule of love in the human heart (amillen-
nial view), or as the eventual fulfillment of the Church's
mission in the world (postmillennial view), or as the dramatic incursion of supernatural power to judge the wicked
and deliver the faithful (premillennial view). Each variety
of interpretation finds support in the New Testament Gospels

themselves. The earliest gospel, Mark, ends abruptly, with the expectation that Jesus was waiting for the disciples in Galilee (16:7-8); and that their present suffering would soon be vindicated in the triumph of the kingdom. In Matthew, however, Jesus leaves his disciples a commission to fulfill before "the end of the age" (28:16-20); and in Luke Jesus even tells a parable about the delay of a king's return to his own country "because they thought that the kingdom of God should immediately appear" (19:11). John drops the language of the future kingdom of God on earth in favor of talk about the present experience of birth "from above" to eternal life (3:1-21). In John, the last gospel written, the hope in the redemption of the world on the "horizontal" plane of history seems to be replaced by the hope in the salvation of the individual believer through a "vertical" relation to the eternal.

Finney was far too committed to a "common sense" reading of the text to accept the "spiritualized" interpretation of amillennialism. As with almost all revivalists, he accepted the claim that Christ would return to the earth. The question is whether that return would be the creative fulfillment of a redemptive process within history or the destructive judgment of a decadent humanity. Finney retained his optimism to the end. He believed in the power of reasonable persuasion, in the inherent human respect for law, in the capacity for fundamental change in social and political institutions, and in the power of the human will to attain moral perfection.

In Finney's later years, however, the voice of his heir to the mantle of leading revivalist was sounding a far different note. "I look upon this world as a wrecked vessel," Dwight L. Moody declared. "God has given me a lifeboat and said to me, 'Moody, save all you can.'"[52] The grand ambition of Finney and those who shared his vision of a perfect society of sanctified individuals on earth had been exchanged for the hope of Christ's return to take the "saved" to heaven. As Moody put it, "God does not propose to reward his children here. He is to reward them up

yonder. We are to work here. We are travelling to the New
Jerusalem . . . . If we don't find everything down here
just as we want it, we shall be satisfied there."[53]

What could Finney say to such an obvious failure of
nerve? Now the hope of heaven itself had become, along with
the notions of original sin and demonic power, another
"excuse" for people to settle for something less than perfection in themselves and in the world for whose final
reform they are held responsible.

NOTES

1. Shumway, Oberliniana, p. 75.
2. Gospel Themes, p. 344.
3. "Men Often Highly Esteem What God Abhors," Gospel
Themes, p. 360.
4. Lectures to Professing Christians (New York: Fleming H.
Revell, 1879), p. 203. Hereinafter referred to as LPC.
5. For example, Finney concludes a sermon on "The
Essential Elements of Christian Experience" with an exhortation to charity based on the utility of good works as a form
of Christian testimony. "Let all the world see that there
is a power and glory in the Gospel, such as human philosophy
never has even approached. Show that the Gospel begets
purity and peace. Show that it enlarges the heart and opens
the hand for the good of all human kind. Show that it
conquers selfishness and transforms the soul from hate to
love" (Gospel Themes, p. 416).
6. Gospel Themes, pp. 320-322, passim.
7. "The Sinner's Doom," The Guilt of Sin, p. 78.
8. Revivalism and Social Reform: American Protestant-
ism on the Eve of the Civil War, original edition, 1957 (New
York: Harper Torchbooks, 1965), p. 142.
9. Finney's comments on 1 John 5, in which it is said
that those "born of God" do not sin, may serve as an example. Jonathan Edwards had taught on the basis of this text

that the believer was indwelt by the sinless principle of holy love which was no other than the Holy Spirit. Finney, on the ground that moral agency in regeneration cannot be compromised by infused virtue, interprets the passage "as strong language used in a qualified sense," indicating merely that the regenerate habitually practice holiness (LST, p. 578). Finney wisely attempts little exegesis of Scripture, preferring to rely upon established commentators for support, such as Adam Clark (1760-1832), a celebrated student of Oriental languages who began as a Methodist itinerant. Finney quotes from his Commentary on the Holy Bible, published in 1810-1826. Finney also borrows from Robert Barclay (1648-1690), whose chief work, Theologiae Verae Christianae Apologia, was a defense of Quaker spirituality, including the possibility of sinlessness. Finney cites both in LST, pp. 448-450.

10. Lectures on Revivals, p. 392.

11. Ibid., p. 395.

12. Ibid., p. 272.

13. Ibid., pp. 400, 403.

14. Ibid., p. 328.

15. Ibid., p. 417.

16. Gilbert H. Barnes and Dwight L. Dummond, eds., Letters of Theodore Dwight Weld, Angelina Grimke Weld, and Sarah Grimke, 1822-1844, vol. 1 (New York: D. Appleton-Century Co., 1934), pp. 14-16.

17. Gilbert H. Barnes, introduction to Weld-Grimke Letters, vol. 1, pp. xvii-xix.

18. Timothy Smith rightly notes that "the issue was the same one he had raised at the revival in Oberlin in 1836: desire versus will, sentiment versus choice" ["The Cross Demands, the Spirit Enables," Christianity Today (February 16, 1979), 25].

19. Lectures on Revivals, p. 118.

20. The Nature of True Virtue, p. 24. Cf. p. 77.

21. Timothy Dwight, Theology; Explained and Defended in a Series of Sermons (Middletown, Connecticut: Clark and Lyman, 1818), vol. III, p. 150.

22. Fairchild, Oberlin: The Colony and the College, p. 90.

23. *Ibid*., p. 93.

24. Wright, *Finney*, p. 240.

25. Fairchild, *Oberlin: The Colony and the College*, p. 93.

26. "The Cross Demands, the Spirit Enables," p. 25.

27. Finney's six lectures were printed as a separate tract, entitled *Guide to the Saviour, or Conditions of Attaining to and Abiding in Entire Holiness of Heart and Life* (Oberlin: James M. Fitch, 1855). In the introduction Finney warns that the lectures "are designed, *not* to define entire sanctification, not to prove its attainability--nor that it has been attained, but simply to indicate the necessary *conditions* or *means* of *continuing* in obedience to God" (p. vi).

28. Quoted in *A Plain Account of Christian Perfection*, original edition, 1766 (London: The Epworth Press, 1960), p. 11. Hereinafter referred to as PA.

29. Timothy Smith argues that the Oberlin faculty was forced, by criticism from Princeton, to "the alternative of acknowledging their conversion to Methodism, or marrying sanctification to the doctrine of natural ability. That they leaned toward the latter course is small surprise" (*Revivalism and Social Reform*, p. 109). Finney's later views of holiness, therefore, increasingly emphasized the responsibility of the believers to sanctify their own hearts, rather than relying on the ecstatic experience of a "second blessing" to purify them from sin. Smith notes that "the two of Finney's *Lectures on Revivals* which were re-written for the edition of 1868, while making the doctrine of sanctification more prominent, stressed growth more than a crisis of experience" (p. 112).

30. *The Interaction of Law and Religion*, pp. 80-94.

31. "Men Often Highly Esteem What God Abhors," *Gospel Themes*, p. 348.

32. H. Richard Niebuhr, *The Kingdom of God in America*, original edition, 1937 (New York: Harper Torchbooks, 1959), p. 158.

33. By heartily endorsing the principle of voluntarism, the New School Presbyterians turned the necessity of disestablishment into the virtue of moral suasion. See George M.

Marsden, The Evangelical Mind and the New School Presbyterian Experience (New Haven, Conn.:   Yale University Press,
1970), pp. 12-17.
    34. The Kingdom of God in America, p. 102.
    35. Charles Cole attributes the failure of the revival-
ists' program to redeem the nation by moral means to their
ignoring such political and economic realities. "In the
last analysis, it was the short sightedness of the reformers
themselves that led to their failure. Endowed with religious zeal and high ideals, they attempted to erase an evil
without regard to the conditions that produced it" (Social
Ideas of the Northern Evangelists, p. 130).
    36. Skeletons, p. 243.
    37. John L. Hammond, "Revivals, Consensus, and
American Political Culture," Journal of the American Academy
of Religion XLVI: 3 (September 1978), 309.
    38. War with Mexico was declared by President James
Polk in 1846 in a dispute over the southwestern boundary of
Texas, which had been annexed into the Union the year before. The fighting lasted until 1848 when Mexico conceded
the land between the Nueces River and the Rio Grande. The
incident was not one of America's finer hours.
    39. Lectures on Revivals, p. 301.
    40. Winthrop S. Hudson, The Great Tradition of the
American Churches (New York: Harper Torchbooks, 1963), p.
93: " . . . the antislavery campaign was based upon a
summons to repentance--personal repentance--on the part of
each individual citizen for his share in the perpetuation of
the system of human bondage." Cf. Cross, Burned-over
District, pp. 211-237; and McLoughlin, Modern Revivalism,
pp. 105-118. Both agree that Finney sought to subordinate
abolition to the revival in the hope that reform would come
through the "personal reformation of the individual male-
factor" (McLoughlin).
    41. In the Skeletons Finney taught that the Devil's
"whole influence is exerted in this world for the promotion
of selfishness" (p. 217).
    42. "The Spirit Not Striving Always," Gospel Themes,
pp. 284f. Finney borrows the image of the seared conscience
from 1 Timothy 4:2.

43. Perhaps the most poignant illustration of the persistent impenitence of a sinner is in the closing appeal of
the sermon entitled, "The Wicked Heart Set to Do Evil." A
hardened convict, condemned to die, refuses to accept a
last-minute pardon, even though it was secured by his own
parents' tearful pleading with the governor. Realizing
finally that all their efforts to persuade their son to
receive the pardon are futile, the parents can only acquiesce to the justice of his execution (Gospel Themes, p.
144). The anecdote demonstrates the tragic lengths to which
free moral agents are allowed to set their own course, even
to destroy themselves, in a moral universe where God does
not intervene to rescue them from the consequences of their
actions.

44. Weld-Grimke Letters, pp. 318f.
45. Ibid., p. 319.
46. Oberlin: Its Origin, Progress and Results, p. 10.
47. Lectures on Revivals, p. 306.
48. Ibid., p. 301.
49. Ibid., p. 308, n. 21.
50. For a concise analysis of the major alternative
interpretations developed in the period immediately following the war, see Ahlstrom, A Religious History of the American People, pp. 681-689.
51. Lectures on Revivals, p. 308, n. 21.
52. Quoted in McLoughlin, Modern Revivalism, p. 257.
53. Ibid., p. 259.

CONCLUSION

While admiring Finney's call for perfection, present-day
readers may be tempted to dismiss his analysis of moral evil
as superficial, preferring to see individual misdeeds within
some larger context of what is sometimes called "systemic
evil." American theology has long been influenced by Walter
Rauschenbusch's argument that a modern "social" conception
of sin includes the idea of a "kingdom of evil," the supra-
personal powers of social and economic institutions which
batter and exploit human life.[1] Reinhold Niebuhr, a theologian whom some politicians occasionally read, added the
claim that the very driving force of all human institutions
is for their own survival and prosperity and that, therefore, the most one can realistically expect from them is the
sort of enlightened self-interest which sometimes includes
charity toward others. Niebuhr devoted a major work to
delineating

> one of the tragedies of the human spirit: its
> inability to conform its collective life to its
> individual ideals. As individuals, men believe
> that they ought to love and serve each other and
> establish justice between each other. As racial,
> economic, and national groups they take for them-
> selves, whatever their power can command.[2]

Niebuhr is credited with reintroducing the myth of
original sin into American theology and politics, using it
as the basis of prophetic criticism. But it is also the
case that his "Christian realism" was all too vulnerable to
the temptation of political expediency and cynicism. Among
other things, his theology led to a certain despair about
transforming human culture into a realm governed by moral

law. Niebuhr insisted on the tragic paradox that it is
necessary to resort to power to accomplish anything in
society, even for the good, but that the use of power is
itself an act of self-assertion that inevitably corrupts the
user. "The man of power," he declared, "though humane
impulse may awaken in him, always remains something of the
beast of prey."[3] The kingdom of God faded away in Niebuhr's
vision to an impossible dream that nevertheless called forth
one's best efforts while it discouraged any hope in their
lasting success.

In Finney's view the goal of history is a comprehensive
system of moral government in which the highest well-being
of all its members is fulfilled through the obedience of
each to its laws. The entire responsibility for the success
or failure of the system rests upon the individual citizens.
The crucial question is whether each will recognize the
claims presented by conscience and will choose to meet those
demands by subordinating private interest to the general
good. What saves Finney's vision from dissipating into the
mists of the always unfinished utilitarian calculus of the
greatest happiness is his specification of what constitutes
the general good, viz., unconditional obedience of each to
the law of moral consciousness common to all. He challenges
those who claim that it is impossible to act according to
moral principles in national, let alone, international
affairs. Do you find in the world, Finney might ask, any
effective evil force other than human will? No matter how
complex the maneuvers of war, it is still necessary for
individuals to pull triggers, strike matches, and string
ropes. The aggregate of the horrors of battle is composed
of thousands of individual acts of greed, fear, cruelty, and
destruction. What is true of war, he implies, is true of
all cases of "collective" evil: each is a collection of
many deliberate decisions to put the individual's private
interests above those of the universe of moral beings. The
catalogue of "man's inhumanity to man," then, contains no
entry which is not sufficiently explained as the result of
individual selfishness.

Although his ambitious faith may appear naively idealistic, Finney did not yield his hope to either sentimental-
ism or apocalypticism, as did later evangelicals. By insis-
ting that the administrative principles of divine government
were accessible to the human mind and will in the moral law,
he maintained the necessity of reasonable and disciplined
means of evangelism. An appeal to the emotions only, which
excites without either informing or reforming, is ruled "out
of court." Finney would have been embarrassed by the sac-
charine sermons of late nineteenth-century evangelists and
absolutely appalled by Billy Sunday's claim to be following
the Lectures on Revivals in his extravagant histrionics.
Although the reports of Finney's early campaigns indicate
that they were not entirely free from excesses, his considered opinion by 1835 was that excited feelings distract
people from the crucial matter of whether they will submit
to moral law. Faith, as he never tired of saying, is a
matter of the will, not of the emotions.

Nor did Finney's hope in the eventual triumph of the
revival through moral means give way to the despair of this
world which cuts the nerve of social reform in premillennialism, like that which Finney encountered in the adventist
teaching of William Miller. By the time of the rise of
fundamentalism the belief in the imminent return of Christ
to bring judgment upon a world sunk into the depths of sin,
far below the reach of moral suasion, had become the last
refuge of evangelical piety. Denying the possibility, let
alone the duty, of perfecting human culture by bringing all
its operations under moral government, the evangelical community began increasingly to narrow the focus of its vision
to the reign of Christ in the believer's heart. The success
of revival began to be measured by the number of converts
alone, and not also by sanctifying changes in political and
social conditions. Finney counted souls too, but he was
also proud to list among the results of his revivals the
closing of taverns, the freeing of slaves, and the election
of honest public officials. Finney was unambiguous about
the Christian's public responsibilities, even in his early
lectures at Oberlin:

> In a popular government politics are an indispen-
> sable part of religion. No man can possibly be
> benevolent or religious without concerning himself
> to a greater or lesser extent with the affairs of
> human government . . . . [Christians] are bound to
> meddle with politics in popular governments, for
> the same reason that they are bound to seek the
> universal good of all men.[4]

For Finney the reign of Christ in the individual heart
should manifest itself in the extension of God's government
over public affairs.

Finney's theology begins in the perception of human
life as governed by intelligible rules, administered by "a
great public magistrate, sustaining infinitely responsible
relations to the moral universe,"[5] and ends in the call for
responsible citizenship under moral government. Inasmuch as
the primary metaphor of Finney's theological vision is the
human world as civil society, he focuses his attention on
the powers and duties of its faithful citizens. Action in a
civil society is regulated in rational and purposive ways by
a system of laws. Thus, one may proceed with a degree of
certainty and optimism toward the goals of the society that
was impossible under the mysterious sovereignty of the mon-
archical deity of Calvinist imagination. In his own time
Finney's theology provided a powerful stimulus to both
revival and reform, precisely because he interpreted the
realm of human action as subject to rational order, and
therefore as responsive to moral suasion as the realm of
nature is to coercive power.

In recent times, when the relation of religious ideals
to political action has again become a prominent topic of
public discourse, Finney's elaborate attempt to construct a
theology faithful to both Christ and culture is worthy of
consideration. At the very least, his vision of universal
moral law as the basis of civil government serves as a
reminder that any "theology of politics" in a democratic
society must draw its interpretive categories from common

human experience. Any attempt to enact a program of national political action based on religious convictions must be
conceived in terms that are accessible and persuasive to all
those affected by it. Perhaps the most pointed lesson here
for contemporary evangelicals is that there can be no legitimate authority for the Christian in political programs
which are imposed upon other citizens against their wills,
even if those programs fulfill worthy goals.

If, as Finney taught, revival and reform, evangelism
and political activism, are both means of "moral suasion,"
then both must move the wills of others by reason and love.
In those ways only can the moral law be proclaimed as the
redeeming gospel. To those who object that human nature and
the forces of history will inevitably defeat such idealistic
measures, Finney's work poses the hard question: If moral
government is ever to be established in the world, by what
other means could it be achieved? It is appropriate that
the study of Finney's theology should leave us with that
urgently practical question.

NOTES

1. A Theology for the Social Gospel, original edition,
1917 (Nashville: Abingdon Press, 1945), pp. 69-94.

2. Moral Man and Immoral Society, original edition,
1932 (New York: Charles Scribner's Sons, 1960), p. 9.

3. Ibid., p. 13.

4. Skeletons, p. 241. Practically the same words can
also be found in the later lectures (LST, P. 218).

5. "On Trusting in the Mercy of God," Gospel Themes,
pp. 22-23.

INDEX

Abelard, 193
Abolition, 7, 73, 238, 259-61, 270; anti-slavery, 125, 260f., 270
Affections, 174-76, 241; as acts of will, 139, 246; benevolent, 57; gracious, 166; legal, 72; sinful, 120, 173
Anselm, 128, 193, 200
Antinomianism, 117, 210, 251; antinomian, 226
Apostasy, 12, 17-25, 29, 37, 172, 177
Apprenticeship in law, 6, 46, 48-53, 70f., 80, 139
Athanasius, 194
Atonement, 6, 119f., 134, 180, 191f., 225; historical types, 193f.; governmental theory of, 120, 195-209
Augustine, 78f., 168, 210
Authority, 37, 80, 84, 93, 102, 111, 130, 217, 276; of the Bible, 82, 133; of God, 6, 61, 178, 198, 225; of law, 47, 54, 135, 203f.; of reason, 18
Autobiography, 76-80
Autonomy, 12, 17f., 24-28, 49, 139, 244

Beardsley, Levi, 39, 42, 111, 180
Beecher, Lyman, 9, 41, 66, 94, 99, 101, 122, 146f., 229, 247
Bellamy, Joseph, 4, 151, 19
Benevolence, 6, 59f., 118, 145, 156, 161, 171f., 177f., 183, 191, 197, 200, 203, 208, 219-21, 225-27, 232, 242, 251f.; disinterested, 143, 205, 241; law of, 61, 141, 178, 226, 248, 254
Berman, Harold, 47, 71, 73, 206-08, 253
Bible, 6, 29, 46, 49, 66, 82, 84f., 95, 97, 103, 127, 130, 133, 144, 151, 168f., 181, 195, 210, 216, 249, 257f., 262f., 265
Blackstone, William, 2, 8, 43, 46f., 50, 52, 54-57, 59f., 69, 101, 131, 134f., 156f., 178, 180f., 189, 205, 207, 216, 219
Boorstin, Daniel, 8, 70

Calvin, John, 102, 118, 130, 193, 210, 254
Calvinism, 6, 18, 25, 30, 41, 61, 80, 93, 106, 119, 146f.;
    "New School", 9f., 67, 93, 101, 117, 120, 122, 149, 152, 177, 196, 210, 235, 247, 255, 269;
    "Old School", 4, 9f., 30, 67, 91, 95, 113-15, 117-124, 136, 139, 142, 152, 161, 167, 188f., 191, 194f., 200, 208-211, 220f.
Chauncy, Charles, 188
Civil War, 56, 259, 261
Cole, Charles, 34, 270
Coleridge, Samuel Taylor, 78, 159
Colton, Calvin, 29, 42, 63-66, 73f., 121
Common Law, 19, 43, 47, 49f., 52, 55, 69, 131, 134, 197
Common sense, 3, 5, 20, 47, 130f., 139, 217, 241f.; in understanding the Bible, 95, 151, 165, 235, 266; in understanding law, 1f., 13, 50;